WATCHMAN, TELL US

Watchman, Tell Us

*John J. Bird and Black Politics in
Post-Civil War Illinois*

Wayne T. Pitard

SOUTHERN ILLINOIS UNIVERSITY PRESS

CARBONDALE

Southern Illinois University Press
www.siupress.com

27 26 25 24   4 3 2 1

Cover illustration and frontispiece: John J. Bird, ca. late 1870s.
Most Worshipful Grand Lodge of Illinois Prince Hall Masons.

ISBN 978-0-8093-3946-4 (paperback)
ISBN 978-0-8093-3947-1 (ebook)
This book has been catalogued with the Library of Congress.

Printed on recycled paper ♻

SIU
Southern Illinois University System

To my family: my wife Angie, daughter Sarah,
son-in-law Alex, new grandson Augi, and daughter Samantha,
for all their support for this project

Watchman, tell us of the night,
What its signs of promise are.
Traveler, o'er yon mountain's height,
See that glory-beaming star!

Watchman, doth its beauteous ray
Aught of joy or hope foretell?
Traveler, yes, it brings the day,
Promised day of Israel.

Watchman, tell us of the night;
Higher yet that star ascends.
Traveler, blessedness and light,
Peace and truth, its course portends.

Watchman, will its beams alone
Gild the spot that gave them birth?
Traveler, ages are its own;
See, it bursts o'er all the earth.

Watchman, tell us of the night,
For the morning seems to dawn.
Traveler, darkness takes its flight;
Doubt and terror are withdrawn.

Watchman, let thy wanderings cease;
Hie thee to thy quiet home.
Traveler, lo, the Prince of Peace,
Lo, the Son of God is come!

> *Watchman, Tell Us of the Night*
> John Bowring (1825)

CONTENTS

Contents

ILLUSTRATIONS

A look at the author's bio in the back of this book might legitimately lead one to wonder why a professor of Hebrew Bible and ancient Near Eastern Religions and director of a museum of world cultures would undertake a biography of a nineteenth-century African American politician from Illinois. This project developed during preparations for a 2017 exhibition at the Spurlock Museum celebrating the sesquicentennial of the University of Illinois. In 2015, while looking for interesting stories and people from the school's formative years that we might highlight in the exhibit, I came across a paragraph in Winton Solberg's monumental history of the university about John J. Bird, an African American who had been appointed to the Board of Trustees of the Illinois Industrial University (the original name of the University of Illinois) in 1873. Solberg noted the remarkable nature of Bird's appointment to this otherwise all-White board at an otherwise all-White university and discussed what he could glean about Bird from the minutes of the board meetings Bird attended during his nine years there. However, he was unable to find much information about Bird that might explain why the governor chose him for this position. He was dependent primarily on a brief, six-line biography published in the 1918 University of Illinois alumni directory, a few references to Bird located in the Illinois State Archives, and an odd record or two.[1]

Thinking that Bird might be a significant person to explore for the exhibit, I began to search for additional information on him but discovered that virtually nothing seemed to be available. No biographies of Bird or articles specifically about him had been published, nor were there any encyclopedia articles, or entries in biographical dictionaries of notable nineteenth-century African Americans. Historians seemed almost completely unaware of him, and since I was a non-expert in Illinois history, I was content at first to assume that beyond his appointment to the university, he had not played a significant role in the larger context of African American life in post–Civil War Illinois. I was wrong.

Still hoping to find at least some information that might help me flesh out the context of his relationship to Illinois Industrial University, I began to examine contemporary sources, first from the southern Illinois city of Cairo, where Bird lived in 1873 when he received his appointment, and then others from Springfield and elsewhere around the state. Working through those documents, I discovered that there was in fact, much, much more to John Bird than I could have imagined, that from the late 1860s to the 1890s this forgotten man had been one of the most significant African American leaders in the state. I also found that through these sources, I was in a position to reconstruct the major lines of his life story.

It is this newly recovered portrait of John Bird and his significance in post–Civil War Illinois history that I thought I should share, in spite of the distance between the area of my academic expertise and the history of nineteenth-century Illinois. I began the project under the impression that I might find enough material to write a good article about Bird, but as I continued to work on it over the past few years, the biography expanded into the current book. It is my hope that I have done his memory some measure of justice.

Numerous people have helped me in this project. I especially wish to offer my heartfelt thanks to Aaron Graham, my colleague at the Spurlock Museum; William Maher, the University of Illinois archivist; Ron Bailey, head of the university's African American Studies Department; Meghan Harmon and the staff at the Abraham Lincoln Presidential Library; Curtis Mann, head of the Sangamon Valley Collection at the Lincoln Library in Springfield; Monica Smith of the Cairo Public Library; Aaron Lisec of the Morris Library Special Collections at the Southern Illinois University; and Brad Bolin at the Illinois State Capitol. I particularly wish to express my deepest appreciation to Preston Ewing of Cairo, Illinois, who undoubtedly knows more about the African American history of that city than anyone living and provided me with a wide range of information; David Joens, director of the Illinois State Archives, who helped me tremendously with recovering letters from and about John Bird in the archives, read my early manuscript, and gave me exceptionally fine advice on how to get it into publishable shape; Jennifer Egan at SIU Press for her tremendous support during the process of reviewing the manuscript; and the anonymous peer reviewers who provided extremely valuable suggestions for improving my work. All of the mistakes and weaknesses in the book, of course, remain my own.

WATCHMAN, TELL US

Introduction

"Watchman, Tell Us"

ON THE AFTERNOON of July 1, 1874, John J. Bird stepped to the podium in the main lecture hall of the new Southern Illinois Normal University in Carbondale to address an august assembly of leaders and citizens from across the state. They were all gathered for the dedication ceremonies of the first state university founded in southern Illinois. Governor John L. Beveridge had already spoken to the convocation, as had the newly inaugurated president of the university, Dr. Robert Allyn; the presidents of Northwestern University and the Bloomington Normal School (later Illinois State University); and the superintendent of the St. Louis public schools. Bird's address was the final speech of the day, and as he stood before the assembled body, many in the audience were certainly disturbed by his presence there, and some were likely outraged, for John Bird was African American, and the audience to whom he spoke was almost entirely White.

Bird's appearance on the stage at this event was unprecedented. Never before had an African American been invited to speak at the inaugural ceremony of a state university in Illinois (or perhaps in any other state in the postwar North). The roster of speakers had certainly been approved by the office of Governor Beveridge; in fact, Bird's inclusion on it was probably at the specific instruction of the Republican governor, who just one year earlier had created a stir by appointing Bird to the Board of Trustees of the Illinois Industrial University (IIU), the state's land grant institution.[1] That, too, had been an unprecedented move, making Bird the first African American ever named to the board of an essentially White institution of higher education in Illinois (and probably in the entire North). Just a month after his appointment to IIU, Bird had also become the first elected African

American judge in the state (and—again—probably in the entire postwar North), when he won election as police magistrate in the busy town of Cairo, his home at the southern tip of the state. So, when he gave his speech in Carbondale, he was already known to much of his audience and was in fact the most prominent African American in southern Illinois.

Bird's invitation to the ceremony had offended many people in Democratic Carbondale. Apparently, some of those unhappy people were members of the local organizing committee for the event. In what seems to have been an attempt to insult Bird, the committee failed to make arrangements for his arrival. While they appointed welcoming committees to meet the other speakers at the train station, reserved hotel rooms for them for the night before the ceremony, and had dinners arranged for them, they did none of these things for Bird. He arrived at the station and found no one there to greet him. He walked to the few hotels in town and discovered that none of them would accept a Black guest. He tried to eat at a restaurant and was turned away. Finally, he walked about two miles out of town to stay with an African American friend for the night.

Perhaps the committee hoped that Bird might be sufficiently offended by this treatment that he would leave Carbondale without speaking. But Bird would not forgo this chance to address what was essentially a captive audience of White elites who needed to hear what he had to say. And thus on that Wednesday, John Bird arrived at the university's building in the morning, attended all of the events of the celebration, and then stood in the packed lecture hall to deliver his speech.

Bird's invitation had asked him to speak on the subject, "The Education of the African Race," and he did so in a powerful, comprehensive manner. In the speech, Bird laid out the scale of the educational crisis among African American citizens nationwide, north and south. He argued that education was a right belonging to every citizen, and he condemned the fact that three out of four African Americans were still illiterate. He went on to describe the long years of slavery in the United States and the recent transition to freedom, but he pointed out that across the nation, particularly in the southern states, violent opposition to education for African Americans was still prevalent and that people of good will needed to oppose that violence. He concluded with a stirring call for his White audience to support the public education of Black children.

One of the most striking moments of Bird's speech came in his discussion of slavery and its eventual overthrow. Describing the horror of enslavement, he quoted from a hymn titled "Watchman, Tell Us of the Night," written by the British diplomat John Bowring in 1825. The hymn was very popular in the United States, appearing in the songbooks of almost every Christian denomination, both White and Black. It was written in the form of a dialogue between a traveler in the night and a watchman. The fearful traveler asks the watchman if he can see signs of approaching dawn in the darkness, and the watchman responds with assurance that indeed the morning star is already visible and that the dawn is coming. In White churches, "Watchman" was generally considered to be a Christmas hymn, describing the dawn of Christ's birth and the promised arrival of his "peace and truth." But African American Christians saw the meaning of the lyrics quite differently. They interpreted the night during which the song begins as the darkness of slavery and the approaching dawn as the advent of freedom. The hymn had become part of the African American observance of the traditional Watch Night celebration on New Year's Eve, particularly after the implementation of the Emancipation Proclamation on January 1, 1863, when Watch Night took on a clear connection with freedom at the arrival of the New Year.

In preparing his speech, Bird knew that the lyrics of "Watchman" would be familiar to his White audience, but he also knew that the African American take on the song would not. He first set the stage for his use of the hymn by describing slavery before quoting its opening lines: "Two hundred and forty-two years of our history in this country was as one long night of darkness and despair. We waited, hoped and prayed. Often times in the gloomiest hour of our sorrow, we would cry, 'Watchman, tell us of the night, what its signs of promise are.'" Bird's audience knew that the watchman's response in the next two lines was hopeful and reassuring: "Traveler, o'er yon mountain's height, See that glory-beaming star!" These lines were what they anticipated hearing next, but Bird subverted their expectations, continuing, "The answer would come back, falling on our ears with redoubled force, 'Perpetual slavery and ignorance is your doom forever.'" Bird's maneuver here in providing the watchman with a deeply pessimistic response to the traveler presumably startled his White audience and powerfully evoked for them the despair of the generations of African Americans who suffered in bondage.

Following this gloomy assessment, however, Bird then picked up on the optimistic viewpoint of the hymn, paralleling African Americans' current situation with the watchman's heralding of the morning star in the first verse (rather than with the full dawning of the new day in the final verse). "The night of our sorrow has past," Bird said, "but it has left its traces upon our hearts and memories. The day star of gladness has loomed up in the horizon before us, and we are marching forward with courage bold to realize the in-estimable blessings that await us."

John Bird's striking use of "Watchman, Tell Us of the Night" in this speech, with its fundamental hopefulness and optimism for the future as personified by the watchman, characterizes in a very vivid way his own lifelong, overarch-ing optimism concerning the struggle for African American rights in post–Civil War America. During his long career, he held to an unshakable faith that eventually African Americans would live beside their White neighbors in a land of equality and justice. Yet also like the watchman in the hymn, he was aware that that day had not yet dawned, and he knew that a great deal of effort, time, persuasion, agitation, and persistence would be necessary to reach that future. He would spend his life fighting for that goal, and in his struggles, John Bird was never the uncertain traveler of the song. He was the watchman.[2]

JOHN J. BIRD (1844–1912), who stood fearlessly at that podium in 1874, has been almost completely forgotten over the course of the past hundred years, but during the final three decades of the nineteenth century he was one of the most prominent and influential African Americans in the state of Illi-nois. He was part of the first generation of Black leaders (also mostly forgot-ten) who struggled to negotiate what was perhaps the most astonishing cultural transformation in the history of the United States, the transition of some four million people from the condition of enslavement to the status of citizen. Between the mid-1860s and the 1890s, this generation sought to solidify and expand the rights that the Thirteenth through Fifteenth Amend-ments to the Constitution had granted to African Americans, and for a while they were surprisingly successful. Working largely within the Republican Party, they pushed for laws that opened the public schools to Black children, enforced the right of all men (not yet women) to vote, forbade discrimina-tion in public places on the basis of color, and allowed African Americans to testify in court and serve on juries. They demanded and received repre-sentation in government offices at the local, state, and federal levels. With

Reconstruction in effect in the South and the Republican Party in the North apparently allied with the Black community, there was, for a while, a genuine optimism among many that African Americans could soon be integrated into American society with full legal and civil rights. This optimism proved to be illusory in the long run. In the South, Reconstruction collapsed by the mid-1870s, and African Americans living in the former Confederacy suffered, through violence and intimidation, the loss of virtually all of the rights that had been affirmed to them. Conditions were better in the North, but in 1883, the Supreme Court overturned the landmark Civil Rights Act of 1875, which had enforced nondiscrimination in public accommodation, and the hard-won progress toward equal rights began to slip backward. Schools that had been integrated slowly became resegregated. Businesses refused to hire African Americans for skilled jobs and also found it easy to deny entrance to African Americans, even in states that had passed their own civil rights laws after 1883. By the 1890s, lynchings and pogroms, which had been significant tools in the South for dominating the Black populace, spread into the northern states. When the U.S. Supreme Court ruled in 1896 that racial segregation in public facilities (the so-called separate-but-equal doctrine) was constitutional, most of the political achievements won by the post–Civil War generation in the North and South had been subverted or abolished by the White establishment, both Republican and Democratic.[3]

During the latter third of the nineteenth century, African Americans constituted only about 2.5 percent of the inhabitants of the northern states. In 1870 Illinois, they were 1.1 percent of the population, making it a challenge for them to have a significant statewide impact on the political landscape. It helped, however, that most Black people gravitated to a few key cities and counties where sometimes they could hold the balance of voting power between the Republican and Democratic Parties. Their largest concentration was in Chicago (3,691 in 1870), where they still constituted only 1.2 percent of the city's three hundred thousand citizens; but they were about 8 percent of the population of the Second and Third Wards, so that their votes could swing certain local and state races. Illinois's second-largest community of African Americans lived at the southernmost tip of the state in the town of Cairo. Built at the confluence of the Ohio and Mississippi Rivers, Cairo had served as the key Union military port for the western theater of the Civil War and beginning in 1862 had become the location of a camp for "contrabands," Black refugees from the fighting that raged in west

Tennessee and farther south. Several thousand came to Cairo until April 1863, when most inhabitants of the camp were relocated near Memphis. However, many of the refugees refused to leave and became the core of the city's postwar African American population. Thus while in 1860 only forty-seven African Americans had lived in Cairo alongside 2,141 Whites, by 1870 there were 1,849 Black citizens in the city, representing 29.5 percent of its total population of 6,267. No other substantial Illinois city possessed an African American community that constituted such a large proportion of its population.[4] When the Fifteenth Amendment opened the franchise to African Americans in 1870, the political dynamic in Cairo changed dramatically, with the new Black voting bloc lifting the small, White Republican minority in town to effective parity with its Democratic counterpart. Because of this, the African American community in Cairo was able to press for its rights in a stronger way than elsewhere in the state. John J. Bird stood at the forefront of this movement, having begun a career there in 1864 that led to his emergence as the most significant and influential African American in southern Illinois.

Bird was not among the 95 percent of Black settlers in Cairo who had fled there from enslavement. Rather, he was a northern, freeborn African American, a member of the small, but vibrant, Black middle class that had for decades pressed the fight against both slavery and the anti-Black laws that existed in the northern states. He arrived in Cairo in 1864, a charismatic, ambitious young man, well educated and politically active, with the specific intention of aiding and organizing this population of refugees into a new, cohesive community. From the beginning, he showed a remarkable facility for working with and gaining the confidence of people from a wide range of cultural backgrounds, both in the Black community and among Whites, including the Republican politicians with whom he worked. His motivations and rationale for focusing his attention on Cairo were intimately bound up in the prevailing ideologies of the Black middle class of the antebellum period, and one cannot understand the direction of Bird's career without an awareness of the culture that produced him.

In recent years, scholars have substantially illuminated the rise of a definable free Black middle class in the northern states during the early decades of the nineteenth century. Composed of the small number of African Americans who were able to gain an education and training to become teachers, small business owners, newspaper editors, ministers, and other professionals, this group arose alongside the larger White middle class that had developed in the wake of the American Revolution, and it adopted many of the same social and cultural ideas.[5]

In the White community, the path to the middle class was usually seen to flow through education, diligence, the seizing of opportunity for financial advancement, the gaining of respectability, the acquisition of property, and for some, participation in the political system. The role of women in this new middle class was focused on the household and family, removing them as much as possible from the world of paid labor and placing them in the same roles that the women of the older elite class had held. The educated Black community adopted these same ideals concerning middle-class life, but the vicious prejudice and discrimination that surrounded African Americans led them to understand the meaning and purpose of a middle-class community in ways quite different from those of the White majority. At its foundation was an insistence upon racial pride, a rejection of the arguments of Black inferiority that infiltrated every aspect of American White culture. As a key element of demonstrating that this prejudice was woefully mistaken, Black leaders—including notables like Frederick Douglass, Maria W. Stewart, and Martin Delany, as well as many ministers and newspaper editors—encouraged African Americans to aspire to exemplify those middle-class values in order to show that African Americans had the same intellectual and moral capacity as White people to live as respectable, accomplished, and useful citizens. They wrote, lectured, and preached that African Americans deserved the same rights as the White majority and that if young, industrious, and dedicated Black men could seize opportunities for education, they could acquire the skills to enter the professional fields and display the appropriate social aptitudes and manners characteristic of cultured society, while the young women could learn how to be model wives, taking care of the family home and the children. The proliferation of these ideas about Black self-improvement and "racial uplift" in African American newspapers, pamphlets, books of instruction in personal conduct, and inspiring narratives of success had a significant impact in creating and sustaining the Black middle class, both before and after the Civil War.[6]

Although scholars previously tended to characterize these antebellum self-improvement writings as having been a bourgeois form of personal politics, focused on individual advancement, essentially unrelated to the Black abolitionist and civil rights movements in the North, recent analyses of this literature have shown convincingly that these two elements often were closely related. The self-improvement writings were not intended solely, or even primarily, as instructions for the mere personal aggrandizement of individuals, but were part of a larger social and political ideology. Erica Ball has shown that, far from encouraging an elitist lifestyle disconnected from the "lower" classes of Black society, the writers of middle-class self-improvement literature usually linked their instruction to the idea that all more fortunate African Americans had a duty to be involved in the fight against slavery and the anti-Black restrictions that became increasingly severe in the northern states during the course of the antebellum period. She has also pointed out that even though an important motivation for adopting middle-class social customs was to oppose the White belief in Black inferiority, the members of the middle class also strongly believed that living such a life was good in and of itself.[7]

The African Methodist Episcopal (AME) Church, the first independent Black denomination in the United States, supported the idea of Black self-improvement and voiced its opposition to slavery and support for the civil rights of free African Americans in the North from its foundation in the late eighteenth century. Its leadership, like many of the more secular writers in the middle-class movement, was certain that clear and rational arguments against slavery and prejudice, coupled with the living examples of educated and cultured individuals within the Black community, would eventually convince enough White people to change their general attitudes toward African Americans, so that equality could be achieved. These themes already appear in a pamphlet published in 1794 by Richard Allen, the AME's first bishop, and Absalom Jones, which described the remarkable role Philadelphia's Black community played in helping desperate White citizens during the yellow fever epidemic of 1793. The pamphlet concluded with a set of appendices that argued against slaveowners' defenses of slavery, encouraged those who suffered in slavery, entreated free African Americans "to consider the obligations we lay under, to help forward the cause of freedom," and finally, thanked their White allies for their support, particularly for their help in educating the city's Black children. These values continued to appear and develop in many of the church's publications.[8]

This version of the Black middle-class ethos profoundly affected John Bird's character, thought, ambitions, career, actions, and relationships with the Illinois African American community. Born in Cincinnati, Ohio, in

1844, the son of a steamboat steward who owned his own house, and then, after his father's death circa 1853, the stepson of a prominent minister of the AME Church who was a strong proponent of education, a "conductor" in the Underground Railroad, and a newspaper editor, he grew up in a household with parents who deeply valued education, integrity, and social and political activism. His stepfather, Augustus Green, and his mother, Catherine, imparted a love for the intellectual, for history, politics, and current affairs to John. They trained him to be an excellent orator and an advocate for civil rights, primarily within the value system of the AME Church's more activist wing. He emerged into adulthood during the Civil War, as the slavery system of the South began to crumble and as tens of thousands of formerly enslaved African American refugees fled to areas controlled by Union forces, usually in need of food, clothing, and shelter, and without a clear legal status—free from slavery yet not citizens and without defined rights.[9] Although the U.S. government made some efforts to shelter many of the "contrabands," their situation often was dire. The tiny northern free Black community, which had until now spoken theoretically about the end of slavery, suddenly found itself faced with a gigantic mission to aid this massive number of newly free people, scattered in camps in areas across the South where Union forces were in control, as well as in a few places inside the northern states.[10] Some members of the educated class, including Bird, chose to join a contraband community to provide leadership for the population, help organize aid to the camps, establish schools for both children and adults, and fight for and protect their new rights from apathetic and ruthless military officers and politicians. Many of the Black northerners who came to the camps were missionaries from the AME Church who deeply believed that God called them to this work.[11] An AME congregation was organized in Cairo in 1863 to aid the contraband community there, attracting a number of Northern church members willing to help, including John Bird.[12] Although he did not follow his stepfather into the ministry, Bird had been immersed in AME culture and values all his life, and he stayed involved with the city's congregation as long as he was there. His mission, however, was consistently more overtly secular and political in nature than that of the church.

As will be seen in the following chapters, Bird's impact on Cairo, Springfield, and the state of Illinois as a whole between the 1860s and the 1890s was profound. His leadership qualities were recognized from the time he first began making extended visits to Cairo in 1864, well before he settled there in

1869. He quickly became the primary voice representing the city's African American community and shaped numerous aspects of its development. Most critically, he established, along with William T. Scott, John Gladney, and others, the largest, most powerful, and most durable civil rights organization in the city. This organization was not centered around Cairo's African American churches, which during the postwar era were hopelessly divided and antagonistic toward each other. Rather, Bird and his partners framed their vision of an active social movement around a more secular concept—the African American Republican clubs. By distinguishing themselves from the religious organizations and focusing the clubs on the goals of voting rights, education, job development, legal equality, and similar issues, they were able to develop a political organization that could unify the community in a way that the churches were unable to do. Since African Americans in Cairo constituted over 60 percent of the Republican vote, they were able to form a united Black caucus that could pressure their White colleagues to recognize the needs of the Black community in a way that was rarely the case anywhere else in Illinois or in most of the other northern states. Thus in southern Illinois, one of the most stridently anti-Black regions in the entire North, John Bird helped usher in a period of expanded civil rights for Cairo's African American community that was exceptional, leading to the early appearance of a Black public school (though segregated) that came to be run by a well-qualified Black principal and Black teachers; numerous African American elected officials in the city and county government over a period of nearly forty years; city jobs and business contracts; and the integration of most public businesses within the city.[13]

By 1870, when African Americans won the right to vote, Bird had already become the leading Black Republican in southern Illinois and was able to help focus the strong voting power of Cairo's African American community to make the Republicans competitive with the Democrats in the city. In 1873, he stunningly became not only the first African American to be elected to a political office in southern Illinois but also the first elected Black judge in the state, setting a profoundly influential precedent in Cairo that inspired two generations of Black office holders. His eloquent oratorical ability dazzled both African Americans and Whites with his considerable control of U.S. history, current affairs, literature, and law, presented with a powerful and dramatic flair. His ability to inspire and (usually) unite the Black community, while also working well with White people, led to his emergence as the most popular Black campaigner for the Republicans in southern Illinois, and he became increasingly well known across the state for his ability to produce electoral results for the party. Between the mid-1870s and the late 1890s, he also became a major statewide figure in the struggle for civil rights as part of the leadership of the Illinois African American convention movement, where his knowledge, eloquence, and writing ability regularly got him placed on the committees assigned to produce the published addresses and resolutions that articulated the issues of most concern to the state's Black communities. When he moved from Cairo to Springfield, Illinois, in 1887, he joined young Sheadrick B. Turner on the fledgling newspaper the *State Capital* as coeditor and then editor, and during the first three years of its existence, he helped develop it into what many contemporaries considered the most influential African American newspaper in the Midwest.[14]

Bird's list of achievements continues: he was the first African American appointed a delegate to a regional political convention (1870) and one of the first to be a delegate to the Illinois state Republican convention (1874). His prominence in the party led Governor John Beveridge to appoint him to the Board of Trustees at IIU (later the University of Illinois), the first Black appointee to an honorific state position and probably the first Black board member of a predominantly White institution of higher education in the entire North. While his 1873 victory in the election for police magistrate was largely possible because three White candidates split the city's White vote, in 1877 he ran for reelection against a single White candidate and still won. In 1879, he was reappointed to the board of IIU, an indication of the regard in which he was held at that institution. He was the first appointee to a federal position with the Cairo post office in 1879 and in 1881 won another election, this time for justice of the peace. However, these successes also took a heavy toll on him, as he continually faced horrific racist backlash from White supremacists across the state. Surviving White newspaper accounts provide some hints at the amount of fury that arose against him at each major step of his career, but the unrecorded reality of the racist pressures on a successful African American during this period was certainly much worse than the newspapers document.

Throughout his public career, Bird was widely admired for his integrity by Republicans and many Democrats. The code of conduct embedded within the Black middle-class ideology imposed a strong obligation on any accomplished man to act as a role model for other African Americans.[15] Bird appears to have pushed himself to be such a model. He donated vast amounts of his time to the causes he believed were important (to the detriment of his family life), and he campaigned for the Republicans across the state and sometimes in Indiana, Kentucky, and Missouri, in election after election, usually without financial compensation. He seems to have been sensitive to the impression some in the Black community had that African American politicians often were more interested in gaining lucrative positions for themselves than they were in the welfare of their fellow citizens. Thus, when push came to shove in the halls of Republican state politics, Bird appears to have refused in several cases in the 1870s to press his own candidacy for a state position in any context in which it might appear that he was compromising the honorableness of his intentions.

Most of Bird's political ideas in the postwar period, as far as they can be reconstructed through his preserved speeches, published letters, and convention work, focused on long-standing equal rights issues that had concerned the African American community in the North since antebellum times—education, voting rights, job and training opportunities, home and property ownership, African American co-ops, emigration, and others. However, the dramatically changed circumstances following the Civil War had transformed the political landscape of the country and allowed African Americans to proceed with a different, more aggressive approach toward civil rights. New Black communities of voting citizens could use their numbers to press for substantive change, and their Black leaders could enter the political arena in a way that had been impossible before the war.

Bird's public political activities and persona seem to conform largely to the ideas expressed by members of the activist side of the AME leadership but accompanied by new adaptations brought on by the dramatically changed circumstances. He strongly believed in the power of rational argumentation and legal action to bring about change at the local, state, and national levels and to disarm White intransigence. He also believed that the only practical path toward gaining a secure state and national legal foundation for African American civil and political rights was through an alliance with the Republican Party, the party that in the Civil War and Reconstruction had shown its support for basic African American causes. He was able to forge cordial associations with a number of the White Radical Republicans in Illinois during the 1860s and 1870s by using his personal charisma, education, and what Karyn Lacy, in her study of contemporary Black upper-middle-class mores in the Washington, D.C., area, called a "tool kit" of behaviors that helped blur the class and color distinctions between them and himself.[16] His goal was to solidify that alliance and protect it from enemies both outside and inside the party. As he gained status within the party, he was able to put increasing pressure on the more conservative Republican elements by encouraging a certain level of local community agitation in the form of strategic rallies, community-wide meetings, and public lectures while also taking on an increasing role in regional or statewide African American conventions to help publicize for a wider audience the issues of acute interest to the Black citizenry. On a few occasions, Bird's disagreements with the Republican establishment escalated into serious conflicts which eventually damaged his standing in the party (see especially the events recounted in chapter 5), but Bird never abandoned his support for it. His political tone was neither quietly accommodationist nor aggressively confrontational, placing him toward the middle of the spectrum— more aggressive than such contemporaries as P. B. S. Pinchback of Louisiana, James H. Magee of Illinois, or Booker T. Washington, but usually less confrontational than his colleagues William T. Scott of Cairo, John G. Jones, or Ida B. Wells-Barnett, both of Chicago. As the Republican Party moved farther away from its support of civil rights, and as movements such as Booker T. Washington's accommodationist ideology gained steam in the 1890s, Bird, like T. Thomas Fortune, W. E. B. Du Bois, and Wells-Barnett, remained steadfast in his insistence that African Americans must remain politically engaged and willing to push for the attainment of equality in America and that higher education was also critical for Black advancement. But for all his dedication to the Republican cause, the Illinois party leadership from the late 1870s onward increasingly failed both him and the African American community.

John Bird spent his adult life essentially in two Illinois cities, Cairo (1864–86) and Springfield (1887–1912). His most profound impact on Illinois politics took place during his years in Cairo, which are the focus of chapters 2 through 6. However, he continued to have a considerable influence during his residence in Springfield, which is documented in chapter 7. During the 1860s and 1870s, Bird focused on building Cairo's Black Republican infrastructure as a means for improving the lives of that community, as well as creating an active network of African American Republican enclaves throughout southern Illinois. Following his confrontations with the party leadership in 1878–80, however, he lost much of his status within the internal party structure and began to explore other ways to influence the Republican agenda. During the 1880s and 1890s he moved in two different directions: (1) he continued and increased his involvement in the leadership of the state Black convention movement, and (2) he took on the editorship of African American newspapers, first in Cairo, then in Springfield. In both of these undertakings, he continually expressed his dedication to the Republican Party while unceasingly urging it not to abandon its former support for the Black cause. As was the case throughout the country, the African American community was unable to contain the return of White supremacist ideology to the political fore in Illinois, in spite of a few successful battles during this period. Bird and his colleagues watched as most of their achievements in civil rights were overturned at the state and national levels, reaching a low point in 1908, when a vicious White attack on the Black population of Springfield destroyed much of the African American business district of the city.

TO DATE, LITTLE scholarship on the nineteenth-century African American communities in either Cairo or Springfield has been published. Early general histories of Cairo by John Lansden and Herman Lantz largely ignored its Black inhabitants, thus providing significantly defective assessments of the period with which we deal.[17] The first serious attempt to study the Cairo community was produced by Joanne Wheeler in a 1982 article in which she analyzed census data and newspaper accounts to conclude that Cairo's Black community had been unusually successful in creating a strong political and social presence in the city, unlike other towns in Illinois and the other borderland states. This study was followed by Christopher K. Hays's unpublished 1996 dissertation (and 1997 published summary article), which attempted to provide a comprehensive social and cultural history of the city from its beginnings until 1930 and made numerous substantial contributions. Largely ignoring Wheeler's characterization of postwar Cairo as a qualified success for the African American community, Hays focused very heavily on the very real struggles Black citizens endured in the postbellum era, thus creating a darker picture of life in Cairo. Seeking to make Cairo a type-site for understanding other border towns along the Ohio, he ignored most of the elements that actually made Cairo unique. He dealt extensively with the chronic labor problems for African Americans in the city but spent little space discussing the community's political organization and presented a seriously distorted view of the history of Black religion and education in Cairo. Bruce Mouser was the first scholar extensively to examine the political landscape of Cairo's Black community in his 2014 biography of William T. Scott, one of Bird's Cairo colleagues, but as his focus was on a person whose relationship with the Republican Party was always problematic, Mouser's portrayal of the political situation was skewed, and his discussion of Bird, while more extensive than any earlier study, was still fragmentary and superficial. Kerry Pimblott's excellent 2017 analysis of the role of Cairo's Black churches in the extraordinary civil rights struggles in the city during the post–World War II era included a brief but insightful study of the earlier history of the city. That same year, Alonzo Ward completed a dissertation on African American labor in Illinois before 1910 that placed the story of Cairo's workers into the larger state context.[18] Some of these scholars recognized aspects of the political and social success of the post–Civil War Black community, but none of them sought to determine the actual means by which this extraordinary situation became a reality. They failed to recognize that the community's potential for creating genuine political and social change was channeled, or framed, primarily by Bird, Scott, and Gladney, into the Black Republican bloc of the city and that this organization was Cairo's main locus of civil rights activism during the three or so decades after the war. A key reason why this central element of the story of Cairo's African American community has been missed, of course, has been the fact that Bird, the primary architect of this extraordinary achievement, has until now remained virtually invisible.

This book has three primary goals. The central one is to reconstruct for the first time the complex story of John Bird's life and extraordinary career. This is important because the rediscovery of Bird's achievements fills a significant lacuna in our understanding of the African American story in nineteenth-century Illinois. Secondly, because it is now possible to place Bird's work into its larger political and social context, the book presents a substantial reevaluation of the previous understandings of Cairo, postwar Illinois's second-largest African American community, examining the process by which it developed the ability to improve its political and social circumstances within a hostile White environment and looking for the first time at the African American community's leadership, including Bird and others, and how that leadership came to impact not just Cairo and southern Illinois but eventually the entire state of Illinois. In order to do this, I also evaluate the activities of several of Bird's colleagues in Cairo, in Springfield, and across the state, and I examine the community as a whole because while an individual can significantly influence a community, it is the community itself that creates the change. Finally, I hope this book will draw more attention to the significant impact that the Black communities and leaders in southern and central Illinois had on the state as a whole during the last third of the nineteenth century and thus extend our historical gaze to the wider experience of African Americans beyond the better-documented region of the city of Chicago.

SOURCES FOR RECONSTRUCTING John Bird's life are substantial but are limited primarily to contemporary published materials. No personal papers survive, and he published little himself. He wrote no books but did compose a number of informative letters for the *Christian Recorder*, the newspaper of the AME Church, and wrote a few to other papers as well. In addition, newspapers published the texts or detailed summaries of some of his major speeches, and the printed proceedings of the state and national "colored conventions" in which he took part contain resolutions he wrote and convention addresses in which he undoubtedly had the primary creative hand. Finally, a few unpublished letters he sent to various governors of Illinois, as well as letters written by others on his behalf, are preserved in the Illinois State Archives in Springfield and provide considerable insight into certain aspects of his life, as well as his thoughts on many of the issues of the day.

However, the primary sources of information about his wide-ranging activities are the numerous reports about him in newspapers. The most valuable of these are the large number of articles found in the *Cairo Bulletin*, the only Cairo newspaper whose issues survive from the time of its founding in 1868 to 1884. Until 1879, publisher/editor John Oberly wrote the majority of these articles.[19] As a White Democrat, Oberly had every reason to portray Bird, the successful Black Republican, in a partisan, negative light, and he did so for a while (1870–72). But by late 1872 Oberly began to write more positively and more regularly about Bird, despite their political differences, and he took an active interest in his career. Thus the Democratic *Bulletin* proves to be a surprisingly strong source concerning Bird through the 1870s, the time when Bird rose to his greatest political prominence. Oberly's development of more progressive views concerning African Americans in the early 1870s, probably due to his association with Bird, also led him to cover the activities of Cairo's Black community more extensively and positively than was the practice at most Illinois newspapers. For Bird's earlier extended visits to Cairo between 1864 and 1868, we have accounts in the *Christian Recorder* and a number of issues of the *Cairo Daily Democrat*, a paper that Oberly had edited from 1865 to 1868, before he established the *Bulletin*. The *Democrat* was a harshly anti-Black newspaper, and its intensely racist coverage of Cairo's African American community often damages its value as a source.

Once Bird moved to Springfield, local sources become less common, although he appeared with some regularity in the two main White Springfield papers, the Republican *Illinois State Journal* and the Democratic *Illinois State Register*. Between the 1870s and 1890s, reports of his activities are found occasionally in the leading Chicago newspapers, as well as in several widely read, quasi-national African American papers, including the *Cleveland Gazette*, the *Washington Bee*, and the *Broad Ax*. Unfortunately, very few African American newspapers published in Illinois between the 1870s and 1890s, which certainly would have covered Bird more extensively, have survived. About fifty issues of the Springfield *State Capital*, with which he was closely connected, still exist from 1891–92, ironically a period when Bird was not on staff (although he appears in them at times). Toward the end of his career, some of his activities are covered in surviving issues of later Springfield African American papers, the *Illinois Record* (1897–99), *Forum* (1906–11), and *Advance Citizen* (1912).

Nineteenth-century newspapers, of course, were not balanced works of history, and their reliability was dependent primarily upon the talents and dispositions of their editors, the intensity of their political slant, their interest in accurate reporting, and what they wanted their readers to be aware of. Even the best newspaper sources provide only a fragmentary view of Bird's extensive activities in politics and in the African American communities of Cairo and Springfield. Thus, even though he often appeared in the *Cairo Bulletin*, it is clear that the paper, under Oberly and his successors, ignored large parts of his work. For example, while a few articles in the *Bulletin* during the 1870s indicate that Bird was the leading force through the decade in the establishment and development of the Cairo public school for African American children, his actual activities in working with the school board and the mayor's office on this issue over these years apparently did not interest Oberly and so were not discussed in the paper. Because of this, detailed information on one of his most significant achievements is actually fairly minimal.

At the same time, one also must evaluate the reliability of reports that newspapers did publish, particularly when they dealt with Black political figures. Many examples of patently false and provocative material about Bird appeared in papers across the state, both Democratic and Republican. However, the *Cairo Bulletin*, during Oberly's editorship in the 1870s, provides a surprising example of a newspaper with a marked level of credibility in its reporting about certain political subjects, including Bird. Oberly, deeply impressed with him, seems to have excluded him in key ways from his standard, highly critical and distorted reporting style on the Republican leadership. While Oberly, for his own political purposes, used the White Republican establishment's reluctance to reward Bird properly for his extraordinary work on behalf of the party to drive a wedge between the Republicans and their Black supporters, it is also clear that his praise of Bird's intelligence, eloquence, and integrity was mostly genuine and in fact sometimes led local and state Democrats to sharply criticize Oberly. Thus, it appears that the *Bulletin*'s generally positive depiction of Bird, coming as it does from an editor who had little or nothing to gain by presenting him that way (as a Republican paper might have done), can be used, with care, as a reasonably helpful source. Oberly's successors at the *Bulletin* from 1879 onward did not possess the same integrity; they ostensibly continued the *Bulletin*'s support of Bird mainly for more cynical partisan purposes.

Information on Bird's private life and family is very spotty, as will be seen in the sporadic nature of their appearance in the following chapters. Standard sources such as census records, city directories, marriage and death certificates, and other documents supplement a few newspaper accounts of his wife and children, as well as his mother. More extensive sources have survived concerning Bird's prominent stepfather, Augustus R. Green. Still, many key aspects of his personal life and experiences remain lost. It seems emblematic of the gaps in our knowledge that, in spite of the hundreds of references to him in all the sources used in this book, not one of them provides the full middle name that his initial, "J.," stood for. Nevertheless, with all these sources, fragmentary as they are, it has been possible to piece together a remarkably substantial biography.

Through my research on Bird, I also became familiar with numerous other remarkable people who lived in Cincinnati, Windsor (Ontario), Cairo, Springfield, Chicago, and elsewhere, who played important roles in Bird's life but like him have also slipped into obscurity. As far as possible within length constraints, I have tried to provide portraits of them and hope that future scholars might someday more fully pull them from the shadows.

Finally, I want to register my frustration over the lack of information in the sources about the many women who played significant roles in Bird's life. His mother Catherine Bird Green, his wife Annie Venerable Bird, her mother Arena Venerable, Fanny Strother, the wife of Rev. Thomas Strother, and Elizabeth Tanner, Annie's closest friend and "sister," all make brief but important appearances here, but they certainly had much larger stories that cannot yet be told.

CHAPTER ONE

"Prepared in Cincinnati, O"

John Bird's Early Days in Ohio and Canada, 1844–1864

J OHN J. BIRD BEGAN his eventful life in January 1844, born to a free middle-class couple who lived in Cincinnati, Ohio, a major metropolitan center that possessed a significant and activist African American community and a strong Black educational system, both private and (by 1849) public. The sources that survive concerning John and his family indicate that it was in this urban environment, with its well-established and vibrant Black cultural institutions, as well as the strong support of his parents, that many key aspects of young John's personality and character began to develop. By the time he and his family moved away from Cincinnati in 1855, the boy had already been immersed into the spiritual and ideological milieu that would profoundly influence his later worldview, his social, educational, and political thought, and his intense call toward public service. All of this would be supplemented by his experiences as a teenager in Zanesville, Ohio, and Windsor, Ontario (1855–64), through which much of his basic persona became solidified. Thus, the overall trajectory of his life, as we will follow it in this book, had already essentially been formed in his youth.

John Bird's Childhood and Education
in Cincinnati, 1844–1855

In the early 1840s, Cincinnati, Ohio, was a booming, bustling commercial center on the rise. Located on the northern bank of the Ohio River about halfway between its source at Pittsburgh and its mouth at Cairo, Illinois, it had emerged in the 1830s as the first major city in the Midwest, growing into a key port for hundreds of steamboats that moved goods and people up and down the river. With a population of 46,338 in 1840, it was the sixth-largest city in the United States. By 1850, the population had mushroomed to 115,435.[1] It was an important center for shipbuilding and pork processing, boasting famous breweries and distilleries, and producing vast amounts of furniture and shoes. It styled itself in those days as the "Queen City of the West," and indeed it was.[2] During the 1840s, Cincinnati also became a great city of immigrants. Thousands of German and Irish families poured into the city, drawn to America by the unrest in the German states and the potato famine in Ireland. By 1850, some thirty thousand Germans and fourteen thousand Irish were permanent residents there.[3]

In addition, Cincinnati was a border city. The small towns of Newport and Covington, Kentucky, sat on the southern bank of the Ohio directly across from the busy port. This border was considerably more significant than just a boundary between two states. Ohio was a free state, and Kentucky was part of the slaveholding South. This proximity brought the issues of race and enslavement to the surface in Cincinnati in a way that did not often occur elsewhere in the North. The city had close economic and cultural ties with the South, as the southern states were major trading partners with the businesses in Cincinnati, and many citizens had deep family ties in the slaveholding states.[4]

Cincinnati also had a substantial African American community. It did not constitute a large percentage of the population—about 5 percent in 1840 and only about 3 percent by 1850—but in raw numbers, it was one of the largest Black settlements in the North. The 1840 census counted 2,258 African Americans, a number that increased to 3,172 by 1850.[5] About 72 percent of Cincinnati's Black population in 1850 had migrated there from the South, mostly from Kentucky and Virginia. A majority of them (about 54 percent) were mixed race and either had been freed outright by their slaveowner/fathers or had been able to buy their own freedom.[6]

It seems clear that African Americans saw Cincinnati as a place of opportunity, but they had no illusions about their status there. Although Cincinnati was in the "free" state of Ohio, that fact did not mean that the city or the state were hospitable toward their African American residents. In fact, conditions there were generally quite hostile. The state itself had passed a series of brutal "Black Laws" in the early 1800s that excluded African Americans from voting, sitting on a jury, testifying in court against a White person, allowing their children to attend public schools, joining the state militia, being treated in state hospitals or other medical facilities, or participating in any types of state welfare. White businesses had the right to deny service to African Americans, and most did. Homes were searched without warrant, and violence against individuals was rarely investigated by the police. Three times, in 1829, 1836, and 1841, White rioters had attacked their Black neighbors, leaving death and destruction in their wake. But even under these terrible circumstances, Cincinnati was a better place to live than the South, and African Americans continued to arrive there, satisfied to take their chances.[7]

As Cincinnati in the 1840s and 1850s did not yet have segregated neighborhoods, African Americans settled all across the city. Being such a small minority, they were always located in neighborhoods that were dominated by White people. However, they did tend to cluster themselves together in small groups of families within the larger neighborhoods. The East End of the city, a crowded, busy mixture of residences, factories, churches, and other public buildings, contained the largest number of Black residents, especially in the First and Ninth Wards. The blocks between Fourth and Eighth Streets south and north and Sycamore Street and the Erie Canal west and east were the location of the institutional and cultural center of Black Cincinnati, where most of the African American churches and schools were situated. In this neighborhood, the city's Black community could gather together and join forces to fight for their collective well-being.[8]

African Americans were sharply restricted in the jobs they could hold in most of the North, including Cincinnati. Factory owners refused to give higher-level positions to Black workers, no matter what their potential might be. The trade associations actively opposed the hiring of African Americans for any positions other than those that were unskilled, and they refused to train Black men in any of the trades. About 85 percent of Cincinnati's Black workers were stuck in unskilled or minimally skilled jobs. However, the other 15 percent were employed in such skilled or semiskilled positions as barbers, carpenters, bricklayers, gardeners, stewards, and cooks.[9]

The size and success of the African American community brought forth a vibrant culture of social activism in Cincinnati that gained considerable attention across the nation. From the 1820s, the community fought against the Black Laws, spoke out for the right to public education and against discrimination in public spaces, and from early on, many were involved in the Underground Railroad. Cincinnati's location on the border with Kentucky made it one of the primary destinations for those escaping enslavement, and its growing African American population, along with a strong White abolitionist network, made it one of the most active centers of the Railroad in the country. In the 1840s, several churches, most notably the Bethel AME Church and the Baker Street (or Union) Baptist Church, were heavily engaged in these activities, at great peril to individuals and to the institutions themselves. Working with the Railroad was dangerous for both Black and White members—those caught aiding fugitive slaves found their lives, families, homes, and businesses in jeopardy. The peril was more marked for African Americans because of their lack of virtually any legal protection when accused. While authorities were usually reluctant to invade the homes of suspected White members of the Railroad without clear evidence, Black homes and vehicles could be searched without any restrictions.[10]

It was into this extraordinary city and community that a young African American couple, John and Catherine Bird, arrived sometime between 1841 and 1843. John had been born about 1818 in Hardin County, Kentucky, south of Louisville, and was a free man in Ohio. Catherine Freeman, born in Lynchburg, Virginia, on August 10, 1820, was also legally free. The two had married in Montgomery County, Ohio (the Dayton area), on June 24, 1841 and moved to Cincinnati before the birth of their first child, John J., on January 30, 1844. The 1850 U.S. Census and other sources provide some key information about the Bird family. In that year, the three were living on the east side of the city in the Ninth Ward, in a house at 218 Broadway, one of the ward's main north-south streets. The neighborhood was one of the poorer in town, but it was also in the cultural center of the African American community. The house, probably a simple frame building, was located on the east side of Broadway, between New and Seventh Streets. The census indicates that Bird owned the house, which was valued at $500, typical of such a home. Besides the family, another young couple lived at the address—they probably rented a room from the Birds. Racially, the census identified John as Black and Catherine and John J. as mulatto. Professionally, Bird was one of the fortunate 15 percent of Cincinnati's Black residents who had a good semiskilled position—he was employed on a steamboat as a steward, a relatively well-paying and prestigious job within the Black community. However, like all jobs on steamboats during that era, it was a dangerous one, and one that probably kept Bird away from home for long periods of time.[11] Sometime in 1851 or 1852, John and Catherine also had a daughter, but her name has not survived.[12]

Although we do not have specific information about John J.'s education during his eleven years in Cincinnati, a few things can be inferred from the general situation involving African American schools in the city and from certain aspects of his later views on education. Most Black children who could attend school began about the age of six, and thus it seems likely, since the Birds appear to have been relatively secure financially, that John would have begun in 1849 or 1850. The school year of 1849–50 represented a milestone for Black education in Cincinnati. Until that year, African American children were excluded from Cincinnati's public schools, and those who received an education did so in private schools, some run by sympathetic White abolitionists and others organized and taught by African Americans, and often related to church congregations. A high school for Black students was established in 1844, financed by Rev. Hiram S. Gilmore, a White philanthropist who constructed a five-roomed building for the school and hired its teachers. It lasted for only five years, but it trained some of Cincinnati's key African American leaders of the 1850s and 1860s. These schools sometimes suffered attacks by Whites who virulently opposed the idea of education for Black children.[13]

The struggle for access to the public schools finally succeeded in 1849 when the legislature passed a law requiring school districts to provide separate public education for African Americans and establishing a separate Black board to oversee the schools, its members to be elected by the African American men of the community.[14] The law was a major achievement for the African American community and their White allies who had agitated for public schooling for over two decades. In spite of serious opposition from the Cincinnati city leadership, including the withholding of funds and the provision of inadequate buildings, the schools opened in 1849 under a Black board led by John I. Gaines and Peter H. Clark.[15] The board continually demanded increased support, but in 1853, the White leadership responded by removing the board, placing the Black schools under the White school board and beginning to replace Black educators with White teachers. This situation lasted for two years, but in the face of constant agitation, the state legislature finally returned control of the schools to a Black-run board.[16]

Young John J. likely received much of his early education in the new public schools. During several of these years, he would have studied under African American teachers, who served as role models for him. The community activism that pressed for school improvements during these combative years likely informed and affected how he viewed education later in his life, when he became involved in the formation of a Black public school in Cairo in the 1860s and 1870s. There he would fight for a segregated school where students were taught in an adequate building by accredited African Americans under the supervision of an African American principal. Bird, like many African Americans, initially was skeptical of integrated schools because he did not trust the White teachers or administrators in them. Although he would eventually change his mind and support integration, for several years he saw the organization of Cincinnati's segregated Black schools under Black control as the preferred model (see chapter 3).

Young John Bird and His Stepfather, Augustus Green

Sometime during 1853, disaster struck the family when it appears that the elder John died at the age of thirty-five, leaving Catherine alone with two young children.[17] About a year later, on October 26, 1854, Catherine married the Rev. Augustus Richardson Green, who from 1852 to 1855 was pastor of the Allen Chapel African Methodist Episcopal Church, the primary AME congregation in Cincinnati.[18] Augustus was a recent widower in his early fifties, and thus more than twenty years older than Catherine.[19] He and his first wife, Rebecca, had had at least five children, four of whom were still at home, so John and his young sister became part of a family with three new stepbrothers and one stepsister, all close to John's age.[20] Reverend Green became the most profoundly formative figure in Bird's young life, and it is impossible to understand the trajectory of John's career and the growth of his political and social thought without a brief look at Green's remarkable life.

In the 1850s when he married Catherine, Green was a highly regarded minister of the AME Church, a powerful orator, a successful evangelist, active in the politics of the church and in the Underground Railroad, and beloved by his congregations. He had become an itinerant minister with the AME Church in the late 1820s or early 1830s and by the 1840s was both a popular preacher and an up-and-coming leader within the administration of the denomination, ordained as an elder in 1842.[21] At the 1844 General Conference of the church held in Pittsburgh, his strong reputation as an educated and thoughtful person led to his appointment to a five-man committee assigned to make substantial revisions to the AME Church's general charter, *The Doctrines and Discipline of the African Methodist Episcopal Church.*[22]

In 1846, he was named pastor of the Allen Chapel's predecessor in Cincinnati, the Bethel AME Church, already long known for its abolitionist activities, and he served there until 1848. His success at Bethel led to substantial growth in the church's membership, which in turn created the necessity of constructing a new, larger building. Green oversaw the legal incorporation of the congregation and the purchase of the land for the construction of Allen Chapel.[23]

In 1848, he left Cincinnati when the national AME leadership called upon him to become the founding editor of the denomination's first official newspaper, the *Christian Herald*, in Pittsburgh. He performed that duty until 1852. Green developed an enduring belief in the power of the African American press to fight for civil rights and to spread knowledge to Black communities across the nation. "What," he wrote, "in the time of a people's struggle for liberty, is the most dreaded by despots? It is the Press—this mighty engine by which the truth can be so rapidly propagated, and countless numbers of enlightened minds are from the deep slumbers of ignorance martialed to assert the truth of the doctrine that, 'wisdom is power.'"[24] Green would put that faith into practice in a series of newspapers he edited in the 1850s and 1860s. In 1852, the *Herald* was moved to Philadelphia and renamed the *Christian Recorder*, which is still published today.[25] At that point, he returned to Cincinnati and became pastor of the recently completed Allen Chapel.

Although Green certainly had been involved with the Underground Railroad for years, our only documented information about his extensive participation in it dates to his ministry at Allen Chapel, between 1852 and 1855.[26] Levi Coffin, the famed abolitionist who led the White network of the Underground Railroad in Cincinnati from 1847 until the end of the Civil War, praised Green's actions in his 1878 memoir. In the book, he recounted two stories that concerned collaborations between himself and Green, depicting the latter as a leader who hid escaped refugees in his home and got them safely out of Cincinnati. These stories provide a dramatic glimpse into the types of humanitarian (and dangerous) activities in which Green and his family (including John) were involved during the prewar years.[27] This early firsthand experience with refugees from the South undoubtedly played a formative role in John's interest in political activism and concern for refugees from enslavement.

Green also became involved in the Black emigrationist movement that particularly emerged following the passage of the Fugitive Slave Law of 1850.

It seems likely that soon after he arrived in Pittsburgh in 1848, he met Martin R. Delany, who would become the leading voice of the movement in the 1850s and would have a profound influence on Green. Delany had been the editor of a Pittsburgh newspaper, the *Mystery*, between 1843 and 1847, when he left it to coedit the famed paper the *North Star*, with Frederick Douglass in Rochester, New York. Shortly thereafter, the *Mystery* had closed, and the AME Church had bought its press to print the *Christian Herald*.[28]

In 1852, Delany published an important book on emigration. He had long despaired that African Americans could ever gain freedom or civil rights in the United States and argued that Black people who were able to do so, whether free or fleeing enslavement, should leave the country and emigrate to Central or South America, where the majority of the population was non-White and thus not prejudiced against people of African descent. He eliminated Canada as an abode for Black emigrants because he was certain that the United States would eventually annex the country.[29] Green was as pessimistic as Delany about the prospects for African Americans in the United States and was increasingly convinced that no African Americans were safe from slaveholders. Thus he also believed that they should leave the country, but he disagreed with Delany about the suitability of Canada. In a pamphlet he published in 1853, perhaps in part as a response to Delany's book, he insisted that Canada was indeed the best place for U.S. Black emigrants to settle. Arguing that land ownership was central to the long-term financial and spiritual well-being of African Americans, he pointed out that the cost of land in Canada was still affordable and that African Americans could purchase property without legal problems there. He strongly disagreed with Delany's fear that Canada would soon become part of the United States and provided arguments opposing that notion. He noted that Canada also offered the opportunity to train and work in professions that were closed to Black men in the United States and that Canada granted the right to vote to all its (male) citizens.[30]

Emigrationist ideology was highly controversial in the northern African American community and was vehemently opposed by most of its leadership, including such notables as Frederick Douglass, John Mercer Langston, and George B. Vashon.[31] In July 1853, Douglass and his allies held a Colored National Convention in Rochester, New York, in which the assembled members called upon White Americans to afford African Americans the civil and political rights that had been granted to themselves. In spite of the convention's opposition to emigrationism, Green decided to participate, hoping to place emigration on the agenda. But he was relegated to a minor role in the convention and was unable to convince the delegates to consider the issue.[32]

After the Rochester convention, Delany, Green, Rev. William Webb of Pittsburgh, and others organized the National Emigration Convention of Colored People held in Cleveland in August 1854 to bring national attention more directly to their cause.[33] Delany was the guiding force of the convention, but Green played a significant role as well, serving on the Credentials, Nominations, and Business Committees. Delany, Green, and Webb also composed the constitution for the newly founded National Board of Commissioners, and they were voted onto the board.[34] In addition, Green was on the committee that produced the most significant document of the convention, "Political Destiny of the Colored People on the American Continent," a powerful expansion of Delany's arguments for encouraging African Americans to emigrate to Central or South America. The document was largely Delany's, but Green and his allies were able to soften Delany's stance on Canada. The report still argued that Canada would inevitably become part of the United States, but unlike Delany's previous publications, it encouraged African Americans to move to Canada West (Ontario), at least as a temporary measure, and to purchase as much land there as they could—Green's argument in his 1853 pamphlet.[35]

The National Emigration Convention of 1854 was a landmark event. It created a long-lasting organization, the National Board of Commissioners, with Delany as its president, that would produce some of the most comprehensive information about the status of African Americans across the United States and would sponsor expeditions to the western islands, Central America, and Africa in search of places to establish new homelands for those ready to emigrate.[36] It opened a much wider debate over the issue and represented a genuine alternative to the path taken by most of the African American leaders up to that time. Green continued to be involved with Delany and the board at least into 1857 and probably longer.[37]

While Green was the pastor of Allen Chapel in Cincinnati, he also established close contacts with pro-emigrationist elements of the Black leadership in Canada West, including the Shadd family, who ran the important Canadian newspaper the *Provincial Freeman*. By 1854, he was the local agent for that paper in Cincinnati, representing it and its ideas in the city and surrounding areas.[38] Toward the end of 1854, Green and the Allen Chapel hosted the extraordinary Mary Ann Shadd, publishing agent and primary public representative of the paper, for a series of three lectures in favor of emigration to Canada, along with a proponent for colonization in Liberia. At the end of three days of debate, the attendees voted to endorse Shadd's position by a wide margin.[39]

The Moves to Zanesville and Windsor, 1855–1864

John's life changed dramatically when in the early fall of 1855, Green was assigned to a new pastorate at Zanesville, Ohio, about 160 miles northeast of Cincinnati. Zanesville was a considerably smaller town, but it had a solid African American population and a significant body of White New England abolitionists.[40] This, along with the city's location on the National Highway and some key rail lines, had made Zanesville another important stop on the Underground Railroad.[41] It is likely that Green and his family continued their deep involvement with that network. In 1856, he established a short-lived newspaper called the *Christian Intelligencer*, which was "devoted to Religion, Anti-slavery, Temperance, Literature, Agriculture, Emigration, Science and Mechanism."[42] The family's departure from Cincinnati probably represented the end of John Bird's formal education, at about the fifth- or sixth-grade level. While Zanesville had begun supporting segregated public primary schooling for African American students in 1853, the city did not provide any secondary classes until the 1870s.[43] Concerning Bird's education, his brief biography published in the *University of Illinois Alumni Record (ARUI)* only states, "Prepared in Cincinnati, O."[44] But Reverend Green had the deep conviction that education was an absolute necessity for African Americans to take their place as citizens in the United States or in Canada, and it seems that he and Catherine took their sons under their wings and educated them themselves through the rest of the 1850s and into the early 1860s.

Green's interest in Canada persisted during the years the family lived in Zanesville, and as early as 1856 he was already expressing an intention to move there.[45] In that year, the AME Church in Canada officially organized itself as a separate legal entity from its parent in the United States and became the British Methodist Episcopal (BME) Church. Green continued his work in Zanesville until December 1859, when he officially gave up his position in the AME Church and moved the family—his four children, James, Elizabeth,

The *True Royalist*, June 21, 1861, 1. Augustus Green edited this
newspaper in Windsor, Canada West (Ontario), and his stepson John
Bird worked on it as a printer, his first experience working on a newspaper.
INK-ODW Newspaper Collection: http://ink.ourontario.ca/viewer
/cecil/focus/ink/newspapers/tr/ree11/00017-xo-yo-zi-ro-o-o.

William, and Richard (his oldest son Alfred M. was already an adult); his
mother, Charity; Catherine, John, and his sister; and a brand new baby son
who belonged to Augustus and Catherine—to Windsor, Canada West, across
the river from Detroit, Michigan, where he became the pastor of a BME congregation.[46] By April 1860, he had started up a weekly newspaper, the *True
Royalist and Weekly Intelligencer*, with his teenage sons James and John, and
(by 1861) William and Richard working as printers.[47] The last surviving issue
of the paper was printed on June 21, 1861, and it seems likely that it did not
last much beyond that date.[48]

　　The move to Canada proved to be traumatic for the Green family. Shortly
after they arrived, John's eight-year-old sister developed what the census calls
"putrid sore throat," probably diphtheria, and died. Then Augustus and

Catherine's infant son succumbed to whooping cough at the age of eight months.[49] As if this weren't heartache enough, in April 1860, Green's seventeen-year-old daughter, Elizabeth, was sexually assaulted. The perpetrator, an African American man, was arrested, but at the trial he insisted that she had consented to his advances, and the court sided with him, setting him free.[50] In August, James, the eldest son, and another of Elizabeth's brothers found her assailant and severely beat him. The two boys were arrested and held for trial, which took place in early October. James was convicted of assault with intent to kill and given a three-year sentence in the penitentiary, while his brother, not named in the news reports (but possibly John, since he was the next oldest), was released because of his age. Many in the African American community thought that James's sentence was too harsh under the circumstances, and in February 1861, John Brown, Jr., son of the famous abolitionist, circulated a petition seeking a pardon for the lad.[51] It is not known whether the petition was successful, but James was still not living at home when the 1861 Canadian census was taken later that year.[52]

In addition to these tragedies, Reverend Green, shortly after arriving in Windsor, had a falling out with Willis Nazrey, the presiding bishop of the BME Church, over the validity of Nazrey's authority within the church. Nazrey had retained his bishop's status in the AME Church, and this was seen by many, including Green, as a problem. The *Discipline* of the AME Church stated that a bishop could not hold any position within another denomination, and now that the BME was legally separate from the AME, Green argued that Nazrey could not be a bishop in both churches. In 1860, Nazrey briefly resigned from the BME to retain his role in the AME but then changed his mind and insisted that he could maintain his authority in both churches. Green and others resisted this idea and argued that Nazrey was not a legitimate bishop in Canada. Green, with his long career in the AME, became the leader of the anti-Nazrey movement. The controversy escalated into a schism in the BME. The AME leadership supported Nazrey in this, and Green's refusal to back down led to his ouster from the BME Church in May 1861. In response, Green established a rival BME denomination in Canada (the British Methodist Episcopal Church of British North America) in July of that year and was elected as its bishop. But Nazrey's support within the AME remained strong, and Green's group was never recognized by the American denomination's leadership, leaving them as outcasts. For Augustus Green, this was a disaster—estranged from the beloved church he had served with honor for some thirty years. But his sense of justice, along with his refusal to compromise, kept him from seeking a rapprochement for seven years. In 1868, he proposed to merge his congregations into the AME (not with the official BME), but the proposal was rejected. At that point, he kept his tiny denomination going (now as the Independent Methodist Episcopal Church) for another nine years before he finally surrendered and dissolved it in 1876.[53]

Thus John spent his late teenage years during a tumultuous period, not only because of the family tragedies and the Civil War raging in the United States but also because of the religious battle that pitted his stepfather against the power of the denomination to which he had dedicated most of his life. He saw firsthand the tremendous cost of maintaining an uncompromising stance toward powerful institutions. While John appears to have supported his father in this controversy (he wrote a letter in 1867 to the *Christian Recorder* defending Green's church), it is probable that his father's disastrous experience in the BME influenced his decision not to enter the ministry.[54] It also likely influenced his decision to moderate his use of confrontation in seeking the goals of equal rights and social justice.

In spite of these disasters, not everything was gloom and doom for John in Windsor. Blacks had legal protection and enjoyed the right to vote in Canada, and he watched his stepfather quickly become a political leader in the Black immigrant community of Windsor during the election campaign of 1861, rallying support for Colonel Arthur Rankin for Parliament.[55] Rankin was a supporter of the Republican government in the United States and even attempted to raise a Canadian regiment to serve in the Union army.[56] John also watched Augustus lead the ceremonies for the Windsor and Chatham Black communities' celebration of the anniversary of the emancipation of enslaved people in the British West Indies.[57]

About the same time that the Greens moved to Windsor, several families from Pittsburgh also immigrated into the area, both into Windsor and into Chatham, a town about fifty miles east.[58] Among those who settled in Windsor was the Venerable family (also spelled Venable, probably reflecting the name's pronunciation). Samuel Venerable and his wife, Arena, arrived in Canada with four children—Annie, age twenty (in the 1861 census), John, fourteen, Samuel A., twelve, and Dennis, six.[59] They had lived in Pittsburgh since at least 1841 and probably had known Augustus during his years living there (1848–52).[60] Samuel and Arena had been delegates to the National Emigration Convention of 1854, and Samuel had been appointed to the Board of

Commissioners established at the conference, as Green had.[61] Although his occupation was listed in the 1850 U.S. Census simply as laborer, he owned their home in Pittsburgh, valued at $600. They joined Green's BME congregation and became loyal supporters when he broke with the bishop in 1861. Samuel, in his late forties, got a job as a sailor on one of the myriad ships steaming through Lake Erie and Lake St. Clair.[62] At least by the early 1870s (likely much earlier), he was also a lay preacher in Green's BME Church.[63] In both census records, Samuel and Arena are listed as illiterate, but, as is often the case with census information, this appears to be mistaken, at least for Arena. Green, in his account of the split with the BME Church, describes a key church meeting in 1861 during which Arena wrote him a note suggesting what he should do at a critical moment, even providing the text of the note.[64] The Venerable family stayed loyal to Green when in 1868 he founded the Independent Methodist Episcopal Church. This closeness to the Green family makes it unsurprising that in 1864 John Bird married Annie Venerable.[65]

Although little documentation survives about John Bird's youth, the family in which he grew up, with its strong roots in the urban Black middle class, provides significant insights into the foundations of his character. It is clear from the preserved records that Augustus Green had a defining impact on John. Green's deep involvement in the struggle for African American rights was critical. John spent years watching his stepfather risk his life in the Underground Railroad, and perhaps John participated himself. John saw Green take courageous stands in the pulpit and in public forums, a trait that John took on himself. Bird's focus on education certainly is related to that of his stepfather, as was the development of his oratorical skills. Green's involvement in the national African American conventions in the 1850s and then in the political life of Windsor, although subordinate to his religious calling, appears to have pulled John most significantly into the life he eventually would lead. Green's dedication to the African American press resonated with John as well. Bird would edit three newspapers himself between 1882 and 1896, making use of the training he received as a teenager at the *True Royalist*. And Green's deep support for the legitimacy of emigration as a potential solution to oppression when there was little hope of progress at home would reverberate with Bird in his thoughts about the Exoduster movement of emigration from the South to the state of Kansas in the late 1870s.

Bird's stepbrothers also entered adulthood under the powerful influence of their father. Augustus's oldest son, Alfred M. Green, born in 1833, became a schoolteacher in Philadelphia and an abolitionist leader who fought against enforcement of the Fugitive Slave Act, actually spending some months in prison for having attempted to rescue Moses Horner, a runaway, from being sent back to his "owner" in 1860. When the Civil War broke out, he became an influential speaker encouraging African Americans to join the Union war effort. One of his early speeches, "Let Us Take Up the Sword," given on April 20, 1861, just after the fall of Fort Sumter, was widely distributed and encouraged many to volunteer. Once the Union army finally began to accept Black soldiers, Green became a recruiter for the famous Fifty-Fourth Massachusetts Colored Infantry and himself joined the 127th U.S. Colored Infantry in August 1864, mustering out at the end of the war as a sergeant-major.[66] After the war, he became a well-regarded AME minister and by 1880 was located at a large church in New Orleans, where he remained for decades as a prominent community leader.[67] He, too, was likely a role model for John. James A. D. Green, the son who spent time in prison in 1860–61, also became a well-regarded minister in the AME Church, and Richard A. Green, two years younger than John, became both a physician and, briefly, the editor and publisher of the *Virginia Star*, in Richmond, Virginia.[68]

CHAPTER TWO

"A Cairoite to Some Extent"

John Bird's Activities in Cairo, Illinois, ca. 1864–1869

THE YEAR 1864 WAS A WATERSHED for John Bird. At twenty years of age, he had spent four years as a Canadian citizen, watching the events of the Civil War unfold to the south. His oldest brother, Alfred, who had never come to live in Windsor, had joined the Union army, and in late 1863–early 1864, his father, Augustus Green, made a tour of the midwestern states to get a sense of what conditions were like for African American refugees and soldiers in the region. During that visit and a subsequent one to Washington, D.C., Augustus became convinced that he and his family were called to aid the formerly enslaved refugees, the "contrabands," who had been gathered into camps along the borders of the war but suffered from great want of food, clothing, shelter, and medical attention. John appears to have agreed with his father, because during the summer he made an extended trip to Cairo, Illinois, to see what he might do to help the large number of refugees who now lived there. This became the first of many such visits over the next four years, during which time, although not a permanent resident of the city, he created for himself a profound leadership role within its Black community. Apparently reluctant to move his family to such a rough, chaotic, and dangerous town (in contrast to Windsor) and a place with a starkly belligerent White population, he nevertheless became a quasi-citizen of Cairo during long stretches each year, helping to create a solid social infrastructure for the city's African Americans well before moving permanently to the city in 1869.

The war and the second half of the 1860s, of course, brought about a series of profound changes for all African Americans in the United States. In the South, emancipation was not a single event that occurred either with the

Emancipation Proclamation or with the defeat of the South but began when increasing numbers of enslaved people, eventually about five hundred thousand, on their own initiatives, fled from their bondage and made their way to freedom by way of the U.S. Army. This is what Du Bois called the "general strike" that crippled the Southern economy and weakened the Confederate war effort. It also represented, as Manning has pointed out, the first time in the history of the country that the federal government, in the form of the U.S. Army, took on a role, although quite tentative, in support of significant numbers of African Americans. The army officially protected the refugees as "free" people, but during the war the government did not have a clear sense of what that "freedom" actually entailed. In "emancipating" them, were they also providing them with any rights of citizenship? This question had not been answered by the end of the war, at which point another 3.5 million people joined their ranks as "freedmen." New questions about rights for African Americans also were asked about the African Americans who already had been "free" in the North and South before the war but who had lived under extremely restrictive laws themselves. For decades, free northern Black people, including many among the small group of middle-class African Americans, had pushed the state and federal governments for equal rights. The end of the war and the abolition of slavery forced the issue, and African Americans now expected change. In the North, the Black leadership began to argue that the valor of the African American troops in the war had shown without doubt that Black people deserved full citizenship and equal rights, and during the second half of the 1860s, that leadership and their allies in the Republican Party pushed through the Thirteenth through Fifteenth Amendments, abolishing slavery, extending citizenship to African Americans, and granting the right of Black men to vote. These amendments, plus the Reconstruction Acts of this period, were revolutionary and appeared to presage a time when Blacks and Whites would live peacefully and equally together.[1]

Those same five years were also the critical period in which the Black inhabitants of Cairo formed themselves into a cohesive community, a process on which John Bird had a dramatic influence. Despite the fact that limited information exists about Bird between 1864 and 1869, it is striking to note that he can already be identified as the primary leader in organizing many basic elements of the community's infrastructure in the city, an infrastructure heavily based on the antebellum Black middle-class ideology. Thus we find him in 1864 already deeply involved in education, while in January 1865 we see him emerge as the leader of Cairo's Black community, delivering a speech sharply denouncing the anti-Black prejudice prevalent in Illinois, and soon afterward joining Henry O. Wagoner, the respected civil rights activist from Chicago, in leading a protest meeting in Cairo to demand that the city's Democratic leaders acknowledge the new legal status of African Americans following the repeal of the Illinois Black Laws. By 1866, he is working with the Reverend Thomas Strother of the AME Church both on education issues and on an interdenominational association for raising funds to establish an African American hospital in Cairo. He is also a cosigner, along with Strother, of the call for a statewide African American convention held in Galesburg that year, the main goal of which was to agitate for voting rights in Illinois and public education for Black students. In 1867, he becomes the president of the Cairo Educational Association's short-lived private free school, and he leads the formation of one of the earliest Illinois lodges of the Prince Hall Masons outside of Chicago, the most significant mutual aid society in African American communities, and becomes its first Worshipful Master.

But perhaps his most significant achievement during the years before the passage of the Fifteenth Amendment was his work within Cairo's Republican Party, as he, William Scott, and John Gladney molded essentially the entire African American community into a unified political organization as the Black majority wing of the city's Republican Party. This organization became the largest and most powerful civil rights institution in Cairo. It was intentionally secular and independent of the city's Black churches, which by 1867 were mired in internal turmoil, and it became the focal point for the community's push toward political, legal, and social rights. After the ratification of the Fifteenth Amendment, this (usually) unified voting bloc was able to make the Republican Party competitive with the Democrats in Cairo and force the White Republican Party members to take their needs and goals seriously. Bird rapidly became the most influential Black Republican in southern Illinois and pushed the party to support a number of political, legal, and social advances for the African American community. Our sources dramatically show him evolve from a mere spectator at party rallies in 1866 to a featured orator in 1869, addressing the faithful alongside a White luminary such as U.S. Representative John A. Logan.

The Green Family and the Civil War

The Greens had lived in Windsor for about a year and a half when the American Civil War began. The outbreak of that conflict dramatically changed the situation for the Canadian immigrants—suddenly the possibility that slavery itself might actually be abolished in the United States seemed real. Even though the federal government refused to characterize the war as a battle against slavery for over a year, most African Americans believed that in the end that must be its result. Large numbers of African Americans immediately volunteered to join the Union army, but the government at first refused to accept Black soldiers. Similarly, many Canadian expatriates who were willing to return to the United States to join the fight were frustrated by the army's policy. It was not until the Emancipation Proclamation went into effect on January 1, 1863, that African Americans were officially allowed to join the armed services, and from that point a steady stream of Black Canadians made their way southward to join the battle. By this time, many of the leaders of the emigrationist movement themselves had changed their minds about the possibility of progress in the United States and were ready to focus on the war effort. This included Martin Delany, the movement's most prominent voice, who was living in Chatham, as well as Augustus Green.[2]

In the latter part of 1863, Augustus and some of his children began to investigate the possibility of returning to the United States to aid both formerly enslaved people who had fled to Union lines and the Black soldiers who were taking part in the war. Letters that Green wrote to the *Christian Recorder* indicate that in late 1863 and early 1864 he made an extended journey toward the "southwestern" part of the United States (Illinois and Missouri) including St. Louis, where he spent time working with both refugees and an African American regiment stationed at the Benton Barracks.[3]

During 1864, friends invited Augustus to come to Washington, D.C., to see firsthand the dire health crisis surrounding the massive number of Black refugees now living in the district and the fact that most of the city's doctors refused to treat African Americans. Overwhelmed by the situation, Green decided that his church had "a full supply of ministers for our work" so that "we gave our entire attention to the practice of medicine."[4] Moving to D.C. in late 1864 with Catherine and their youngest son, Richard, now eighteen, Augustus began, at the age of sixty-three, to study medicine, most likely becoming affiliated with the Contraband Hospital in Washington.[5] Soon

Richard also decided to become a physician. Augustus in one of his writings mentions studying medicine together with Richard in 1866.[6] The 1867 *Washington City Directory* is the first to list Augustus as a practicing physician, while Richard is still identified as a student.[7]

The Town of Cairo, Illinois

In 1864, John was now twenty years old and still living in Windsor, but he became convinced that he, too, should get involved in the refugee crisis. Perhaps he had heard about Cairo from Augustus, who likely visited there during his journey to the region early in the year, or perhaps John had even accompanied his stepfather on that trip and had seen the situation himself. What is certain is that in the early summer of 1864 John Bird made an extended visit to Cairo to see what he could do there. Like Washington, D.C., where Augustus and Catherine moved later that year, Cairo was a town where numerous African American refugees, mostly women, children, and the elderly, had settled, in this case escaping from the war's western front, in search of freedom, safety, and work and in desperate need of assistance. While Augustus turned to medicine and spiritual guidance to help the fugitives, John saw his primary mission in education and in political and legal advocacy.[8]

Cairo was a dramatically different kind of place from any that Bird had lived in before. Although it was a river town like Cincinnati, it was much smaller and considerably more primitive, and it had had virtually no pre–Civil War existence. Its location at the convergence of the Ohio and Mississippi Rivers had suggested to many people that it possessed the potential to become a major transportation hub, and developers had attempted unsuccessfully to create a viable town there twice, in 1818–19 and from 1836 to 1846. The second venture had been heavily dependent on the success of a plan to construct a railroad from Cairo northward through the length of Illinois. This would make Cairo the southern terminus for the transport of goods to and from the north by rail, connecting with ships traveling up and down the Mississippi and the Ohio. By 1840, Cairo had a population of about two thousand, composed mostly of people who worked for the company that had undertaken the town's development. But the railroad did not materialize, and the company and its investors were quickly in financial trouble, leading to the cessation of most commercial activity and the depopulation of the town.[9] Charles Dickens visited Cairo during his trip to America in 1842 as he traveled by steamboat from Pittsburgh to St. Louis. His impression of Cairo was decidedly negative: "A dismal swamp, on which the half-built houses rot away: cleared here and there for the space of a few yards; and teeming, then, with rank, unwholesome vegetation, in whose baleful shade the wretched wanderers who are tempted hither droop, and die, and lay their bones . . . a hotbed of disease, an ugly sepulchre, a grave uncheered by any gleam of promise: a place without one single quality, in earth or air or water, to commend it: such is this dismal Cairo."[10]

The company went bankrupt in 1846, and a new one took over development of the town shortly afterward but did not begin selling residential and commercial lots until December 1853. The Illinois Central Railroad finally was built and began service in late 1855 between Cairo and Chicago, and northwestward to Galena, allowing for significant civic expansion during the second half of the 1850s. It was officially incorporated as a city in February 1857. While in 1850 the population of Cairo had dwindled to a mere 242, by 1860 it had rebounded to 2,188, about the size it briefly had been twenty years before. But there was only a tiny antebellum African American presence in Cairo; the 1860 census listed a mere forty-seven Black residents. The Civil War, however, dramatically changed the town's demographics.[11]

Cairo's prewar culture was strongly influenced by and sympathetic toward the South, which is not surprising, since it was surrounded to the east and west by the slave states of Kentucky and Missouri, and most of its native-born occupants in the 1850s were southerners. The inhabitants of the city overwhelmingly supported the Democratic Party, the pro-slavery, anti-Black party that dominated the central and southern parts of Illinois, as well as the secessionist South. When the war broke out in April 1861, Governor Richard Yates and the military commanders in Washington, D.C. were not certain of the loyalty of southern Illinois and feared that it might attempt to break away from the state and join the Confederacy, handing Cairo, with its strategic importance, to the enemy. On direct orders from the secretary of war, Yates immediately sent newly mustered troops to the town to make sure it stayed in Union hands. From that point onward, Cairo became a key Union military stronghold and supply depot for the western campaign. General Ulysses S. Grant arrived in September 1861 to take command of Fort Defiance, built during the summer just south of town, and from Cairo he began his long quest to secure the Mississippi for the Union.[12] Throughout the war, Cairo was the focal point for troop movements along the Mississippi,

A commercial street in Cairo with Union military barracks
in the distance, c. 1861. Library of Congress, call number:
LOT 14046, no. 04[P7P]; control number: 20116466.

including fresh troops heading south to battle, as well as wounded and released soldiers heading home. In March 1862, the United States Sanitary
Commission founded a Soldiers' Home at Cairo, which over the following
three years hosted nearly two hundred thousand wounded and convalescing
soldiers. Hundreds of thousands of other active troops passed through Cairo
during the course of the war.[13]

The arrival of the military in Cairo transformed the tiny village into a
frontier boomtown by mid-1862. The army at Fort Defiance and the navy
that took control of the port on the Ohio River side of the city had great
need for equipment and provisions for the prosecution of the war. Entrepreneurs poured into town and established new manufacturing and supply
businesses to supplement the few that had originated before the war. To ful-
fill the military contracts, they required numerous semiskilled and unskilled laborers, and workers poured into Cairo, attracted by the possibility
of steady work. Cheap and flimsy housing sprouted up along the muddy
streets to the west of the business district that had grown up near the water-
front on the Ohio River side.[14]

Shortly after the war began, a number of fugitives from slavery began to make their way across the rivers from Kentucky and Missouri into Cairo, where the army formally protected them as "contrabands." But the trickle of Black refugees increased to a flood beginning in mid-1862, as Grant and his troops pushed their campaign southward. Unable to build secure refugee camps within hostile territory, Grant began sending those who reached his lines, mostly the women, children and the elderly, up the Mississippi on the steamboats that brought supplies to him from Cairo, while keeping the younger men with him to support the troops. Cairo did not welcome the refugees; most of its citizens made it clear that they did not want them there. Supplies of food and clothing were very slow to arrive, and no shelter was arranged for them until the late fall, after Rev. James B. Rogers was placed in charge of setting up a contraband camp, the only one located in a Northern "free" state. As winter approached, and after considerable effort, he received permission to take over a dilapidated set of barracks on the western side of the city. With the refugees doing most of the work, the barracks were consolidated and converted into a habitable camp during the winter. The army set up a minimal hospital for the contrabands, and nongovernmental aid groups began providing a variety of services. Two White Quakers, Job Hadley and his wife (her name is not preserved in the records), arrived in December to establish a school in the camp. Although they departed some three months later, the "contraband school" continued to function until the end of the war.[15] Many of the refugees, however, refused to move into the camp when it opened, particularly those who had already found work in the wartime economy of Cairo at the military installations in the town, on the busy wharves, and on the railroads.[16]

At first, the military authorities planned to move as many refugees as possible farther north where they might find employment by replacing the young men now in the army, particularly on farms. Although a small number of people were successfully placed in Illinois and other states along the upper Mississippi, the plan was mostly met with vicious opposition from White communities, politicians, and newspapers.[17] Several cities held protest meetings, insisting that the state uphold its Black Laws, which forbade the migration of African Americans into Illinois, and newspapers and politicians fulminated against the "threat" of Black men taking away White jobs. With this opposition, the plan was abandoned. By early 1863, the Black population in Cairo had reached about five thousand, and the army stopped sending new refugees to the camp. In April, the Freedmen's Commission announced a new program to resettle Cairo's African American community farther south on two strongly fortified islands in the Mississippi. However, a significant number of the refugees refused to leave. When the transfer took place, between one and two thousand contrabands stayed in Cairo, determined, in spite of considerable hardship, to make their lives there.[18]

In 1864, the African American community in Cairo remained in a situation of great uncertainty. It stood at a precarious in-between point, no longer an official contraband camp but with a large population of former refugees living across the city still without any defined rights or legal protections. The government had largely washed its hands of those who had refused to move to the island camps farther south, although families were allowed to continue living in the barracks, and the contraband hospital and school remained open until the end of the war. On the other hand, the military made no further efforts to protect the community from the hostile White population. Private aid societies did what they could to provide supplies of food and clothing for the needy, but many who could not work were left to the mercy of Cairo's often belligerent city government. Their needs were largely ignored, since the majority of Cairo's political and financial leadership were Democrats who had continually opposed the presence of the refugees.[19] A special census ordered by the city council in December 1864 showed that the total population of Cairo had quadrupled since 1860, rising to 8,569 of which 2,083, or 24.3 percent, were African Americans. There was no residential segregation at this time in Cairo, and its Black residents were spread fairly evenly across the city's four wards (Ward 1, 447; Ward 2, 567; Ward 3, 442; Ward 4, 627). This type of residential integration continued into the 1890s.[20]

Coming mostly from a rural, agricultural background, the contrabands attempted to adjust to this more urbanized setting. Confined to the lowest-paid and most difficult jobs in the city, Black men and women found employment in the military installations, businesses that supplied the latter, in the homes of the newly wealthy White elite, and in the saloons and bordellos in the southeastern part of town. Unlike African Americans in other Northern cities like Cincinnati, Philadelphia, or Chicago, Cairo's refugees suffered from an almost complete absence of established antebellum Black institutions and community leadership that might have helped ground and support them. And until the end of the war, they had no certainty that they would be allowed to stay permanently in the city. In spite of this, some African Americans took steps toward creating lasting organizations—the first church outside the camp, an AME congregation, was established in the spring of 1863 in the home of James and Maria Renfrow, with eight members, and having grown dramatically by early 1864, it had converted a house in town into a church building and briefly operated a private day school.[21]

Cairo had other problems that affected the African American population. It was a rough, ugly frontier town, made chaotic by the military presence and the constant movement of thousands of troops in and out. The vice industry that served the soldiers attracted a great deal of petty and violent crime, and law enforcement was lax. African Americans were commonly the victims of this type of activity. Residential housing was mostly substandard, and the majority of African Americans not in the contraband camp lived in poorly built rooming houses. There was also a major natural problem that plagued Cairo for decades: the city lay in a depression that was accentuated by the high levees built to protect it from the rivers on its east and west sides. When the weather was rainy or when either of the rivers rose, the ground inside quickly became saturated and turned into mud. This placed several of the residential areas in periodic jeopardy, and even in the business district of the city, the streets would often become impassable. Raised wooden boardwalks were built for pedestrians, but these would be submerged at times. Anthony Trollope, the British novelist and travel writer, visited Cairo in February 1862 and called it "of all towns in America the most desolate."[22] In spite of all these serious adversities, the African American community remained.

While the vast majority of Black citizens of Cairo had arrived there from the South, a small number of Northern African Americans moved into the city during the 1860s as well, most of them to find jobs, but some coming to aid the formerly enslaved in a variety of ways. Several of these Northerners—ministers, educators, and even saloon owners—became a major part of Cairo's first generation of Black leadership, and John Bird was one of them.[23]

John Bird's Early Visits to Cairo, 1864–1865

The Illinois to which John Bird traveled in 1864 was neither a hospitable nor a safe place for an African American person to visit. In fact, it was perhaps the most extremely anti-Black state in the "free" North.[24] In 1853, its state legislature had passed a set of "Black Laws" that effectively closed its borders to African American immigration. No incoming Black person could stay in the state for more than ten days without being liable to arrest and fine. If the defendant could not pay the fine, the authorities were allowed to sell that individual at auction into involuntary servitude for a determined period. The few free Black people already living in the state had very limited rights and faced continual hostility from Whites. This attitude did not decline with the outbreak of the war. In January 1862, a state constitutional convention, controlled by Democrats, designed a new constitution and separately proposed an additional amendment that would enshrine within the constitution itself both the ban on Black immigration and the law forbidding African Americans the right to vote or hold public office. In a referendum held in June, the state's citizens rejected the new constitution but still supported the separate anti-Black amendment with 71 percent of the vote. The region of southern Illinois, popularly (and with some biblical irony) referred to as "Egypt," favored it with 94 percent of its vote.[25] While the Black Laws did not become part of the constitution, they remained in effect, and in January 1864 the Illinois Supreme Court pronounced the provision of the law allowing for the sale of African American defendants as constitutional.[26]

John Bird also arrived in Cairo that summer at a disheartening moment for the national Republican Party, when support for the war effort appeared to be waning and many were convinced that Lincoln would lose the presidency in the November election. Democratic politicians and newspapers viciously denounced the Emancipation Proclamation and those Republicans who supported full emancipation of the enslaved. They also pointed to the contraband community in Cairo as a prime example of a Republican plot to bring a wave of Black people into Illinois that would overwhelm the White population. With a substantial number of Democrats campaigning on a platform of immediately suspending the war and negotiating a peace with the Confederacy, it was possible that, in spite of all the lives and effort expended on the war, slavery might survive and even that all the refugees might be sent back to their old masters.[27] Thus Cairo's African Americans found themselves looking at an extremely uncertain future, surrounded by White hostility. But John Bird, twenty years old, educated, and confident, arrived with a developed sense of how to build a strong community there.

Surviving documents describing his activities in Cairo between 1864 and 1868, while he was only a part-time resident of the city, are not numerous, but they provide clear indications of the deep impact Bird made in the city. They show that he almost immediately became the most influential leader of the Black community. They also show him already acting upon the primary concerns that would characterize his entire career: education, social justice, civil rights, the law, and the Republican Party. This is illustrated in his first documented appearance in Cairo, which occurs in a report sent to the *Christian Recorder* by "An Observer." It described a special celebration on July 4, 1864, in honor of the teachers and students of the contraband school. Among the featured events of the day was an "oration by John J. Bird, of Canada." The fact that he was asked to speak at this gathering suggests that he had come to Cairo with a special interest in the community's education situation, a passion that would lead to some of his most significant contributions to the city. This speech also indicates that although young, he already had well-developed oratorical skills, which would play a significant role in his rise to prominence.[28]

Bird returned to Windsor shortly after this event and married Annie Venerable in August. It may be that he used his visit to Cairo in part to consider whether the city might be an appropriate home for the new couple, but it seems that he decided it was not for now. On the other hand, his trip clearly convinced him that he had an important role to play there and that he needed to return soon. Bird was back in Cairo before the end of 1864 for a stay that lasted at least until May 1865. By the beginning of 1865, it appears that he was already regarded by many Black Cairoites as a valued leader in their community. In January, he sent the *Christian Recorder* an account of the community's New Year's Day celebration, commemorating the second anniversary of the implementation of the Emancipation Proclamation, an event held at the contraband school featuring both African American and White participants, including the respected Black Chicago minister George H. Newburne and the superintendent of the Freedmen's Schools, Mr. Cooley, as speakers. The celebration included other speeches, with one by Mrs. Foster, the head teacher of the school, followed by Bird, who gave an address titled "The Future of the African Race on the Continent of America," and then Lieutenant-Colonel Allen, a White abolitionist. Bird interestingly describes his own speech only through the reaction to it by Allen. The officer, according to Bird, "thought the gentleman who preceded him was somewhat pointed, in his ideas on some subjects. My readers are, no doubt, aware what those subjects are—'Slavery' and 'Prejudice.' Our mission is to proclaim the whole truth, so we are not to blame if we tread on some folk's toes."[29] This passage provides a sense of Bird's self-assuredness about his abilities to articulate the issues of the day.

That same month, the Illinois General Assembly, after years of pressure from the Black and abolitionist communities, finally began to debate a bill repealing the state's odious Black Laws. In Chicago, John Jones, the most influential African American in Illinois and longtime leader of the campaign for repeal, and his colleagues Henry O. Wagoner and Rev. Abraham Hall organized, as part of their intense lobbying effort, petition drives across the state to inundate the legislators with signatures, Black and White, demanding repeal.[30] However, apparently no petition arrived from the community in Cairo. In January 1865, the *Christian Recorder* published a letter from a Chicago correspondent, known only as "Ruth," that criticized the Black population of southern Illinois for this lapse, and Bird responded to Ruth's comments with a letter in defense of Cairo and the other southern communities. Unfortunately, neither of these two letters survives in the incomplete set of existing copies of the *Christian Recorder*, but they are both described in Ruth's reply to Bird's letter, which included a sharp attack on Bird, whom she clearly saw as an upstart outsider, saying in part, "It appears he has assumed the responsibility for all Egypt, which in the opinion of Ruth, is more than any one individual can successfully maintain. Had the Cairoites wanted to assist in the great work, why did they not do so, led on by Bird, who in his own opinion could have organized an association in Cairo."[31] Although her criticism of Bird judges him harshly for his perceived hubris, it seems clear that Bird felt in a position to speak for the Cairo community as their advocate in this debate.

On January 24, 1865, the legislature repealed the Black Laws that had barred African American immigration and Black access to the courts, and on February 7, Governor Richard Oglesby signed the bill into law, actions that were greeted with great joy in the African American community. This dramatic change for Black people living in Illinois had a more immediate impact on them than the congressional passage of the Thirteenth Amendment on January 31.[32] For most of the Black residents of Cairo, the repeal was revolutionary—for the first time since they arrived in Illinois, their presence in the state did not make them lawbreakers, and they were no longer potentially subject to arrest and possible sale.

However, many White local authorities in southern Illinois were furious at this turn of events and defiantly resisted the changes in whatever ways they could. In Cairo, this noncompliance centered on a rejection of the African Americans' new right to testify in court and bring lawsuits against White people. Bird described the situation in a letter to the *Christian Recorder*:

> The sentiment of the people here does not appear to change with the times. They have been governed so long by barbarous usages, that to degrade and oppress the Black man, has become a second nature with them. It degrades their dignity to recognize them in their new relations to this State. Civil officials have already gone so far as to say, in regard to our exercising our oath, that though in the repeal of the Black Laws we have a right to testify on oath, it will be some time before we shall exercise that privilege in Cairo, and when we do, they will no longer serve in their respective stations. Loud talking for a copperhead snake.[33]

The fight against this official lawlessness became the Cairo Black community's first civil rights campaign and young John Bird's initiation into full-scale political organization. But he did not have to learn how to do this on his own—he had significant help from a veteran of such campaigns. In March, Henry O. Wagoner, a leading civil rights activist in Chicago and a close associate of John Jones in the movement to repeal the Black Laws, traveled to Cairo to help organize the resistance to those officials and train the young leadership of the community, including Bird, on the tactics used by Jones and his allies. Wagoner employed a three-pronged approach here: he made clear to his opponents the legality of his case, then called for a mass protest meeting, which culminated in a move to use publicity to push back on the White leadership in the city. From Cairo, he wrote to the Illinois secretary of state, Sharon Tyndale, a Republican, to obtain an official ruling on whether the law of Illinois now allowed African Americans to "sue out a warrant against a White man." Tyndale responded to him that in his judgment, the act "gives the negro the right to testify under oath." With this letter as ammunition, the Black citizens of Cairo held a protest meeting at the AME church on March 23, where Wagoner took a back seat to Bird, who was elected chair. Wagoner acted as secretary and took part with two others in drafting the meeting's resolution, which was to make sure that the situation that led to the protest and the letter from Tyndale were published and publicized in the city and beyond.[34] It is clear from this proceeding that Bird was already seen as the political leader within the community, and it seems likely that the

Henry O. Wagoner, a Chicago civil rights leader, came to Cairo in 1865 to help Bird and the Black community learn protest techniques. From William J. Simmons, *Men of Mark: Eminent, Progressive and Rising.* Cleveland: G. M. Rewell, 1887. Reprinted Arno Press & New York Times, 1968, after 680.

training he received from this veteran of the civil rights movement had a deep impact on him. In Jones and Wagoner, he saw two secular political leaders who emphasized the power of the law and the use of legal arguments and moral persuasion, and who had used public mobilization in meetings, speeches, conventions, petitions, and other such means to break down opposition to equal rights. This certainly influenced and confirmed the way that Bird focused his own approach to civil rights advocacy and added to his desire to continue his work on behalf of the community in Cairo.

It is doubtful that this protest had an immediate effect on the White Cairo leadership, because the political dominance of the Democrats in the city and region could insulate them from certain rulings from Springfield. But that did not dissuade Bird and his colleagues from continuing to press for their rights. As the war moved toward its end in April 1865, Bird wrote of the political context the Black community was in: "Much excitement prevailed here on Monday the 3d inst., having received despatches [*sic*] that Richmond, the Confederate capitol [*sic*] and rebel stronghold was in possession of our troops—Guns were fired, flags hoisted and quite a display of patriotism was exhibited by the loyal few of the community. The copperhead organ (*Cairo Daily Democrat*) true to its principles, had its flag half mast, emblematic of its solemn grief for secesh fatality."[35]

Bird was still in Cairo in May 1865, when he provided a brief obituary to the *Christian Recorder* about the death of Cairo's first appointed AME minister, Rev. George Jacobs.[36] His six-month presence had brought some leadership and planning to the refugee population, but the community was hurt by the end of the war, the subsequent withdrawal of the military with its many jobs, and the shutting down of the contraband hospital and school. In September 1865, Alma Baker and Phillip C. Tolford, two White missionaries who had taken over teaching at the privately funded freedmen's school that succeeded the contraband school, wrote a letter to Brigadier General John W. Sprague, the assistant commissioner of the Freedmen's Bureau for the region, imploring him to reopen a medical facility for the African American community, which now had no place in Cairo that would serve it. They excoriated the city authorities about their lack of concern for the African Americans and charged that steamboat operators were hiring Black workers and then throwing them off the boat at Cairo without pay if they got sick. Sprague did not respond, and the Cairo office of the bureau closed in early December 1865.[37]

Bird's Activities in Postwar Cairo, 1866–1868

Bird reappeared in the *Christian Recorder* in December writing an obituary from Windsor for a member of his stepfather's congregation.[38] He was not in Cairo on January 1, 1866, when the Black community held its Emancipation Day celebration with speeches from local dignitaries, including Reverend Houston, a Baptist minister; John Gladney, a member of the AME congregation; and Phillip Tolford, the White teacher at the Freedmen's School. Also speaking was Rev. Henry Young of Windsor, a leader in Augustus Green's church.[39]

Bird returned to Cairo for another extended stay by February. While he had been gone, the Rev. Thomas Strother had arrived to take charge of the AME congregation, accompanied by his remarkable wife, Fanny. Strother, in his mid-fifties, was a well-respected, activist minister, who had been involved in establishing churches across the Midwest and had become a trustee of

Wilberforce University when it was purchased by the AME in 1863. During the war, he had served churches in Terre Haute, Indiana, and Louisville, Kentucky, and moved to Cairo in December 1865.[40] Thomas and Fanny had been intimately involved in opening schools in the churches they served during the war, so when they arrived in Cairo, they naturally took charge of reestablishing the closed AME one. Fanny almost immediately opened a night school at the AME church to serve both children and adults, and soon reopened the day school. The Strothers' school became one of six for Black students that had sprung up in the city, some connected to the new Black Baptist churches that had emerged in 1865, and others run by charity organizations like the Freedmen's Aid Society school under Phillip Tolford. By early 1866, the day schools in Cairo were serving between three and four hundred students.[41]

John Bird quickly came to admire the Strothers. They shared common values, not just religiously but also with regard to political priorities and methods for achieving them. The Strothers acted as mentors for Bird in the manner by which they were able to unify opposing groups to work for a common cause. This they did shortly after their arrival in Cairo, as they became aware of the dire medical situation that had resulted from the closing of the government contraband hospital in mid-1865. Almost immediately they began working to form a community-wide benevolent association designed to organize care for the sick and to raise money for an African American hospital, and by early 1866 had managed to unite the leadership of Cairo's Black Baptist churches and the AME congregation for this purpose.[42] In his reports to the *Christian Recorder* on the schools and churches of Cairo in 1866, Thomas showed himself to have little interest in sectarianism, placing all his discussions in the context of the entire community, describing the Baptist, AME, and secular schools as "our" schools, and opening a description of the town's Black churches with "We have four churches in our city." In a dispatch from Cairo to the *Christian Recorder* in early 1866, Bird praised Strother's abilities: "Too much credit or praise cannot be given Rev. Strother for his efforts in this community, which have been the means of bringing about a successful, and I trust a permanent union among the people here. Through his untiring zeal, the churches have been caused to lay aside sectarian ideas, and are laboring ardently and harmoniously to effect the object for which the society was organized."[43]

Bird certainly worked with Strother on the medical association, and the two also joined together during the summer of 1866 to help organize the Illinois State Convention of Colored Men held in Galesburg October 16–18. They were the only Cairoite signers of the official call for the convention, the purpose of which was to pressure the Illinois state legislature to pass laws concerning three key political issues not resolved by the repeal of the Black Laws: African Americans' right to vote, the right to public education for their children, and the right to serve on juries. Not being a citizen of Illinois in 1866, Bird did not attend the convention, but Strother played a significant role in it. At the convention, the fifty-six delegates adopted an address that laid out the legal, moral, and Christian arguments for the passage of such laws.[44] While the convention mobilized many African Americans and perhaps a few White Republicans to push for granting these rights by state law, it would take the congressional passage of the Fifteenth Amendment to begin to break the logjam.[45]

As the new postwar era took hold, the initial euphoria over the Northern victory was tempered by the struggle in Washington between President Andrew Johnson and the so-called Radical Republicans. Outraged over Johnson's leniency toward former Confederate leaders and the southern states' passage of "Black Codes" that re-created a system of White domination differing only marginally from slavery, the Republicans passed the Civil Rights Act of 1866 over Johnson's veto as the first major attack on his Reconstruction policies. The act, designed to strike down the Black Codes, enumerated several significant rights for African Americans, including the right to make contracts, to sue, be parties and give evidence, to own property, and to have "full and equal benefit of all laws and proceedings for the security of person and property." They also moved to pass what became the Fourteenth Amendment, granting citizenship to all people born in the United States. Johnson responded by embarking on a speaking tour across the North in August and September to rouse his Democratic base before the fall congressional election.[46]

While Johnson was on tour, southern leaders who had supported the Union during the war but in many cases had been removed from office, threatened physically by the former Confederates who now controlled the southern states, and forced to leave their home states, held a convention in Philadelphia, September 3–7, to expose the disastrous situation that Johnson's policies had unleashed upon both loyal Whites and African Americans in the South. Delegates from the former Confederate states passed a resolution that included a call for the enfranchisement of African Americans. Following the convention, several delegates were sent on a speaking tour that duplicated the itinerary of Johnson's campaign swing to undercut his message and support the Republican agenda. The tour proved very successful.[47]

Bird traveled to Chicago (either from Windsor or Cairo) to attend both Johnson's and the Southern Loyalists' visits there. He heard the speech Johnson made from the balcony of the Sherman House on September 5. In a letter to the *Christian Recorder*, he described the enthusiasm not of Johnson's supporters but of the large number of protesters who loudly shouted "Grant, Grant, Grant," throughout Johnson's short speech. Bird was also in Chicago for the Southern Loyalists' visit on October 1–2 and witnessed the massive display of support for them from the Republican faithful of the city. He was present on the evening of October 1 at the initial public speeches the delegation made at the Tremont House and also the following day, when they spoke at Lake Park. In his letter, Bird particularly mentioned the speech of Paschal B. Randolph of New Orleans, a physician and the only official African American delegate to the Loyalist Convention. Bird found the Southern Loyalists, with their insistence upon Black suffrage, inspirational: "Their radical views (far in advance of our Northern friends) on the suffrage question were received with unbounded applause, and have been the means of inaugurating a new line of policy on the suffrage question, which will become engrafted in the subsequent platform of Illinois Republicanism."[48]

But his enthusiasm for the strength of the Republicans in Chicago was tempered by his knowledge of the much more hostile atmosphere against African American rights in Cairo. From Chicago, the Loyalists divided into seven groups that went to speak in small towns across the state between October 3 and 6. One of the groups arrived in Cairo on October 5. This meeting proved to be the only one in Illinois at which the local Democrats felt strong enough in their control of the city administration to actually disrupt it. Well before the time for the presentation, Democrats entered the Atheneum auditorium and stationed themselves in seats around the hall. One went on stage and tore down the anti-Johnson banner that flew behind the podium. Shortly after the event began, Colonel J. Stancel of Texas started to deliver an address, when the Democrats began heckling the speaker, shouting pro-Johnson slogans. Colonel Stancel refused to end his speech, and the shouting got louder. Some, but not all, of the women in the audience were frightened—the *Chicago Tribune* reported that "L. Lewis, of the Cairo *Democrat*, was unceremoniously hustled out of the gallery by certain ladies, who were annoyed by his unmannerly actions and boisterous manifestations." But the police refused to intervene, and the Democratic city leaders in the audience did nothing to stop the commotion. Finally, after Stancel finished, the other scheduled speakers decided it was hopeless to continue, and the meeting was adjourned prematurely.[49]

Bird, who had had high hopes for this event, was incensed. "And thus it is," he wrote in his account to the *Christian Recorder*, "that in a land of liberty, of free speech and free men, at a lawful assemblage of men, men who love loyalty better than treason, Union men, White or Black, better than traitors; men who believe that the ballot is the safeguard of our liberties, the hand of tyranny grasps us by the throat with all the force and power of the dark ages. . . . How much longer shall loyal meetings be broken up by such unprincipled and godless men?"[50]

The Republican triumph in the 1866 elections marked the beginning of a period of about a decade in which it genuinely appeared possible that African Americans might eventually be accepted into American society as full and equal members. Dramatic reforms followed one after another from Congress—the Reconstruction Acts in 1867 that required enfranchisement of Black males in the former Confederate states before their return to the Union; the adoption of the Fourteenth Amendment to the U.S. Constitution in 1868; congressional passage in 1869 of the Fifteenth Amendment instituting voting rights for all African Americans; its ratification in the spring of 1870; and the passage of the Civil Rights Act of 1875, which required equal access to public accommodations and transportation and forbade the exclusion of African Americans from serving on juries. These changes opened significant opportunities for Black people, including, after 1870, in local and state politics, areas to which Bird found himself drawn. Many of these changes were slow to be felt in Democratic Cairo during the latter third of the 1860s, but the Fifteenth Amendment transformed the city dramatically.

In the postwar 1860s, Cairo itself developed from its ugly, wartime hardscrabble character into a more appealing small town. Many entrepreneurs, convinced that the city had a great future, moved in and founded shops, lumberyards, iron works, theaters, furniture makers, warehouses, and other businesses.[51] Beginning in 1866, the city government made substantial improvements to Cairo's infrastructure, including bringing in trainloads of soil and gravel to raise the ground level of the lower parts of town so that the mud issues from which it suffered were somewhat abated.[52] In the spring of

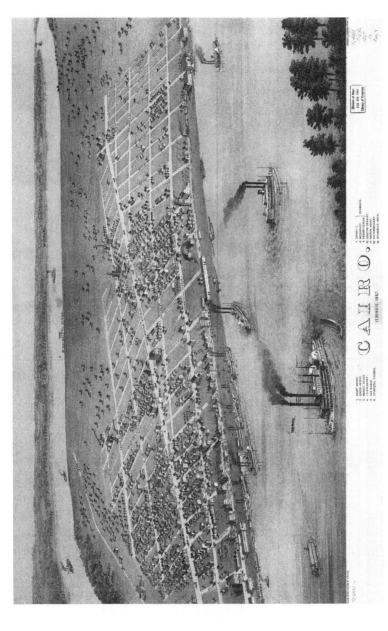

Panoramic map of Cairo, Illinois, 1867, provides a sense of the development of the town. Chicago: Chicago Lithographing Co. Library of Congress, call number: G4104.C15A3 1867 .R8; control number: 73693346.

1866, Bird could report, somewhat hyperbolically, "Much progress has been made among the Cairoites, White, and Black, since I last wrote you, or even since you passed through here. The dark muddy Cairo that you saw has almost in appearance, been transformed into an Eastern city of wealth, grandeur, and highly social and intellectual accomplishments. The streets are being filled, the sidewalks have been raised, and the city is lighted with gas."[53] In addition, the federal government began construction of a substantial new customhouse that would boast a modern post office and a federal courtroom as well.[54]

But the social and economic conditions of the Black community only marginally improved. With the expanding economy, many African Americans were able to find jobs in Cairo, but, as during the war, generally in the lowest-paid positions available. They also came into conflict with White workers who provoked violence on the job.[55] Violent incidents also occurred outside the workplace. For example, in July 1867, four Whites, two men and two women, disrupted a worship service at the AME church. Reverend Strother confronted the four and persuaded three of them to leave, but one of the men pulled a pistol and threatened the congregation. Once Strother convinced him to depart, the minister locked the front door, which apparently angered the belligerent one, who returned and pounded on and kicked the door. Unable to reenter, he then shot a round through it, hitting one of the congregants in the face.[56]

In the presence of this kind of insecurity, along with continued poverty and sickness, the African American community organized itself in various ways to protect the vulnerable. As previously noted, the churches, at least in 1866, united to form an association to raise funds for an African American hospital, and it is highly probable that the women of the various congregations formed groups to visit the sick and aid the poor. In 1867, John Bird oversaw another significant step in the development of the institutional infrastructure of the community by engineering the establishment of a Prince Hall Masonic Lodge in the city. Chartered by the newly established Grand Lodge of Illinois in Chicago, Lincoln Lodge No. 5 became the first major African American fraternal organization in Cairo. Such organizations played vital roles in Black communities across the country in the postwar period, acting as emotional support systems for Black men and women and providing mutual aid to members' families, including death and illness insurance. The Masons focused on numerous things that appealed to Bird, including an insistence upon racial pride, Black respectability, education, and moral re-sponsibility. The Masons also provided an extensive mechanism for net-working with other lodges and their leaders, including the main lodge in Chicago, where John Jones and his colleagues had been the primary forces behind the Masons during the antebellum period. Finally, the Prince Hall Masons were very active in the equal rights struggle of the late 1860s and sup-ported the types of political tactics that appealed to Bird. His primary role in the founding of the Cairo lodge is clear in the fact that he was named its first Worshipful Master, even though he was not a full-time resident of the city at this point, a position that he held for the next five years.[57]

The Weakness of Black Church Leadership in Cairo and Its Consequences

One of the most striking elements of the story of Cairo's early African Amer-ican community is the dominance of essentially secular leaders such as Bird in the fight for equal rights during the 1860s and 1870s and the relative lack of input from the city's Black church leadership. The Black church was gen-erally the central social organization within African American communities and the institutional base from which the civil rights movements of the nine-teenth and twentieth centuries most often emerged. Black ministers have been among the most important leaders of these movements from the time of the Revolutionary War until the present day.[58] Kerry Pimblott, in her ex-cellent account of the powerful role of Cairo's churches and their leaders in the civil rights struggle of the late 1960s and early 1970s, naturally assumed that the early churches of Cairo played a similar part in the post–Civil War era, but the evidence appears to dispute that interpretation.[59]

There are several reasons why Cairo's churches failed to take a leadership position during the early postwar period. To begin with, there was no cul-tural infrastructure for African Americans in Cairo before the Civil War, and no established Black churches existed in the city, as Cairo's tiny antebellum African American population did not have the critical mass to create stable social institutions. The chaos and uncertainty of the war years made it im-possible for the refugees who arrived after 1862 to establish any sense of per-manence about their situation, so those who brought their religion with them (mostly Baptists) simply practiced it wherever they could within the area of the contraband camp. In 1864, however, the federal government constructed a building for the refugees that could accommodate about 350 people for both educational and religious purposes.[60] The only successful permanent church founded outside the camp during the war was the AME group in 1863, which grew quickly enough to be able to purchase and remodel a house into a church building later in the year and receive a certified pastor by the end of 1864. In 1865, however, a proliferation of small Baptist congregations sprang up within the city, meeting in houses or borrowed spaces, some quickly disbanding, while new ones emerged. By 1867, three somewhat larger and more stable Baptist congregations had been organized, joining the single AME church as the community's religious centers: the First Missionary Baptist Church, whose pastor Thomas J. Shores would play a complex role in this period; the Second Free-Will Baptist Church (later New Hope), with Nelson Ricks as its pastor; and the Second Missionary Baptist Church (later Antioch), overseen by Jacob Bradley.[61] Strikingly, none of these ministers, all of whom led their congregations into the 1880s and beyond, played a leadership role in the early civil rights movement in Cairo. Neither Ricks nor Bradley ever appears in surviving records of the 1860s and 1870s as having been politically active, and although Shores was involved in Republican politics primarily between 1868 and 1872, he was never part of the Black Republican leadership.[62] In addition to the lack of activism among the Baptist pastors, the AME church leadership suffered from a structural problem in dealing with local politics. National church policy dictated that pastors should not stay with a single congregation for more than two years. Because of this, it appears that during their tenures, most of Cairo's AME pastors did not get deeply involved in the political situation either (Strother was the primary exception).

But the problems went deeper than just the ministers' decisions to focus on their pastoral duties rather than external political issues. Although Reverend Strother initially had been successful in negotiating a period of interdenominational cooperation in 1866, by the fall of 1867 this fragile ecumenicism had collapsed into an extended period of internecine strife. Most of the conflict swirled around Reverend Shores, beginning with the latter's attempt to undermine Strother's plans to create a private free school for Cairo's poorest Black children and continuing with a brazen effort to lure away members of Bradley's congregation to his own. Each of these actions by Shores initiated an escalating conflict that broke into large public disputes between him and the minister he had attacked, leading in each case to a series of angry letters sent to the *Democrat* or the *Bulletin*, accusing each other of numerous unethical practices and crimes. In fact, Shores and Bradley seem to have been constantly embroiled in conflicts and were occasionally expelled from their churches and ministerial associations yet managed somehow to return and hold onto their congregations.[63] Reverend Ricks and his church seem to have remained on the sidelines and stayed out of the clashes between the other two Baptist congregations. Sources say little about Ricks until he finally took a dramatic stand on the condition of the city's Black school in 1883, discussed in chapter 6. Thus, the pastors who took charge of the few churches that flourished through this period were generally not up to the task of creating a unifying Christian political message that would allow the congregations to work together for the betterment of the community.

This unhealthy ecclesiastical situation meant that if the fight for equality were to be waged, it would need to be taken up by people from elsewhere in the community. This made it relatively easy for more secular leaders such as John Bird, John Gladney, and William Scott to step in. Bird and Scott were both free middle-class northerners from Ohio, and Gladney was a native of Arkansas, literate, and a natural businessman. They recognized during the late 1860s that the city's Republican Party offered a rare opportunity for Cairo's Black community that few northern cities could rival. They saw that with the ratification of the Fifteenth Amendment, the number of eligible Black Republican voters in Cairo would dwarf that of the city's White Republicans and would also bring the very weak party into virtual parity with the dominant Democrats. Bird and his colleagues understood that if the Black community could be unified by an enthusiastic allegiance to the party, regardless of their church affiliation, they could make demands on the party that were considerably more comprehensive than most Black communities elsewhere in Illinois could propose. And these young men, all in their twenties, had the charisma, eloquence, vision, and organizational skills to form a powerful social and political organization that could pull the community together around the idealized principles that were being articulated by the Radical branch of the Republican Party. In doing this, they pulled off a feat that was essentially the reverse of what the African American civil rights leaders in Cairo achieved in the 1960s. Instead of having vibrant church leaders who were able to frame a powerful civil rights organization by merging the contemporary, secular Black power ideology into an activist Christian, church-related context, Bird and his colleagues took some aspects of Black church ideology from a relatively passive

William T. Scott was John Bird's colleague and sometime political enemy
from Bird's earliest days in Cairo until his death in 1912. From I. Garland Penn,
The Afro-American Press and Its Editors, Springfield MA: Willey & Co 1891, 129.

religious context and channeled that spirituality into a vibrant, secular
political organization.[64]

The Postwar African American Schools
in Cairo, 1865–1870

Securing education for Cairo's African American children was one of John
Bird's central goals during the second half of the 1860s. Although the city's
surviving newspapers rarely mentioned the Black community's early private
schools or the leaders of its campaign calling for African American public education, his leadership in an 1867 attempt to form a private free school in
Cairo, discussed below, along with the reports on Bird's leadership on these
issues from 1870 onward indicate that he was already established as one of
the primary forces in that struggle during these years.

In the postwar 1860s, Illinois's school law required the state to provide a
public-school education to all White children, while not explicitly forbidding
public education for Black children. Thus, Chicago had allowed Black students into the schools early in their existence. Elsewhere in the state, a few

small- and midsized Illinois towns, including Alton, Bloomington, Decatur, Galesburg, Jacksonville, Normal, Peoria, Quincy, and Springfield, financed segregated public schools for Black children in the 1850s and 1860s. In all of those towns, the African American population was small, constituting between 0.5 percent and 5.6 percent of their total populations, with only three of these Black communities in 1870 numbering more than five hundred (Quincy with 1,073 Black citizens, 4.5 percent of the city's population; Springfield with 808, 4.6 percent; and Galesburg with 575, 5.6 percent).[65] Thus the size of their African American student bodies was modest. In fact, Robert McCaul estimates that in 1866, only about four hundred to six hundred Black students attended public schools in Illinois, out of about six thousand of school age in the state.[66]

Cairo's African American community was faced with problems that were unique in the state. Unlike the towns that had opened their schools to Black children, Cairo's African American population was much larger (1,849 in 1870) and constituted 29.5 percent of the city's inhabitants, so that the number of potential new students there (between 350 and 500) and their percentage of the total student body were enormous in comparison. To bring that many children into the public school system would require more financial investment in Cairo than in other cities. The White Democratic majority vehemently opposed the very concept of Black public education, particularly the thought of integrated schools, and they were unwilling to pay more taxes to support a separate Black public school. These opponents fulminated against the idea in speeches and newspapers, stoking fear of integration, which they charged would ultimately lead to the destruction of the public school system itself and warning that of the vast sums of money that the school board would demand were it to happen, none of it would be paid for by African American taxes.[67] This hostile political environment, along with the lack of a mandate from the state, made the efforts of the Cairo Black community to establish a public school for its children a long and complex process. Its eventual success in doing so in 1871, the year before the state legislature passed its first law mandating public education for African Americans, was an extraordinary achievement.

The development of private Black schools in Cairo during the early postwar years played a significant formative role in the eventual arrival of the public free school. Many gaps in the surviving records make a full account of this subject difficult, but its main outlines can be reconstructed. Our earliest information about the schools appears in an October 1866 letter from Reverend Strother to the *Christian Recorder*, in which he reported that there were six day schools in the city, three taught by African American teachers and three by White instructors, with a combined enrollment of about three hundred students. Strother and his wife Fanny taught the AME school, plus a night class. Sources indicate that another school was operated by the relatively short-lived Mt. Orange Free Will Baptist Church under Rev. Jeff Huston (or Houston) and his daughter, and the Freedmen's Aid Society ran a third, with the White teacher Phillip Tolford, who had taught in Cairo since 1865. Other Cairo churches, probably including White ones, likely accounted for the other three. It seems, however, that by the end of 1866, some of the White Baptist churches joined with the Home Mission Society, a large Baptist organization that provided the congregations with a substantial grant that allowed them to obtain property on Walnut Street at the southeastern corner of the intersection with Nineteenth Street and construct a two-story frame schoolhouse, which presumably was used to consolidate several of the day schools into one. The Mission Society covered the bulk of the cost of the building.[68]

The Strothers, however, had their own plans concerning the expansion of their school. Most of the students in the church-related schools were children of congregation members who paid a modest tuition. However, these schools were only reaching part of the children living in Cairo. This situation concerned the Strothers, as Thomas wrote to the *Christian Recorder*: "The only thing we regret is, the large number of children running about our streets, who recently came from the South, and who are, as yet, unable to be educated. Will not our State Legislature do something for our benefit? As yet we have received no aid from it."[69] In 1866, Strother contacted Newton Bateman, the state superintendent of public instruction and an active proponent of public education for African American students, and learned that there was little chance that the legislature would remove the term "white" from the state's school law in the foreseeable future. Having also heard directly from Joel G. Morgan, Alexander County's superintendent of schools, that Cairo's leadership would never willingly open the schools to Black children, Strother and Bird decided to seek financial support from the Black community and sympathetic Whites to create a private free school for children whose parents could not afford educational costs. Although they apparently obtained pledges from several interested Whites, they were unable to raise sufficient funds to open the school during the 1866–67 school year. Thus, they planned to try again in the fall of 1867.[70]

Those plans were short circuited by Rev. Thomas J. Shores, who became minister of the First Missionary Baptist Church, probably in late 1866 or early 1867. Born in Virginia about 1817, Shores proved to be a divisive figure in the African American community, both religiously and politically. An army chaplain during the war, he was imposing and charismatic but also impulsive, egotistical, and intimidating. Shores took firm control of his congregation and made it a personal power base from which he attacked the leaders of other Black congregations in the city and region as easily and often as he fought members of the White establishment.[71] In August, Reverend Strother announced a community meeting to be held September 3 at the AME building to discuss the plans for the free school. Shores, who apparently had taken a strong dislike to the popular AME minister, decided that he would beat Strother to the punch. He invited Superintendent Morgan to address an open meeting on the general subject of Black education on August 30, four days before Strother's gathering. Morgan gave a standard speech, reiterating to the crowd (falsely) that state law forbade local authorities from using government funds to support public education for African American students and encouraging the community members to raise their own money toward a privately funded free school. Shores then rose and announced that he and others were now organizing a free school to be called the Colored Union School of Cairo. On September 9, Shores and his supporters met to elect three school directors, who then hired Shores to be the school's teacher and set October 7 as opening day for classes.[72]

Strother had been working on his project for months, was raising money to place the school on a firm financial foundation, and had worked with Morgan on an educational constitution, including the establishment of bonds and security for all donations made to the school. To him, Shores's unexpected announcement of a competing school was offensive and detrimental to all the work he and his colleagues, including Bird, had done. He met with Superintendent Morgan and several prominent White leaders to get their endorsement for his project, as opposed to that of Shores, and apparently was successful. On September 16, Strother led a meeting at the Cairo City Hall, in which supporters of his school established the Cairo Educational Association, approved its constitution, and chose the officers for the proposed free school. John Bird was elected president of the school, while Superintendent

Morgan became its treasurer and John Gladney was appointed to the association's seven-member Board of Directors.[73] On September 22, the association published a statement in the *Cairo Daily Democrat* publicly announcing its formation and goals for getting the school off the ground. The leaders of the association called upon the White community to support their efforts and indicated their exasperation concerning Shores's attempt to preempt their school, blasting him for his near total lack of organization. They also expressed bemusement that Shores himself had been hired as the school's teacher, stating, "Our candid opinion is that he does not know the English alphabet to-day as a teacher should know it." The latter charge appears to be confirmed both by Shores's 1880 census entry, which marked him as able to read but unable to write, and by his Last Will in 1882, which he signed with an X.[74]

The criticism of Shores and his project led to a series of angry letters to the *Daily Democrat* between Shores and Strother that quickly degenerated into vicious ad hominem attacks.[75] John Oberly, the editor, took a smug pleasure in publishing these angry letters, always on his front page. The publicity clearly injured the credibility of both parties and helped damage both schools.[76] Shores's school quickly devolved into a fiasco. The minister, having made little headway in raising money, held a fundraiser on September 24, which received enough income to open the school in a room of the Mt. Orange Baptist Church in early October.[77] But, having rushed precipitously into the project without securing it financially, he apparently ran short of money almost immediately.

In danger of having to close the school, Shores devised a new plan to get the funds, apparently without making any attempt to rally support from other parts of the community. On Friday, October 12, a number of Shores's supporters gathered at the White elementary school on Thirteenth Street and demanded that their children be allowed to attend the school. This event caused a huge stir in the White community, and the next day, according to the *Cairo Daily Democrat*, Shores spoke to the Cairo school director and "demanded that the colored children should either be allowed to attend the public schools on an even footing with the White children, or else the White taxpayers of the city should support the colored schools."[78] The newspaper's description of the second part of Shores's demands may be a racially motivated distortion by its editor, John Oberly. It seems unlikely that Shores was actually insisting that the school board use tax money to support a Black public school. In 1867, even though the entire African American community supported the idea of universal public education, no one believed that such a thing could happen in southern Illinois without the state changing its current law to force such a change. The account indicates that Shores was specifically talking about his school with the school director when he made his demands, and although it is possible that he gave the ultimatum recorded in the *Cairo Daily Democrat*, it seems more likely that he rather used the threat of Black students joining the established White schools as a means to demand private donations for his school from Cairo's wealthy White elite. There is no evidence that Shores had ever publicly advocated for Black public free schools beyond the *Cairo Daily Democrat*'s account of this incident; his focus in 1867 was the founding of a private school over which he had full control.[79] The Democratic *Cairo Daily Democrat*, however, saw this incident as an opportunity to rally the anti-Black sentiments of the population against an influential leader in the Black community. Oberly likely inflated Shores's demands to help shift his previous portrayal of Shores as a harmless buffoon into that of a serious menace to Cairo's way of life and its public schools' very existence.

The *Democrat*, however, did not stop there. Oberly and his coeditor Moses B. Harrell went so far as to threaten violence against those who pushed this concept: "If we were Principle [*sic*] of the public schools we should very probably supply ourselves with a lignum vitae base ball bat, and answer all such demands as their impertinence might demand. The question must be squarely, even indignantly, met." On Shores himself, the *Democrat* wrote, "If this man Shores persists in his mischief-making, he may become the object of attentions that will render it entirely agreeable for him to domicil [*sic*] in some other locality." Such threats immediately quashed Shores and his brief movement. By October 20, Superintendent Morgan had revoked his teaching certificate, and his free school collapsed.[80] He never again attempted this type of provocative agitation, a tactic that in any case had no support among the other African American leaders in Cairo through the 1870s, and he and his congregation essentially disappear from the surviving newspapers during 1868–69.

Caught up in the vicious reaction to Shores's demonstration, Strother and the officers and board of the Cairo Educational Association found their project now in peril. The board met in mid-October and produced a series of resolutions that they sent to the *Democrat*, carefully disassociating themselves from Shores, his school, and the "party or parties who have intruded on the sanctity of the Public Schools (White) of this community, by attempting to gain admission for colored children." They again asked the White citizens of Cairo to contribute "willingly and liberally to the cause of education—a cause indispensable to the growth and prosperity of a free people." The most significant resolution, however, had to do with the reasons why they did not ask for public funding of their school for now: "*Resolved,* That we regard the school law, in reference to persons of color, as valid, and do not feel disposed or inclined to make incursions on it as it now exists; but on the contrary will wait with patience until the wise and generous legislature of this State see proper to so amend the law, as to give us the benefit of the school fund."[81] Thus the association did not attempt to argue for universal public education in this context, but focused attention on the future, when they hoped the law of the state would shift in their favor. But even with this conciliatory tone, it is not clear whether the association was able to repair the damage this conflict had caused. There is, unfortunately, little evidence to indicate how long the association's school lasted. In September, as soon as Strother and Shores decided to stop sending letters to the *Democrat*, the paper, our only source, totally lost interest in the story of Black free schools, ignoring that aspect even in its coverage of Shores's actions in October, where it shifted the focus of Shores's "transgression" onto the dual bugaboos of integrated schools and higher taxes for White citizens, ignoring the free schools. All that can be said with certainty is that the Cairo Educational Association was still active at least in November, when it placed an advertisement in the *Democrat*, signed by Bird as president, announcing a fundraising dinner.[82] One indication that the school existed for a time is found in the posthumous biography of Bird in the University of Illinois's *Alumni Record* of 1913, which states that Bird "organized the first free sch. System for negroes in Ill., and was Supt." This section most probably refers to the events described here. The reference to "Ill" here is certainly a mistake for "Cairo," since, as mentioned above, Illinois had earlier free schools in the 1850s and early 1860s. It seems unlikely that this moment in Bird's career would loom so large as it does in this short biography if the school had been too ephemeral.[83]

Following this incident, little information survives about the education situation in the African American community until the end of 1868. Sources indicate that the Baptist school on Walnut, the Freedmen's Aid Society's school, and the AME Church's schools under Fanny and Thomas Strother continued to operate. Thomas served as pastor of the AME congregation in Cairo for nearly three years, a long term in one location for an AME minister. In the fall of 1868, Strother and the congregation apparently asked the leaders of the district to allow him to stay yet another year, but they were refused, and the district sent a new pastor. The Strothers, however, were not ready to leave Cairo, and Thomas declined to accept any new appointments for two years, while he and Fanny continued to work in the community, particularly with the AME's school, as well as in other political and social activities.[84]

The Baptist school that operated at Walnut between Eighteenth and Nineteenth Streets became a pivotal point in the move toward a public school for Black students. In order to sustain itself financially, the owners had allowed Rev. Jacob Bradley to make use of the building as a church on evenings and weekends. Bradley, like Shores, was a controversial and volatile man who repeatedly alienated the other Baptist congregations in town but had a fierce following within his congregation. Late in 1867 Phillip Tolford, the White minister and teacher in charge of the Freedmen's Aid Society school, made an effort to oust Bradley's congregation and take over the Walnut Street building for his school, his intention likely being to merge the two schools into one. Bradley naturally objected to this situation and was apparently able to continue using the building for about a year. However, Tolford, a Baptist himself, apparently had the support of the Home Mission Society and the local congregations that owned the building, and eventually he was successful at dislodging Bradley and his parishioners at the end of 1868. The day after Tolford took possession of the property, the building and parsonage were destroyed in a fire, probably arson. Tolford and those in the community who supported him constructed a temporary structure on the grounds that was used for the rest of the school year, and by mid-June 1869 the local Baptist churches had raised enough money to begin erecting a new building.[85]

Bird, Strother, and others saw the construction of the new school building as an opportunity to use political and legal means to take a step toward capturing state resources for African American students. It appears that they recognized this as an opportunity to apply for state educational funds through Section 80 of the education law, which provided that "in townships in which there shall be persons of color, the board of education shall allow such persons a portion of the school fund, equal to the amount of taxes collected for school purposes from such persons of color in their respective townships."[86]

The Black community could use these funds for whatever educational purpose it wished. While most Black populations outside Chicago were too small to accumulate significant money from the education fund, Cairo was different—by 1869 several of its Black citizens paid substantial taxes. Although the funds were not sufficient to erect an independent structure, they could be used to supplement the Baptist reconstruction project and create a larger, higher-quality building. The *Bulletin*, apparently once again trying to stir up White resentment, began referring to the school as having been built by the "government," usually ignoring the large private contribution, which this time came largely from Black Baptist organizations, and never mentioning that the state money itself came completely from African American taxes. On its completion, the paper provided a general description of the new school: "about thirty by sixty feet, one story, with a ten-foot basement. It can be made to accommodate about two hundred pupils."[87] Classes began in early September 1869, but despite a push to place Reverend Strother in charge of the new building, the Baptists retained Tolford as schoolmaster.[88] However, this victory in securing the state education funds inspired the Black community to increase its calls for the city school board to create a Black public school.

John Bird and the Rise of Black Republicanism in Cairo

During John Bird's early years visiting Cairo, he had become a community leader, focusing on things that centered specifically on the concerns delineated by the antebellum middle-class ideology on which he had been raised. He had supported efforts to improve the education of Black children in the city, given speeches, worked on raising funds for a Black hospital, supported the call for an African American convention in Galesburg, led a protest meeting against the actions of the city leadership, and established a critical fraternal organization in the city. But during this period, he also led a movement to create something that had been completely impossible before the war: the foundation of an African American wing of an established, national political party in Cairo that, when unified, could hold substantial power within the local and county political structure.

African Americans had maintained both hope and skepticism concerning the Republican Party of the 1850s and early 1860s. They were pleased with Lincoln's antislavery sentiments but were insulted by his early embrace of the idea of the removal of emancipated Black people from the United States to Africa. Views began to change when he issued the Emancipation Proclamation and as the abolition of slavery finally became an official policy of the government. With the postwar passage of the Thirteenth and Fourteenth Amendments, and the Civil Rights Act of 1866, many African Americans began to believe that the Republican Party was moving toward the establishment of full political and legal equality and felt deeply supportive of it. The party curried that support during the late 1860s. The Reconstruction Acts had required universal male suffrage in the states of the former Confederacy but had done nothing to establish it in the northern "free" states. Illinois Republicans talked about extending the franchise to Black men after their big election win in 1866, but even with substantial majorities in the state legislature and the governorship, they were unable to unify behind that cause until after Congress passed the Fifteenth Amendment in February 1869.[89] But by 1868 the White Republicans in Cairo were beginning to mobilize Black support in the city in anticipation of their eventual eligibility to vote.

Sources show that Bird was interested in the mechanics of the Republican Party early in the postwar period. Although the first explicit reference to his embrace of the cause appears in his 1866 description of his trips to Chicago to see President Johnson and the Southern Loyalists, it seems probable that his support for the party long predated that. That support is also evident in a *Cairo Daily Democrat* article that describes an African American celebration of July 4, 1867, at which Bird gave a speech. The main ceremony of the day was chaired by Strother, and although there were no local Republican leaders in attendance, one White visiting minister, Reverend Joy, took part. The speeches began with Reverend Shores reading the Declaration of Independence and giving the opening oration. He was followed by four others, with Bird and Reverend Joy, who perhaps represented the party, at the end. The *Cairo Daily Democrat* only commented on the final two speakers: "Joy has white skin. J. J. Bird has black skin. Bird made a temperate and well-prepared address. Joy made a fool of himself." The *Cairo Daily Democrat*'s attack on Joy, who likely supported the Radical Republican agenda, is expected, but it is surprising that the paper would print anything positive about a Black orator who certainly espoused ideas similar to those of Joy. This is the first indication in print that John Oberly, the newspaper's editor, had taken note of Bird's abilities and rhetorical skills. Oberly's interest in Bird would play a very important role in the political lives of both men over the next decade. After the speeches, a committee made up of Bird, Strother, and R. Robinson produced resolutions that clearly indicated their support of the Republican Party. The two key resolutions were as follows: "That the principles inculcated in that document [the Declaration], will, if strictly adhered to, and rigidly enforced have a tendency to promote the happiness and welfare of all men, establish just and wholesome laws for the good government of mankind, and bring about that civil and political equality which is the strength and glory of our 'Republican Institutions'" and "That we firmly endorse the reconstruction policy of Congress, and believe it will, if properly enforced, calm and quiet the disturbed elements of our common country."[90]

Before the summer of 1868, the political and social activities of Bird and the other African Americans of Cairo were undertaken with little or no obvious input from the Republican Party. In the political structure of Illinois, Republicans saw Black people as spectators of the scene—they could support the party but did not have an active role within it. That began to change as the national party pushed toward the passage of the Fifteenth Amendment. The White Republican leadership in Cairo had good reason to believe, as Bird and his colleagues did, that a united Black wing of the party could revolutionize their political position in the city and county. Cairo's postwar population was declining, but it had lost considerably more Whites than Blacks: between 1865 and 1870, it lost about 27 percent of its people (from 8,569 to 6,267), but with a loss of only 11 percent of its Black inhabitants (2,083 to 1,849), as opposed to 32 percent of its Whites. Thus by 1870, the African American community accounted for 29.5 percent of the population, allowing its voting power a chance to break the Democratic stranglehold on the city, if its members were unified and motivated.[91] Thus the Republican leadership began to meet with leaders of the Black community including Bird, Strother, John Gladney, William T. Scott, and Reverend Shores about organizing potentially eligible Black voters into a Republican club in preparation for the time they would be able to exercise the franchise.[92] They also tentatively began to incorporate Black people into Republican public events. On October 1, a large reunion of the Union troops from the region was held in Cairo, with at least some participation by African Americans in the celebration. The event was very much a Republican affair and was dominated by a three-hour speech by John A. Logan, a native of southern Illinois, a well-regarded general in the war, a former intensely anti-Black Democrat who underwent a conversion to the Radical Republican view during the war and now Republican U.S. representative. Bird was present at the event and in a letter to *Christian Recorder* called Logan's speech "one of the most eloquent, masterly and unanswerable arguments I ever heard." He also expressed optimism about the future of the Republicans in Cairo: "Modern Democracy [i.e., the Democratic Party], which has triumphed over the true principles of American ideas and institutions in this locality, is, I am proud to say, on the wane, and the people rising to the dignity of the high calling, are espousing the cause of Republicanism, which is in these times, the representative of liberty and justice untrammeled and unimpaired."[93] Thus, when the party began to engage with Cairo's Black community, Bird was ready to become involved.

John Bird and two other men, William T. Scott and John Gladney, had the most powerful impact on the long-term development of the Black Republican wing in Cairo. Scott was, like Bird, an Ohio native, born in Newark in 1839. He moved to Cincinnati in 1857, where he studied in the city's African American high school for two years before taking a job as a barber on a riverboat. In 1863, he volunteered for the navy and was stationed at Cairo, where he served as a steward on a receiving vessel that was permanently docked along the Ohio River levee. When his eighteen-month commission was over, he stayed in Cairo. During the war, Scott had befriended William P. Halliday, one of the city's wealthiest men, who loaned him funds to set up a bail bondsman business and purchase a saloon. Very quickly the industrious Scott became one of the wealthiest African Americans in town. In many ways, Scott was like Bird: educated, a good speaker, interested in politics, influential in the Black community, and well connected with parts of the White community. Both were deeply involved with Black fraternal orders such as the Masons and the Oddfellows, and Republican leaders saw both as important persons to cultivate for the party. But for all their similarities, the two were strikingly different people. Bird was respectable, cultivating the middle-class image of integrity and morality, while Scott lived life on the legal and moral edge, sometimes outraging both the White and African American communities. His flamboyant style made him appealing to some and appalling to others. Bird and Scott were both important to the Republicans because each had a different constituency within the Black community. However, because of his choice of occupation, with drinking, gambling, and prostitution never far from his public persona, the party's leaders were reluctant to fully embrace Scott. They preferred Bird as a representative of the party, more regularly appointing him as delegate to county, congressional, and state Republican conventions. Scott never won elected office in the city or county government, while Bird succeeded in doing so repeatedly. Although both began their political lives as ardent Republicans, Scott became disillusioned with the party toward the end of the 1870s and became a political enemy of Bird, culminating in a complete break in their friendship in 1882 as Scott began a political shift toward the Democrats, something that Bird could not accept.[94]

John Gladney held a slightly lower status than Bird and Scott within the Black Republican wing but was still quite important. Born like Bird in 1844, he was a native of Arkansas and was already living in Cairo in 1865, when his name appears in that year's state census. His early history is unknown, but by the mid-1860s he was literate and exhibiting leadership qualities in the community. He became a close associate and friend of Bird and also got involved in community activism during the early postwar years. He was one of the orators at the Cairo Emancipation Day celebration on January 1, 1866, and he became one of the board members of the Cairo Educational Association, organized by Reverend Strother to form his free school in 1867. He also worked extensively in the local AME church, leading its Sunday School program for years, and was a leader of the fraternal organization, the Free Benevolent Sons of America. Although he started out as a laborer in Cairo, he was able to open his own business in the early 1870s and by 1872 had a contract with the city hauling lumber and then garbage. Following Bird's groundbreaking election to the office of police magistrate in April 1873, Gladney ran for and became the city's first elected Black county constable that November. He remained involved in law enforcement during most of his subsequent years in Cairo, before he moved to Springfield, Illinois, about 1890. Although less visible in the sources, Gladney certainly played a significant role with Bird and Scott from the earliest days of the Black Republican wing.[95]

In 1868, when the opportunity arose to form a Black organization within the Republican Party, these three young men stepped forward to inspire and mobilize an entire community still struggling with poverty, unemployment, underemployment, lack of education, and weak social and religious organizations. They also had to deal with the fact that it would be necessary for them to engage virtually all the eligible voters in the community for the Republican Party to attain sufficient strength to defeat the Cairo Democrats in any election. Thus, every vote counted, and there was little room for disunity. Forming the organization of this new social movement and creating a successful collective action plan would be complex. Unlike many social movements as described in the literature concerning framing process, this one began at a remarkably optimistic moment in African American life. It was different from most protest movements, in that while it was based on the long-standing insistence upon rectifying enduring grievances suffered by African Americans, it also was based on an invitation to ally their movement with the dominant political party in the country as the means to do that. For African Americans, this had never happened before. For the Cairo Black community, such a prospect was remarkably appealing: the new Black Republican wing would be significantly larger than its partner, the White Republicans, constituting 60 percent of the party to the latter's 40 percent. This gave them considerable power to press their agenda. However, that power was by no means complete. The two wings had to work together to create about 50 percent of the electorate. Thus, it was critical for them to cooperate with one another in order to have any chance of gaining and holding power in Cairo. Either wing could veto the proposals of the other. In addition, of course, was the fact that the White, established, still racist, wing of the party had strong assumptions that they were in charge and that the Black wing, although larger, should and would follow their orders. The latter did not always happen. Sometimes the two groups had different priorities, and thus negotiation and compromise were necessary. But in the late 1860s, the major agendas of the Republican Party and the African American community had enough overlap that a collaboration between the two seemed plausible. Bird and his colleagues would find it a challenge to work with their White counterparts, but they were able to inspire the African American community with a vision of a better life through Republican principles well enough to motivate a large Black vote for the party most of the time.[96]

The White Republican wing in Cairo was small, consisting of about two hundred voters and their families. It was led primarily by several local lawyers, most of whom supported the Radical Republican agenda. Most prominent appear to have been Daniel W. Munn, a local attorney who in 1866 had become the first Republican from southern Illinois to be elected to the Illinois state senate; his law partner Patrick H. Pope; and another attorney, David T. Linegar.[97] Linegar had been an early convert to the party, and it seems, from the few surviving newspaper accounts that focused on Cairo's Republican

David T. Linegar, a Cairo lawyer who became Bird's closest
White Republican ally during the 1860s until 1874, when he switched
allegiance to the Democrats. Detail from a collage of the 32nd
General Assembly House of Representatives, 1881. Abraham Lincoln
Presidential Museum and Library, #29428. SVFOZ_32GAHouse.

Party in 1868–70, that he was the most involved in helping organize and support the African American wing. These attorneys made great efforts to secure African American support for the Republican cause in Cairo. They also very quickly realized that Bird was an unusually strong leader and orator and began to make use of him at various rallies where they spoke to Black and perhaps mixed crowds. His appearance on the podium alongside White Republican leaders created much controversy in southern Illinois.

It was during this period, when he had taken on so many responsibilities, that John Bird decided that shuttling between Cairo and Windsor was no longer practical. In his October 1868 report to the *Christian Recorder*, Bird had called himself "a Cairoite to some extent," but in early 1869 he became one in reality. In so doing, he brought his family to a place where he was already an established leader in the community, maintaining solid relationships with many people, both Black and White. He, his wife, Annie, and their two sons, John William, born in 1866, and Egbert, born in 1868, settled into a rented house on the south side of Twelfth Street between Walnut and Cedar Avenues, not far from the former site of the contraband camp. Soon he got a job with the Illinois Central Railroad as a Pullman porter, a good but time-consuming position that he held at least until 1873.[98] From this point on, Bird's political career was sharply on the rise, and he became a force to be reckoned with in the city itself and in the Republican Party of Illinois.

Shortly after he settled in, Bird launched an additional project: he began to study law with one of the Republican attorneys, likely David Linegar, with whom he seemed closest in the early 1870s. This proved to be a critical moment in Bird's career, for although he was never admitted to the state bar, this training gave him significant advantages in his ability to argue for civil rights, as well as the credibility he needed in 1873 to run for police magistrate.[99] At the same time, the Republicans began to deploy him for speeches at rallies and events across southern Illinois. Few of these are mentioned in the Democratic *Bulletin*, our only local source, but editor Oberly described Bird in May of 1869 thusly: "the negro Bird, who has at frequent intervals, played the orator among the colored people of Cairo, and who, once upon a time, addressed that class from the same stand occupied by Olney and Linegar, and made the best speech of the occasion."[100]

On August 1, 1869, Bird gave his most important address to date at a celebration of West Indies emancipation in Carbondale at which the main speaker of the day was Congressman John Logan, whom Bird had described with such admiration to the *Christian Recorder* just a year earlier. Many downstate Democratic newspapers, including the *Illinois State Register* of Springfield, found it alarming and disgusting that a Black man should share the same podium with an important White official like Logan.[101] The *Bulletin* "defended" Bird's appearance there, with a primary political intent to insult Logan. Speaking of Bird, Oberly wrote, "The colored man referred to is the General's peer in every respect. He is more polished; a better scholar; a more eloquent speaker than the General, and a more intelligent politician. When the colored men of Illinois become electors and capable of holding office Bird will hold as long a pole as Logan; and will go for all the official fruit in view. If Logan, Linegar and Munn care about official honors in the future they should proceed to suppress Bird. He is a black bird with good strong wings, and is sure to fly high."[102] Oberly clearly used Bird's appearance on the podium to denigrate Logan (i.e., a Black man is superior to him as a speaker and a politician), and he concluded with the old canard, a warning to the Republicans—and his own Democratic readers—that the Fifteenth Amendment, if ratified, would lead to Black politicians dominating White citizens.[103] His praise of Bird might simply have been for political effect. However, in light of Oberly's earlier, consistent praise of Bird's abilities, one might wonder whether Oberly would have made these comparisons between Logan and Bird (rather than lampooning his speech as a fiasco, the method usually employed against Black speakers in Democratic papers) unless he actually considered Bird to be polished, a good scholar, an eloquent speaker, and an intelligent politician. But whatever intentions Oberly had in saying these things about him in the paper, for twenty-five-year-old John Bird, this experience, speaking on stage alongside a respected White Republican congressman in anti-Black Democratic southern Illinois, must have felt like a good indication that, in the words of the "Watchman" hymn, the political morning for African Americans was truly beginning to dawn.

CHAPTER THREE

"The Colored People Intend to Stay"

John Bird's Rise in Cairo Politics, 1870–1872

T HE RATIFICATION OF THE Fifteenth Amendment giving African Americans the elective franchise was a major milestone in the brief "golden age" of African American rights in the northern states that lasted from the late 1860s into the 1880s—not that Black people received full acceptance into American legal, political, and social culture during this period, but they made unprecedented strides that would not be replicated in quality for about three quarters of a century afterward. In Illinois, where African Americans in 1870 represented a mere 1.1 percent of the population, their political impact was somewhat muted, but it was felt noticeably in Chicago's Second and Third Wards, where their numbers allowed them to hold the balance of power in some elections. Their influence was considerably more marked in Cairo, where their voting power, directed in favor of the Republican Party, was sufficient to turn a previously Democratic stronghold into a viable two-party city. Three other cities, Galesburg, Springfield, and Quincy, had Black inhabitants that accounted for about five percent of the population, which limited but did not eliminate their political influence, and several rural counties in southern Illinois and near St. Louis had substantial Black populations that had notable successes within several small towns.[1]

Enfranchisement dramatically changed Cairo during the 1870s. John Bird and his colleagues William Scott, John Gladney, and others led the efforts to motivate the 350 to 400 eligible Black voters to participate in the elections of the early 1870s that brought Republican candidates into city, county, and state positions. It was now possible for the Black community to successfully press city leaders to establish an African American public school and force many businesses to open their doors to Black patrons. From the moment the ballot became available to them, the idea of electing African Americans to political office in Illinois also became a major goal, a key symbolic one—a visible manifestation of African Americans' ascent to citizenship and leadership within the predominant White society. In 1871, John Jones of Chicago became the first African American to win an election in Illinois when he gained a seat on the Cook County board. In Cairo, however, many of the White Republicans, while happy to accept African Americans' votes for the party, were reluctant to give theirs to a Black Republican candidate, and this delayed the appearance of a Black office holder in the city until 1873, when John Bird broke that barrier. The city's political and social improvements were tempered by the fact that Bird and the Black Republican leadership found it largely impossible to affect the huge issue of labor discrimination against African Americans, particularly in view of the fact that the majority of businesses in Cairo were owned by Democrats, who were strongly inclined to keep Black workers in the lowest jobs and were largely untouchable.[2]

John Bird entered 1870 not just as the head of the Black Republican wing but also as their primary representative to the local White party leadership. He used his considerable skills at interfacing with Whites to gain increasing influence within the inner circle and found himself taking part in internal party organizational matters. In addition, he made himself invaluable to the Republicans by regularly speaking at rallies around southern Illinois and western Kentucky and helping organize other Black communities to take advantage of their right to vote. He also learned quickly how to make use of his political clout in party meetings to force the White leaders to take the wishes of their African American constituents seriously. During the two years following enfranchisement, he became experienced in dealing with the many complications of keeping an organization like the Black Republican club both unified and motivated. He also had to counter external political challenges to his community from the city's Democratic leadership as they heightened their attempts to stoke anti-Black fear among their White constituents and developed means to suppress the Black vote in early elections.

The First Election and the Push for an African American Public School

By early February 1870, the requisite number of states had ratified the Fifteenth Amendment, so that its inclusion in the Constitution was assured. As it became clear that the amendment would become effective on March 30, the Cairo Republican Party focused on the next city election, a small one on April 11 for a member ("director") of the school board and a school trustee, as the first test for the strength of the new Black Republican wing's organization. This election was an appropriate one for the situation, since it was related to the highest political priority among the leadership and members of the Black community after the advent of voting rights: the establishment of public education for their children. But Bird and his colleagues faced several challenges during the months leading up to the election, both internal and external, that would ultimately determine the success of this movement.

Cairo's Democrats seem to have underestimated how successful Bird and his colleagues would be in motivating the Black voters of the city. One important reason for this was that until early April, the city leadership had no intention of implementing the requirements of the Fifteenth Amendment for the election at all. The *Bulletin* had largely ignored the rise of the Black Republican club and the building of its organization from the time of its founding in mid-1868 until the beginning of 1870. At that point, the paper, confident in the Democratic control over the city, began to report on a few political topics related to the Black Republican wing, such as dissension within the organization from Reverend Shores, a speech that Bird gave in Columbus, Kentucky, and preparations in the Black community for a celebration of the ratification of the Fifteenth Amendment scheduled for April 12, the day after the election.

The basic unity within the African American Republican wing faced some internal conflict during the weeks preceding April 11, dissension that was led by Rev. Thomas Shores. By early 1870, the minister seems to have become displeased with Bird and the other young leaders and with his own sense of being relegated to a minor role within the party. Thus, as he had done in 1867 when he subverted Reverend Strother's free school project at the last minute, Shores broke with the Black Republican club led by Bird in early March, one month before the election, in a clear bid to seize control of the Black wing of the party. His campaign began on March 4 with a not-so-subtle attempt to center the upcoming election around himself, by announcing that all Black voters should come to his church to "register" so that he could determine the community's voting strength. This proved to be a failure when few people showed up. Two days later, he announced that he was calling a mass meeting of all African American citizens of the city for the purpose of forming a new

Republican club separate from the original one. The meeting was held on March 9, but according to the *Bulletin*, only thirty to forty people showed up, presumably mostly members of his own congregation. Although this proved to be an unsuccessful rebellion, it certainly was an unhelpful distraction for the established club in preparing for the upcoming election. It is not clear how long Shores's separate club existed.[3]

A more serious challenge, however, was posed by the city leaders. Apparently as a response to the ratification of the Fifteenth Amendment, several of the Democrats decided to slow the city's implementation of it through illegitimate bureaucratic obstruction with regard to the April election. On March 30, Oberly nonchalantly wrote in an article about the election that "the machinery of the Amendment cannot probably be got into working order by the 11th." Democratic threats of such obstruction regarding the amendment were relatively common in other places, too, that spring. But the new, expanded Republican Party of Cairo was apparently ready to oppose this action. By April 7, without any discussion of how the "machinery of the Amendment" had been fixed, it was clear in the *Bulletin* that African Americans would be voting on April 11.[4]

The contest for the school directorship in Cairo was between the Republican candidate, I. M. Warwick, who was active in temperance causes, and the incumbent, Claiborne Winston, a local real estate agent and Democrat running as an Independent.[5] On Election Day, the African American voters turned out in force. The *Bulletin* reported that by 1:00 PM at least 250 of the 500 votes that had been cast were cast by Black voters. By closing, it was many more. Eight hundred and forty-seven ballots were cast, "fully three times the number that are ordinarily polled here at elections of that nature," wrote the *Bulletin*. "The reason for this is, chiefly, that the enfranchised Africans, having an opportunity to vote, availed themselves of it . . . the colored voters, almost to a man, voting for [Warwick]." Warwick handily defeated his opponent, 454 to 321.[6] The election was an impressive show of the Black Republican wing's power in Cairo and of Bird's organizational skill at getting the voters to the polls. It was also a wake-up call to the Democrats that their control of city politics was no longer firm.

The following day, the African American citizens held a massive Fifteenth Amendment celebration that became a seminal event for the Black community of Cairo and the surrounding region. Conceived in February, apparently by John Bird and William Scott, the first public organizational meeting for the celebration was held at the AME church on February 15, with no evidence of White participation. Bird and his colleagues intended this to be a huge and memorable event. Indeed, they modeled it on the grand reunion of the Union veterans from across the region that had been held in Cairo in 1868, where Bird had heard and admired Logan's impressive speech. They invited the Black citizens of the entire region to take part in the celebration. By March 17, the White Republican leadership was also on board and involved. At a mass meeting that evening, David Linegar and Bird spoke to the assembly about the plans for the celebration.[7] The event was set for April 12, the day after the local election, perhaps in part to distinguish it from a mere political rally. Indeed, it would be much more than that.

On the morning of the 12th, the activities began with the firing of cannon, followed by a parade through the city that stretched about a half-mile in length. A large wagon led the procession, holding thirty-six young African American girls in white dresses with red wreaths around their heads and blue sashes, each of which named one of the states, while another young woman stood with them representing the goddess Liberty. Two years earlier at the veterans' reunion, a similar collection of girls had ridden in its parade, but they had all been White. Those who attended both events must have felt the power of this day's symbolism. Behind the wagon were columns of African American men, nearly a thousand strong, carrying banners in honor of the occasion. Crowds, Black and White, lined the streets through the town. Even Oberly appeared genuinely impressed with the parade, describing it movingly in the *Bulletin* without a hint of his well-known sarcasm and beginning his account, "This day will long live in the memory of the Cairo colored people." Following the parade, the people assembled to hear speeches by Linegar and Bird. Because the crowd was too large to fit in the building reserved for the speeches, the program was moved outside to an open area. In the evening, the Black community hosted a well-attended fair, which concluded with a few other speeches, including two by William Scott and the Reverend Jeff Huston. The celebration was a huge success for the entire community, and a particular triumph for Bird as its lead organizer.[8]

The speech Bird gave before the crowd assembled at the celebration is the earliest of his for which we have some sense of its content. David Linegar, who had worked tirelessly to support Bird and the new Black Republicans, gave the first afternoon oration, and then Bird spoke to the crowd. The *Bulletin* published much of Linegar's speech ("except his reference to the rights and necessities of the Blacks in educational matters") and a partial account of Bird's.[9] It is clear that Bird designed the speech with a mixed audience of Blacks and Whites in mind and that the subject of highest priority in it was public education for African American children.

He opened with a recognition of the appropriateness of celebrating the day: "Was it not meet, then, that the colored men of America should give out an expression of happiness and exultation, at their birth into a free and equal manhood—their accession to the lawfully recognized title of American citizens?" He then thanked the generations of abolitionists who, "through obloquy, derision and danger, were pioneer soldiers in the struggle through which the colored man achieved the liberty which he cherishes as such a Heaven-sent blessing."[10] He went on to praise Abraham Lincoln and John Brown, before turning to the main issue of his speech: public education for African American children. This subject was very controversial in southern Illinois, with most Democrats and many Republicans still deeply opposed to the idea. As Bird made this speech in Cairo, the Illinois Constitutional Convention, forging an updated constitution for the state in Springfield, was still debating whether the new Article on Education in it should expand the mandate for public education to include African Americans, and in spite of a Republican majority, there was no certainty in April that that would happen. In fact, the wording finally adopted on May 9 did not explicitly mandate that Black children must be educated.

Referring back to Linegar's comments on Black education (the section of that speech the *Bulletin* had omitted from its coverage), Bird stated that the African American community in Cairo, while insisting upon the right to public education of its children, did not seek to integrate the public schools: "They desire no such thing, and have not asked it. They do ask, however, that the colored children be enumerated, and that when educated in *separate* schools they shall share, pro rata, of the public school fund. The colored people can establish and maintain their own schools, provide their own teachers and prefer to do so; but they ask and shall insist that the same laws that provide for the education of the white man's child shall extend to the child of the black man." As a model of such a successful segregated school system, Bird pointed to the schools in Ohio, "among the best disciplined and most flourishing of the land—as evidence of the ability of colored citizens to educate their own children, (separate and apart from the white, and without even the assistance of white teachers) when placed on an equal footing with other citizens."[11] No doubt Bird used this example because he had experienced the African American public schools in Cincinnati during his childhood. He had been a student during the years when the Black community had successfully fought for control over its schools, wresting them from White educators who often did not have African American students' best interests at heart. The issue of whether Black students were better off in White-controlled, integrated schools or in Black-controlled, separate ones was quite controversial in the Black community in the years after the war, and Bird supported the latter for Cairo in 1870.[12] He would later change his mind, but at this time there was an element of practicality in Bird's position. The intensity of the anti-integrationist hysteria in Cairo, fanned by the Democratic newspapers in town, made segregated schools appear to be the only plausible option that the Black community could propose as it negotiated with the White school board and city leaders, who still denied that there was any legal obligation to fund public education for African Americans. Defusing a clear flashpoint around mixed-race schools seemed to him the best strategy.[13]

In the final part of his speech, Bird turned, "in a spirit of bitter vindictiveness" according to Oberly, to the Democratic Party, and "warned the colored people against its wiles and machinations. He only wanted the democrats to let the colored people alone." He criticized them for their continued support of African colonization. "They wanted the colored people out of the country. 'Now, the colored folks,' continued the speaker, 'are well satisfied with this country; it is their native land, and beneath its soil the bones of their ancestors had rested for years and ages; and if the democrats didn't like the fellowship; if the presence of colored people here is obnoxious to them, *they may leave the country themselves, for the colored people intend to stay* [italics Oberly's]."[14]

This speech was the opening salvo of an intense campaign in Cairo by the African American community to establish a public school for its children. The campaign was somewhat buttressed by the adoption of Illinois's new state constitution in 1870, which brought some pressure to bear on school boards across the state. But the compromise language of the critical phrase in the Education Article requiring school districts to provide public schools "whereby all children of this State may receive a good common school education" allowed the anti-Black forces to argue that Black children were not necessarily included in the words "all children." It took the General Assembly two years to finally define the phrase inclusively in its revision of the state school laws under the guidance of State Superintendent Bateman. The new law, which passed on April 1, 1872, explicitly required school officials to make public schooling accessible to Black children, although it allowed the individual districts to determine whether Black children would attend integrated or segregated schools.[15] The African American community in Cairo, however, did not wait for the legislature to act and continued to press for a school. Although the *Bulletin* provides spotty information about the process by which this happened, there can be little doubt that Bird was the leader of this push.

The decision to establish an African American school was made by the three elected Cairo "school directors" (i.e., the school board) in the summer of 1871. I. M. Warwick, whom the Black Republicans of Cairo had helped make a school director in their first election, resigned in January 1871, after one year of his two-year term.[16] Thus in the 1871 election, held April 3, two of the three positions on the board were open. Only three candidates emerged, and the two winners were Daniel Hurd, a Radical Republican, and Moses B. Harrell, the intensely racist, unreconstructed Democratic editor now of the *Daily News*, who was fiercely opposed to the extension of any public funds to educate African Americans.[17] But the Black community and its leaders were able to convince Hurd and Joseph B. Reed, the incumbent director, that the city had an obligation to educate its children. In addition, Oberly of the *Bulletin*, who as late as the end of 1870 had contributed heavily to the hysteria about the dangers of Black children in the public schools, changed his mind on the subject and began to support the idea of a segregated public school for Cairo in 1871.[18] In August, despite Harrell's opposition, the two directors agreed to take over the operating costs of Tolford's school on Walnut, paying rent for the building and hiring Tolford to run the new public school, along with two subordinate teachers. A year later, the board purchased the Walnut Street school building to be the official "colored school." They also paid the AME church on Fourteenth Street to use their school for any potential overflow.[19] The board had feared that 500 students would arrive at the door, but about 250 actually enrolled in the first year. While most of the African American community was pleased with the city's decision to create an official public school, many were less happy about the directors' decision to hire the White Tolford and his White assistants to be in charge of it. According to letters sent to the *Bulletin*, the Black community was not consulted at all about who should fill the position, and most wanted an African American for the role. It is clear that many African Americans did not particularly trust Tolford.[20]

Even after the board's decision had been made, Moses Harrell continued to fulminate against the Black community. In an editorial in his paper on September 11, 1871, and in an angry letter to Oberly's *Bulletin* two days later, he argued that Cairo's African Americans were, as a class, "non-taxpaying and non-producing," that the new school imposed a massive financial burden on the White citizens of the city, that African Americans added to the costs of Cairo's crime and "pauper burdens," and that they collectively contributed less than $25 a year in taxes to the city. His solution was to argue that African Americans should not be given jobs in Cairo and that rather they should be encouraged to leave the city.[21]

Oberly, who less than a year before had been sympathetic toward much of this argumentation, responded with a surprisingly sharp rebuke of Harrell and an extraordinary point-by-point refutation of each assertion, which provides a number of insights into the Black community of Cairo in 1871 and illuminates Oberly's slowly evolving position regarding the city's African American citizens. While granting that "as a class," the Black citizens of Cairo—including the women and children—were nonpaying and nonproducing citizens, he pointed out that "as a class," the White citizens similarly were also nontaxpaying and nonproducing. Against Harrell's argument that Cairo's taxpayers would pay for poor Black students, he pointed out that taxpayers paid also for poor White children to attend school. "Indeed, Mr. Harrell's argument is an argument against the public school system which is based on the idea that the poorest is entitled to an education and the wealth of the country must pay for it." While granting that the African American community increased the costs of law enforcement, Oberly argued for a different solution: "They have not the opportunities to obtain labor that White men have, and, since Satan finds some wicked work for idle hands to do, they are too often in difficulties. In this fact we see reason why work should be furnished to them if possible." Finally, he sharply disputed Harrell's charge that the Black community provided less than $25 per year in city taxes: "We can name eleven colored men of Cairo who have paid into the city treasury this year over six hundred dollars, and this is not near all that pay taxes." He pointed out that the many families who rented their homes paid taxes indirectly through their rent.[22] This defense is quite striking from a Democratic newspaper in southern Illinois in 1871, and although Oberly maintained racist attitudes in areas of social equality, his shift in terms of public education and eventually the idea of African Americans holding political office put him

John H. Oberly, editor of the Democratic newspaper the *Cairo Bulletin*,
ca. 1869–70, when he was mayor of the city. In spite of their political differences,
Bird and Oberly eventually became friends, and Oberly softened his stances on
some issues related to African Americans. Located in Cairo, Illinois, City Hall.

in a minority within his party. Bird probably played a role in Oberly's evolving positions in this period, even though Oberly found him politically offensive at the same time.

In spite of the opposition to it within the White community, the "colored
public school" opened in the fall. However, things got off to a shaky start almost immediately. The simmering problem of the board's hiring of White
teachers for the school exploded in early December with an incident between Tolford and a teenaged African American student. Alice Jackson, the
daughter of the AME minister William Jackson, charged that during a class
taught by one of the other White teachers, a boy got into trouble and while
punishing him, the teacher said that "she wished the children were back in
slavery with their masters." Disturbed by this, Miss Jackson told some people
after school what the teacher had said. When Tolford found out, he pulled
Miss Jackson aside and demanded that she recant her accusation. When she
refused, he whipped her with a rawhide lash across the shoulders.[23] Upon
hearing about this, her outraged parents had Tolford arrested, and he was

brought before the police magistrate's court over the situation. Tolford told a different version of the story, in which Miss Jackson "had made some remarks about Mr. T. out of school hours, at which he took offense. He called the young lady to an account for it. She denied that she had said 'any such thing,' but a number of the other pupils were willing to testify that she had used the language. Mr. T. in order to make her acknowledge that she had used offensive language, applied the lash." Judge Fredoline Bross sided with the principal and dismissed the charges, but the Black community was not willing to let this go.[24] On the December 11, a mass meeting was held in which the citizens called for the firing of the teachers involved, protesting "against the employment of teachers over colored children who are unworthy of the position they hold, who seek not their elevation, but would, if possible, plunge them into ignorance and degradation far worse than that from which they have just emerged."[25] But when the school board met to discuss the situation, they sided with Tolford. He would remain the head teacher of the school into 1874.[26]

John Bird's Growing Political Influence, 1870–1872

The surviving sources concerning Bird between 1870 and 1872, while fragmentary, clearly show the influence he had during this time in both the Black community and the Republican Party in Cairo. If the White Republicans had expected the Black wing docilely to follow their political lead, they were very quickly disabused of that idea. At a meeting of the Republican leadership on April 11, 1870, the day of the school election, Bird showed a willingness to use his community's clout to veto a proposal his White Republican colleagues were considering that he thought was not in the interest of the African American citizens of Cairo. While it was clear to all that the addition of Black votes to the Republican side in the city had pulled the party to near parity with the Democrats, it was also clear that the numbers were very close.[27] As the White leadership looked toward the larger election in November, it met with a number of disaffected Democrats who had sought to run for office but had been refused by their party. These Democrats offered to switch party allegiance and bring over with them a set of voters, if they were placed on the ballot as Republicans. Although the leadership was suspicious of the Democrats' offer, they also thought this alliance could enhance their chances for power. But at the meeting, Bird rose and blasted this proposed alliance:

"Mr. Linegar has said that he is willing to apply to Democrats the rule of the Methodist church, and admit them into the Republican party on probation, and that if they act with becoming propriety while occupants of the probationary seats, that he will consent to take them into full membership; but I say to you, we, the colored people, will not consent to the adoption of such a rule. Allow a Democrat to come into the Republican party! Well, be it so; but I beg you to allow them to come in only *ninety days after death!*"[28] It appears that the White Republicans backed down on this issue and that the Democrats were not welcomed in after all.[29]

Bird's skills as a voting rights activist were called upon at this time across the region. A few days before the Cairo election, Bird traveled south to speak to a mixed mass meeting in Columbus, Kentucky, using the occasion to try out the speech he would make in Cairo on the 12th. Part of the function of his visit likely was to strategize with the town's large Black community (1,094 African Americans out of 2,573 people), concerning the fact that the Democrats who controlled the city government were planning to ignore the Fifteenth Amendment at their city election in May, as Cairo's city officials had attempted to do.[30] In fact, on the same day the *Columbus Dispatch* reported on Bird's speech (it particularly noted his "good English language"), it also printed an editorial arguing against observing the amendment.[31] This effort, like the one in Cairo, was thwarted, although no details survive, and by late April, the Republicans fielded a slate of candidates for city offices. In order to inspire Columbus's Black community to take advantage of their new right, Bird worked with their leaders to hold a Fifteenth Amendment celebration in the city on May 5, two days before the election. Between seven hundred and eight hundred people attended the event, and Bird gave one of the two keynote speeches.[32] The election was a triumph for Columbus's Black community and the Republican Party, who took most of the contested offices.[33]

On May 21, the Alexander County Republicans met in Cairo to choose their delegates to attend the convention to nominate the Republican candidate for U.S. Congress from the Thirteenth District. At the meeting, they chose Bird to serve on its Resolutions Committee and then appointed him as one of the four delegates from Alexander County to the congressional convention. This appointment made him the first and only African American to attend a district Republican convention as a delegate, certainly in southern Illinois but perhaps in the entire state.[34] The convention was held in mid-June, and Daniel Munn, one of Cairo's Republican leaders, was nominated for Congress, with Bird's support.[35]

The school board election in April 1870 had been small. The first real test of the new Republican strength in Cairo was the November 8 election, which included contests for U.S. representative, a few statewide offices, the local members of the state senate and house, and several county offices. During the summer and fall, Bird, Gladney, Scott, Shores, and others worked intensely to encourage the African American vote for the Republican ticket. Bird traveled to several counties in support of Munn and the other statewide candidates.[36] A good sense of his campaign style comes from the complete text of a speech Bird delivered at a rally in Cairo on October 31, published in the *Christian Recorder*. The opening paragraph indicates that the audience was a mixed one of Black and White attendees. The address covered the wide range of national campaign issues, using carefully constructed arguments, based on a substantial analysis of historical information and legal reasoning. After a brief introduction, Bird began with an examination of the Democratic Party's rule over the country during the years leading up to the Civil War, focusing particularly on the administrations of Franklin Pierce and James Buchanan during the 1850s. He criticized both their shameful records toward African Americans and their dismal economic performance. He also discussed the Supreme Court's Dred Scott decision, an early secessionist threat made by Robert B. Lee (Robert E.'s grandfather) in 1790, and the deeds of John C. Calhoun, whom he called "the Archbishop of nullification," to emphasize the Democratic Party's long-standing anti-Black and secessionist tendencies. He blasted Buchanan for refusing, during the last months of his presidency, to oppose the secession of the first states and laid the blame for the war on that failure. Responding to a speech by Munn's Democratic opponent, incumbent John Crebs, in which the latter insisted "that the democratic party did not pass any resolutions for or against the rebellion," Bird gave specific examples showing that the party passed numerous resolutions opposing the war in 1863–64.

In the second half of the speech, Bird turned to the record of the Republican Party, defending Lincoln's understanding of the Constitution with regard to secession and his administration's financial record. He then looked at the reduction of the federal debt and of taxes during the first sixteen months of President Grant's administration and explained why he supported the

Republican policy of tariffs on foreign goods. The climax of the speech provided a detailed argument that—contrary to the beliefs of Chief Justice Taney, Stephen A. Douglas, and other Democrats—African Americans were in fact legal citizens of the United States well before the Fourteenth Amendment was ratified, that during the American War of Independence, Black men served as soldiers against the British and were specifically recognized as citizens in New Hampshire, Massachusetts, New York, New Jersey, and North Carolina during the late eighteenth century when the Constitution was ratified, and that the early constitutions of those states made no discrimination against free Black people into the 1820s. Bird closed by contrasting the two parties, describing the Republican Party thusly: "All the peace and prosperity of our country to-day, is attributable to the undying devotion of the republican party to the objects of the fathers of this glorious republic. The republican party was an eminent necessity, and fortunate for our government, fortunate for justice, liberty, and humanity, that it came into existence." In contrast, he said, the Democrats "moulded and fashioned the government to suit a heinous prejudice, and a system of slavery more cruel and wicked than any known in the annals of history." The breadth and clarity of his historical arguments and his ability to address the wide range of contemporary Republican issues, while never losing sight of the key concerns of his largely African American audiences, illustrate why he was such a popular speaker.[37]

But all the labor that Bird and his colleagues put into the campaign largely came to naught, as the Democrats in Cairo worked to counter the Black Republican impact. Their strategies are clearly visible in the *Bulletin*. Within four days of the school election in April, Oberly was already charging that many of the Black votes in that election were illegally cast by African Americans shipped in from out of town. This would become a regular theme among the Democrats. In addition, Oberly continued to whip up anti-Black fear among the White voters of Cairo by focusing much of his coverage on Reverend Shores. For the White community, Shores's march to the White school in the fall of 1867 had made him the epitome of the dangerous Black revolutionary. Beginning in early 1870, Oberly resurrected this image of Shores, determined to make him the face of Black Republicanism. He consistently and falsely portrayed Shores as the dominant force in the African American community, malignant and powerful enough to hold even the White Republican leadership under his sway.[38] It is clear that Oberly could not effectively use the actual Black leaders—Bird, whom he called the "leader of the respectable portion of the colored Radicals of Cairo," Gladney, or even saloon-owner Scott—to create the kind of anti-Black reaction that he could by using Shores as the boogeyman.[39]

In spite of the Black community providing about 325 votes for the Republican candidates across Alexander County, the Democrats swept almost all the offices in the election, including the congressional seat. Nationwide, this election, the midterm of President Grant's first administration, saw Democrats make significant gains in several states, in part because the electorate was reacting against the Fifteenth Amendment and other pro–African American advances that had occurred during Grant's first two years. In Alexander County, Crebs defeated Munn for Congress 959 to 804, and William B. Anderson defeated John A. Logan for the office of congressman-at-large by 922 to 844.[40] However, there is considerable evidence from the *Bulletin* itself that part of the Democrats' success came because they deliberately used their power to suppress the Black vote in Cairo during the polling. On October 21, Oberly charged that the Republicans were "colonizing Kentucky and Missouri negroes" into the county for the purpose of illegal voting and demanded that the Democratic leaders take steps to intervene. On Election Day, the Democratic judges acted to keep large numbers of African Americans from voting, and Oberly praised Cairo mayor Thomas Wilson and John Q. Harmon, the election judges in Cairo's two districts, for having excluded many African Americans from the polls as illegal voters, when actually, only six Black men were charged with the crime in the entire city. The Republicans bitterly accused the Democrats of significant voter suppression. Oberly also obliquely described a confrontation between the two Reverends Strother and Bradley and the election judges, which suggests that the ministers had challenged this type of action. With these widespread voter irregularities, this election did not settle the issue of the full impact of an unrestricted Black vote in Cairo. Even with the suppression, the Republican votes in the city itself were much closer to the Democrats than the latter might have hoped, with the margins of the Democratic victories in Cairo averaging only around twenty or so votes out of over one thousand. This meant that in a fair election the Republicans easily might have an edge but that neither party could be certain of regular victories.[41]

By the time of the next city election in February 1871, no one felt confident about either party's chances—the Democrats had split into two factions, and the Republicans still feared a close loss similar to the one in November.

While Bird and the other leaders had supported the White candidates in 1870 (although there apparently had been a small write-in campaign to elect Shores as a justice of the peace and Scott as a constable in the November election), in 1871 they were ready for the Republicans to put an African American on the local ticket.[42] However, the party was not.[43] By early February, neither party had fielded a slate of candidates, but it was clear to the African American community that the Republicans would not nominate a Black candidate. In light of this, some leaders, primarily William T. Scott and Reverend Shores, met to consider whether to field a separate African American slate for the election.[44] In the end they decided not to proceed, but Scott put himself forward as an independent candidate for city marshal.[45]

On February 22, shortly before the election, a number of White Republican and Democratic leaders held a joint meeting and decided to put together a combined slate of candidates for the city offices that was presented to the public as the "Citizens' Party."[46] John Oberly, who played a leading role in organizing the ticket, described in the *Bulletin* the two reasons that he supported this process: (1) the Democrats were too divided among themselves to present a united front against the Republicans, and (2) the current (Democratic) city administration was under the influence of several unsavory bosses (the "Grasshopper Party") who ran the liquor and vice businesses of Cairo.[47] The Republicans' motivations for taking part are not articulated in surviving sources but almost certainly centered on the fear that they would be shut out of every office, as had happened in November. The Citizens' ticket was composed of a balance of three Republican nominees, including John M. Lansden for the plum office of mayor, and four Democrats, and on February 28, it handily won the election. With 334 votes, Scott came in a distant second to the Citizens' Party candidate Andrew Cain's 693.[48] The Citizens' Party had co-opted most of the White Republican vote, and left Scott with a substantial but insufficient number of Black (and perhaps some White) votes to win the election.

Unlike Scott, Bird bided his time before putting himself forward for office, making himself increasingly valuable to the Republican leadership in a variety of ways. On May 9, 1871, he and three other Black speakers, including John Gladney, addressed an African American picnic celebration, probably in support of the party.[49] In June his name appeared on a petition with over one thousand signatures from the citizens of Cairo to the County Court asking that it restore a contract that offered county bonds to support the construction of a new railroad for the town. The petition, perhaps the first such civic petition to solicit African Americans as signees, included the signatures of Bird, Scott, Gladney, and Reverend Bradley.[50] In October, the Republicans of the First State Senatorial District (Alexander, Pulaski, and Union Counties) called a special convention to nominate a candidate for the state senate to replace an incumbent who had died. Bird was chosen as one of the four Alexander County delegates to this convention.[51]

Bird worked extensively for the Republican ticket in the November 1871 election. The *Bulletin* reported on a rally for the Black community held on November 3, the Friday preceding Election Day, at which Bird was the main speaker. Oberly, increasingly antagonistic toward Bird, provided this distorted description of the relationships between Bird and the other Black leaders: "Bird is a venomous fellow, and talks gall and wormwood. He has a smattering of politics, and domineers over his fellow citizens of the Black color, while he in turn is domineered by the White radical clique of Cairo. Rev. Mr. Shores don't [*sic*] knuckle to him, but Freeman, Scott and Gladney very meekly follow where the self-assured Bird leads. He told them on Friday night that they must vote to-day for Miller and Mertz, and they dare not disobey him."[52] Oberly is correct in describing Bird as the leader of the Black wing, as well as showing the division between Bird, Scott, and Gladney on one side and Shores on the other. However, his characterization of Bird as "domineering" over his compatriots is doubtful. In spite of their hard work on the campaign, the Republicans again lost to the Democrats in the fall election in Cairo.[53]

Also in 1871, Bird made his first foray onto the national African American political scene. After a call was issued for a National Convention of Colored People to be held in St. Louis, Bird joined with John B. Dawson and R. C. Warren to organize the Illinois delegation for the conference. The goals of the convention were to choose the most appropriate date for an annual celebration of emancipation and full citizenship, to determine "whether the colored people favor female suffrage" and to determine the "policy to be pursued by the colored people in the coming campaign of 1872." At a mass meeting of the local community on August 25 at the AME church, the majority (apparently including Bird and Gladney) voted in favor of female suffrage.[54] However, these goals do not seem to have inspired much enthusiasm around the country, and the convention proved to be fairly insignificant in the history of Black Conventions. Sixty-seven delegates assembled on September 22, 1871, almost all of them from the states surrounding Missouri. Bird, a young man and a relative newcomer to the larger political scene, played an active but not leading part in the conference. The attendees passed a resolution calling for annual freedom celebrations to be held on both January 1 and July 4, and another supporting the Republican Party and President Grant's nomination for reelection in 1872, both supported by Bird. Apparently, no decision was made at the convention about female suffrage.[55]

Bird's loyalty to the Republican Party became particularly important in 1872, when two elections created considerable controversy in Cairo's African American community. The first was a local race for police magistrate in February. The Democratic and Republican leaders once again produced a combined "Citizens' slate" that included Fredoline Bross, the Democratic incumbent, for the office of magistrate. But another White Democrat, Claiborne Winston, ran for the position as an independent, campaigning hard for the Black vote. Winston was popular among some in the African American community because he had sold the land upon which three of Cairo's African American churches were built at a steep discount, and he was known as a good landlord who charged reasonable rent to Black families. However, the White Republican leadership had been very happy with the outcome of the first Citizens' Ticket and wanted its members to vote for all its candidates, including Bross. Several Black leaders supported Winston, including William Scott and Reverend Shores, while Bird and Gladney joined the Republican leadership in supporting Bross.[56] In the election, the Citizens' Ticket once again won, and Bross defeated Winston, 677 to 545. No data exist to indicate how many Black votes went to each candidate, but likely the community was divided on the issue.[57]

The second divisive race was the presidential election in November 1872. The Republican Party split over President Grant's support of the Radical Republican agenda and the substantial scandals that had dogged his administration. The dissidents formed a new party called the Liberal Republicans, which, while supporting the recent constitutional amendments, opposed the continued federal enforcement of those amendments with troops in the South. Instead, they called for the end of political restrictions on former rebels and the return of authority for handling enforcement of the laws to the southern states. At their national convention in May, the Liberals nominated as their presidential candidate Horace Greeley, who, although he had been an important abolitionist and Radical Republican voice in the 1850s and 1860s, had now come to support the policies found in the platform.

Grant, representing the supporters of Reconstruction, easily won the nomination of the "stalwart" faction of the party in June. In a surprise move, the Democrats supported Greeley as their nominee, too, so as not to divide the anti-Grant vote.[58] Thus, in an extraordinary situation, two figures who were beloved in the African American community were running against each other for president. Many Black Republicans had been disheartened by the corruption scandals that had marred the end of Grant's first term and turned toward Greeley.

The only Black leader in Cairo who decided to support Greeley was Reverend Shores. He attended the Eighteenth District Liberal Republican Convention on April 25, where he was named an alternate to the national convention in Cincinnati and soon became a delegate.[59] Bird, along with Gladney and Scott, stayed faithful to the party and its Radical agenda. All of them actively campaigned for Grant. Although details are scarce, it appears that, as in 1870, Bird in particular made speaking tours around several of the southern counties. This election proved quite different from the two previous November votes—the Republicans swept the election in Alexander County, including Cairo. In the city, Grant defeated Greeley by a convincing total of 774 to 678, a margin that indicates that Bird and his colleagues kept the vast majority of the Black Republicans faithful to the Grant side.[60] After this election, Shores seems to have largely disassociated himself from politics and never again appears in the *Bulletin* within a Republican context until his death in 1882. His last hurrah was in 1880 when he ran for police magistrate in Cairo following Bird's retirement from the position but garnered only ninety votes out of the 1,055 cast.[61]

The Liberal Republicans also nominated their own slate of candidates for statewide offices, including Gustave Koerner for governor, who was also supported by the Democrats. In this situation, the stalwart Republicans called upon Richard Oglesby, the popular governor from the immediate postwar era (1865–69), to run for the office, even though they expected the state legislature to elect him U.S. senator from Illinois in the same year. As part of this plan, John Lourie Beveridge, who had served in the war as a colonel in the Seventeenth Illinois Cavalry and had left as a brigadier general, was nominated for lieutenant governor on the understanding that he would replace Oglesby as soon as the latter left for the Senate. Oglesby triumphed over Koerner in the election, with Cairo going for him, 764 to 692. Isaac Clements, the Republican candidate for U.S. representative from the Eighteenth (formerly the Thirteenth) District, defeated his Democratic opponent, both across the district and in Cairo by a margin of ninety-seven. All of this would have been impossible without a strong turnout from the African American community, and Bird had again played a key role in securing those votes.[62]

Before 1872, Oberly had often lumped Bird in with the other Black leaders he sharply criticized, but he found it difficult simply to dismiss him. During this election year, he began occasionally to write of him with a grudging admiration. In describing the speeches of several Black Republicans at a mass meeting on February 23, Oberly wrote, "Of the orators Bird was, of course, the most eloquent."[63] He also quoted William Scott calling Bird "the eagle orator of Egypt . . . I cannot pretend to cope with him in eloquence and elegance of diction."[64] By September of that year, Oberly further softened his stance on Bird, in one article calling him "a really clever colored man of some sense" and commenting about Bird's support for Grant, "We know Mr. Bird to have a good deal of sense, although he is a little venomous, but we have confidence in the effects of time. We have no doubt Bird will be all right on the political issues before the lapse of many years. He is too sensible, and we believe too honest a negro to persist in walking along a crooked path, in which he is compelled to trample in the filth of political corruption and mischievous principles."[65] Oberly would be disappointed in his hope that Bird might ever leave the Republican Party.

CHAPTER FOUR

"The Morning Seems to Dawn"

John Bird's Increasing Role in the Republican Party, 1873–1878

THE 1870S REPRESENTED THE HIGH POINT of Bird's career as a singular force within the Republican Party of southern Illinois, a period during which he grew in political influence and prestige in a fashion unparalleled by any other African American in the region and became well-known across the state. In 1873, not only was he the first African American in Illinois to be appointed to an honorific statewide position (as a member of the Board of Trustees of the Illinois Industrial University, later the University of Illinois), but he also became the first African American elected to a public office in southern Illinois, when he won the post of police magistrate in Cairo, which also made him the first Black judge in the history of the state. The following year, he was invited to give a speech at the opening ceremony of the Southern Illinois Normal University, another unprecedented honor for an African American. During this decade, the evidence indicates that he was the primary representative of Cairo's Black community in pressing for improvement in the city's African American school, working closely with the school superintendents to develop it into a remarkably strong institution, eventually run by a well-qualified Black principal and certified Black teachers. These achievements reflect his ability to use his education, charisma, eloquence, integrity, and organizational abilities to influence both African Americans and Whites in the fight for equal rights. The strength of his position in both communities was illustrated in 1877, when he was reelected to the police magistracy, and in 1879, when he received reappointment to the Industrial University's board. During this decade, he worked constantly for the Republican cause, rallying support for the party within

Cairo's African American community, traveling across the state to speak at rallies, and attending county, regional, and state Republican conventions. But as the White Republicans began pulling away from their commitment to civil rights in the later 1870s, Bird was not afraid to criticize the party, while always insisting upon his loyalty to the Republican ideals that had been embodied in the early postwar period. It was also during this decade that he began to move into leadership roles within the Black convention movement, a part he would play for the next two decades.

Bird's influence can be seen in the improvements that Cairo's African American community saw in the city's political, educational, and social structures during these years. While problems of prejudice were still substantial, particularly in the job market, many elements of Cairo's public structure opened up to the African American community. They were still free to live in any part of the city, as had been the case in the 1860s, and with the exception of a few very wealthy blocks, mostly in the newer, northern section of the city, there were no segregated neighborhoods. Most streets were occupied by a mixture of Black and White households. About one third of White families had Black neighbors next door, and many apartment buildings and rooming houses accepted occupants of both races.[1] Many of the hotels, including the St. Charles, Cairo's finest, were open to African American patrons, as were several of the restaurants. The theaters and public meeting places such as Scheel's Washington Hall, Phillis' Hall, and the Atheneum were also integrated, and audiences of Black and White citizens were common, though usually segregated within the auditorium.[2] By the middle of the decade, the school board was one of the few in Illinois that came close to treating the segregated African American school on an equivalent footing with the White schools. And following Bird's election to the police magistracy in 1873, other African Americans ran for and won political office in Cairo and Alexander County. Cairo became an appealing city for African Americans to settle in, so that as the population increased between 1870 and 1880 from 6,267 to 9,011, the number of Black citizens increased from 1,849 to 3,349, thereby rising from 29 percent of the city's inhabitants to 37 percent.[3]

Bird's achievements played out, however, during a time when the federal government's active stance toward ensuring the civil rights of African Americans began to wane and collapse. Most White Republicans, tired of dealing with Reconstruction in the South and the "negro question" as a whole, began to shift their focus away from African American rights to other political interests. The ominous midterm election of 1874, when Democrats took control of the House of Representatives as well as many northern governorships and state legislatures, was followed in 1876 by the disputed election of Republican Rutherford Hayes, which brought the already severely weakened Reconstruction era to an end and resulted in the disastrous loss of rights for African Americans in the Old South. In the northern states, Black communities did not suffer as deeply as their southern counterparts. There, in fact, these years generally represented a time of continued marginal improvement in the political, civil, and social status of the region's small Black population. Enfranchisement was largely protected in those states, and while the national White Republican establishment steadily backed away from expanding and enforcing civil rights after 1875, most state governments did little to diminish what had been accomplished.[4] In several parts of Illinois, African Americans were able to maintain at least some political influence during the mid-1870s.[5]

At the same time, the majority of northern African Americans continued to suffer from severe economic discrimination, excluded from any but the most menial jobs, living in substandard housing, made even worse by a nationwide depression that began in 1873 and continued about five years. As many manufacturing businesses shrank or closed, Black workers were usually the first to be let go, and those who retained jobs now received even lower pay than before the collapse. The economic disaster allowed the Republican Party to take its focus off the issues surrounding Black rights and onto other economic issues. Dominated by the rising postwar business tycoons, the Republican leadership in the big cities shifted toward anti-union, anti-regulation, pro-railroad policies.[6]

During these years, many members of the northern Democratic Party, stigmatized as having supported the South during the war, attempted to rehabilitate their image among White voters with the New Departure campaign, in which they supported some civil rights legislation at the state and local levels, while still calling for the removal of federal troops from the South and the reinstatement of all former Confederates to full citizenship, and assuring northern voters that southern White Democrats would uphold the constitutional rights of African Americans. This strategy eventually proved to be quite successful for the party.[7] Of course, the southern Democrats had no intention of preserving African American rights, and during the 1870s they seized control of the former Confederacy through intimidation and violence.

The African American community in the North fought ferociously to hold onto the advances they had made, while voicing their outrage at the Republicans' abandonment of their people in the South.

Bird's Appointment to the Board of Illinois Industrial University

The remarkable events of early 1873 came on the heels of the substantial 1872 Republican victory in previously Democratic Alexander County. Bird and his colleagues had proven themselves as valuable organizers of Cairo's Black Republican wing and strong campaigners across the region in a turbulent year, with Bird in particular gaining the confidence of the White Republican leadership. This was certainly a major factor in his appointment to the board of trustees of the Illinois Industrial University (IIU) in March.

The Illinois Industrial University had been established at Urbana in February 1867 as the state's Land Grant institution. Under the capable guidance of Regent John Milton Gregory, it early developed characteristics of a comprehensive university while focusing heavily on the twin pillars of the Land Grant Act—agriculture and engineering. The original establishment law for the university designated a thirty-two-member board of trustees, composed of four ex officio and twenty-eight members appointed by the governor, one member from each of the thirteen congressional districts, and five members from each of the three "Grand Legal Judicial Divisions" (North, Central, and South). As the state grew in the late 1860s and early 1870s, the number of congressional districts increased and the board expanded to thirty-eight members. Those appointed to the board were generally prominent businessmen, lawyers, educators, and farmers, mostly in their forties or older.[8]

In January 1873, Richard Oglesby, who had won the election for governor in November, accepted the office of U.S. senator from the state legislature and passed the governorship to Lieutenant Governor John Lourie Beveridge.[9] Among Beveridge's early duties was to fill a number of seats on the university's board. There was only one opening in the Southern District in 1873, the position of Isaac S. Mahan, who had resigned, leaving the need for a two-year replacement. On March 4, 1873, Governor Beveridge announced to the Illinois Senate his selection of the new board members. For the replacement position, Beveridge, in a bold move, named John J. Bird (misspelled Byrd in his list).[10] This was a historic event—Bird became the first African American appointed to a statewide, honorific office by an Illinois governor.[11] He also became the first African American ever appointed as a trustee of a predominantly White institution of higher education in Illinois, and perhaps in the United States.[12]

Beveridge's decision to appoint Bird to this prestigious position was remarkable and provocative. Not only was Bird an African American, but he was also only twenty-nine years old, and he was still a Pullman porter for the Illinois Central Railroad, a unique occupation for a university trustee. There were certainly several distinguished White Republicans in southern Illinois who had sought the post and were disappointed, and the designation of an African American from the most Democratic part of the state seemed destined to create a stir. But the White Republican leadership in Cairo, who must have recommended Bird to Governor Beveridge, apparently saw the opening at IIU as an appropriate way to reward Bird in light of his faithful and successful service to the party. The appointment also was an excellent fit for Bird because of his long interest in education, his work in fighting for Cairo's Black public school, and his own scholarly achievements, eloquence, and oratorical skills. The governor, however, initially appears to have made this appointment without any fanfare concerning Bird's racial identity, and the state's newspapers, including those in Cairo, Urbana, and Chicago, seem to have missed or ignored the story.

Bird's first meeting on the board took place on March 11, 1873 in Urbana, and he was sworn in with the other new members. He was assigned to two committees: the Military Committee and the Library and Apparatus Committee. The former produced a report for the board, while the second examined the report on the library furnished by Regent Gregory. Bird, speaking for the latter committee, offered a motion to authorize Gregory to revise his library report in preparation for its public inspection.[13]

This first meeting appears to have been a success for Bird, but the meeting could have been his last one. In May 1873, the Illinois legislature passed a major bill that reorganized several parts of the university's structure, including the board of trustees. It reduced the number of appointed trustees from thirty-four to nine, citing the bulkiness and inefficiency of the large board. All the members were released, and the governor was to choose three from each of the Grand Judicial Divisions to fill the new board. Beveridge did not officially announce his choices until July 1, 1873, while the General Assembly, which was required to confirm the nominees, was not in session. From the

Southern Division, he chose A. M. Brown of Villa Ridge, a judge and horti-culturalist, one of the original trustees from 1867; James P. Slade of Belle-ville, the St. Clair County superintendent of schools, who had come onto the board in 1869; and John Bird, who by now had become police magistrate in Cairo.[14] This second appointment of Bird to the board rather than one of the several White trustees who lost their positions indicates the significance Beveridge placed on having the presence of Bird in the university structure. At the time, however, Beveridge and his colleagues apparently still did not feel politically secure enough to publicize this appointment until after the legislature confirmed it, and again, with the exception of the *Cairo Bulletin*, which now reported on Bird's position, noting the significant fact that he was Black, newspapers such as the Chicago *Inter Ocean* simply listed Bird among the nominees with no reference to his race.[15]

Although the new board had begun meeting in July 1873, the appointments were officially confirmed only in the Senate's next session, on February 12, 1874. With no indication of Bird's race, the request for concurrence on the appointments passed unanimously out of the Committee on State Charita-ble and Educational Institutions. In the full Senate, it passed by a vote of thirty-three to two.[16] Only in the days after the vote did conservative Democrats learn that they had voted unknowingly to confirm an African American to the board. Suddenly Bird's race became a major topic of discus-sion and an issue across the state. The *Illinois State Journal* was typical of Re-publican papers in supporting the appointment, while also reporting happily on the outrage within the other party that followed this discovery:

> The Bourbon Democrats have been sore wroth for a few days by reason of having unconsciously voted to confirm the nomination of the Gov-ernor of Mr. J. J. Bird as Trustee of Industrial University at Champaign. Mr. Bird is a colored man, a conductor of the Pullman Sleeping Car Company on the Illinois Central Railway. He resides in Cairo, and has the respect even of that Democratic Egyptian country. He was nomi-nated by the Governor just as if he was a common man. In the due course of business he was confirmed, and that too, direful calamity! in part by such good old Democratic votes as Senators Archer, Casey and others of the same stripe.[17]

Although the *Journal* and many other Republican papers expressed a great deal of delight over the story, the Democrats were seriously angered at the

State of Illinois
  Champaign. Co. SS.

          We, and each of us
do solemnly swear that we will support
the Constitution of the United States, and
the Constitution of the State of Illinois, and
that we will faithfully discharge the duties of the office of Trustee of the Illinois
Industrial University according to the
best of our ability

Geo. H. Kenower.   John L. Beveridge
                          John E. Reynolds
                          J. H. Pickrell
                          J. A. Sabin
                          James P. Slade
                          A. M. Brown
                          Emory Cobb
                          S. Gardner

Subscribed and sworn to   J. J. Bird
before me this 10th day   R. B. Mason
of July A D 1873   J. T. Fountain
          J. H. Hess J.P.

                          Alexander Blackburn
Subscribed and sworn to before me this
eleventh day of July A D 1873
          J. H. Hess J.P.
and subscribed and sworn to before me by
J. J. Bird and R B Mason this 15th day of
August A D 1873
                    J. H. Hess J.P.

Board of Trustees Oath of Office, Illinois Industrial University, July 1873,
signed by Bird, who became the first Black trustee of the university. University
of Illinois Archives, record series 1/1/5, box 1, folder: Trustees' Oaths.

appointment. However, it was a done deed, and they were unable to reverse their votes.

Bird was not able to attend the first meeting of the new board on July 10, 1873. During the meeting, the members chose lots to determine the length of term for each (two, four, or six years, in order to create staggered terms). Bird received a six-year appointment.[18] He was present at the next two meetings on August 14 and September 23, 1873, but does not appear in the minutes of either session. He missed the following one on December 10. From then on, he attended about half of the meetings over the next five years, a smaller percentage than most of the trustees. His position as police magistrate and his constant activities on behalf of the Republican Party likely made it difficult for him to attend the meetings regularly, but he was well enough regarded at the university that in 1879 Governor Shelby Cullom reappointed him to a second six-year term on the board.[19]

Very little information about Bird's activities on the board has survived, since the newspapers, even in Urbana, showed little interest in the board and produced virtually no independent reporting on it, instead simply printing parts of its official minutes, if anything. Those minutes provide only a surface veneer of the workings of the board, which included participation in committees outside the meeting times, political lobbying of local state legislators and others in support of the university, and interactions with the public across their regions, including especially farmers, in order to bring their attention to the achievements of the university and the programs it offered.[20] Undoubtedly Bird was actively involved in these aspects in Alexander and surrounding counties.

Although there is little information about Bird's visits to Urbana-Champaign, what exists indicates that he became well known in the city. On September 13, 1876, the *Champaign County Gazette* noted that Bird would be speaking that night at Barrett Hall, the leading auditorium in town, which had hosted Susan B. Anthony, Mark Twain, Frederick Douglass, and other major notables in recent years. His speech was the first item in column 1 of the front page, and the item only said, "Bird, in Barrett hall, tonight." This was followed at the end of column 2, with another notice stating, "Go to Barrett hall tonight and hear J. J. Bird, of Cairo." Both of these clearly assume that the *Gazette*'s Republican readers were quite familiar with him and knew the kind of message he would be delivering. The next week, the *Gazette* reported that his lecture, largely on the political situation, was well attended by both Blacks and Whites.[21]

The board of trustees had substantial power over the development of the university, and the records show that the majority of the board members were in fundamental ways at odds with the educational philosophy of the university's regent. From the beginning Gregory had argued that IIU should be more than simply a trade school for farmers and engineers, as the board majority viewed it, and that it should be a true university, a center of learning, with research interests in a wide range of fields, including the sciences, humanities, and the arts. No documentation indicates where Bird stood on these issues, but with his well-known interests in history, political thought, and even music, it seems likely that he belonged to the pro-Gregory faction. The board, however, remained dominated by members who had little conception of the role of higher education in the late nineteenth century. Solberg, in his study of the early days of IIU, argued that while Gregory continued to expand his vision of the university during the 1870s, many of the board members maintained their narrow views. Fortunately for the university, by the time Gregory retired in 1880, his larger vision had won the day.[22]

According to current evidence, Bird was the first African American to be affiliated with the Industrial University. The earliest certain Black employee was L. H. Walden, who was hired in 1879 as a part-time groundskeeper, then as full time, 1890–95 (Bird's trustee position was honorary and therefore uncompensated).[23] Currently, University of Illinois sources list Jonathan A. Rogan, who enrolled in 1887–88, as the first known Black student. Information on Rogan comes from a 1937 card file list of identified African American students and a 1940 study of the Black presence at the university, both compiled and written by Albert R. Lee, chief clerk in the University President's Office and unofficial dean of African American students during the early twentieth century.[24] It is unlikely that Rogan was the university's first Black student, but probable rather that Lee could find no relevant data for the years preceding 1887. Bird himself strongly indicated there were students there during his time in a convention address in 1883, where he explicitly described the Land Grant institution of the state as a college "wherein the co-education of the races, and the co-education of the sexes are encouraged, promoted, and practiced." Thus, it is likely that African Americans attended IIU well before 1887 but simply were not identified in surviving university records by their race. This was the case at the University of Michigan, where historian Elizabeth G. Brown was able to identify two Black students who enrolled at Michigan in 1868 only by finding near-contemporary references to them in non-university sources.[25]

Judge John J. Bird

Just weeks after receiving the trusteeship from Governor Beveridge, Bird achieved a second astonishing victory by becoming the first African American to be elected to office in Alexander County and the first African American judge in the state of Illinois. It was a position for which he was imminently prepared, with his recent legal studies, wide-ranging education, analytical skills, and organizational prowess. The process by which he accomplished this extraordinary feat was complex. Pressure had been mounting on the local Republican leadership to nominate an African American candidate for local office since 1871. They had not supported William Scott that year when he ran for city marshal against the combined Democratic and Republican Citizens' Ticket candidate. In late March of 1872, Scott and Reverend Shores announced they would run for school trustee and school director, but before the election on April 8, they withdrew, likely under pressure from the Republican leadership.[26] In the fall, the Black community pushed hard to have John Gladney nominated as the Republican candidate for Alexander County sheriff, but this, too, seems to have been vetoed.[27] Events developed differently, however, during the run-up to the municipal election held on April 15, 1873. On March 16, the first announcements of candidacies for city positions appeared in the *Bulletin*, including one concerning William F. Pitcher, co-owner of a hardware store and a Democrat, running for police magistrate. Cairo employed two magistrates, who served for a four-year term, but only one position was up for election in 1873. Two weeks later, there were three additional declared candidates: the Democratic incumbent, Bryan Shannessy, a longtime resident of Cairo; James Ryan, an Irish highway foreman; and Charles Mehner, a Cairo police officer. In early April, James Summerwell, a former policeman and city health officer, and Joseph McKenzie, owner of a furniture factory and longtime Democratic activist, joined the race.

On April 11, the leading Republicans and Democrats once again met to choose a Citizens' Ticket for the election. The collaboration had been successful in 1871 and 1872, but this year things did not work out as well. Neither of the two candidates who had announced for mayor were satisfactory to a majority of the people at the meeting, so another candidate had to be found. This took a very long time. Finally, Colonel John Wood, a Republican, accepted the nomination. But after that arduous process, no one had the taste for trying to hammer out candidates for the other positions, so the Citizens' Ticket only forwarded a candidate for mayor. Until this point, Bird had made no announcement of his intention to run for office, but now, on April 13, just two days before the election, Bird placed an advertisement in the *Bulletin* that he was running for police magistrate.[28] It is likely that Bird waited to see what happened with the Citizens' Ticket. When they decided not to field a candidate for the position he wanted, he felt free to join the race without having to run against his own party, as Scott had done in 1871. It is probable that he had the support of the White Republican leadership, because as soon as he appeared on the ballot, three of the six other candidates dropped out of the race. Oberly in the *Bulletin*, faced with the first serious Black candidate for office, took a cautiously complimentary tone concerning Bird's entry into the race: "Mr. Bird is eminently well qualified for the position, and should the voters of Cairo give the office to him, he promises to do the best he can to fill it to the satisfaction of every one."[29] Thus on Election Day, Bird was in the running against three White men, all Democrats. The results showed that the election was largely a two-person race between John Bird and James Ryan, but the other two candidates siphoned off enough White Democratic votes to give Bird the victory, with a vote of 496 to Ryan's 431, Shannessy's 180, Pitcher's 132, and McKenzie, who had already withdrawn, 39. Bird won hefty margins in the First, Third, and Fifth Wards, while losing to Ryan by narrower margins in the Second and Fourth. Certainly he received most of the African American ballots, which probably amounted to between 325 and 375 votes, but in the First Ward in particular, where fewer Black families lived, it is clear that he received numerous White votes as well. His victory was news across the state.[30]

Bird was sworn into his new position on April 29, 1873, and took up court on May 1 at the magistrate's office that Shannessy (the judge he replaced) had used, at the northeast corner of Washington Avenue and Twelfth Street.[31] His first case was that of a White Irishman, Patrick Maloney, who was accused of the theft of a horse blanket. Bird bound Maloney over to the city jail to await the impaneling of a grand jury.[32]

Although John Bird was not the first African American to be elected a judge in the United States, his election was historic nonetheless. In the South

The State Register of Justices of the Peace and Police Magistrates, Alexander County, shows the official entry (line 1) concerning John Bird's election and reelection as Cairo's police magistrate in 1873 and 1877. Illinois State Archives, record series: 103/077.

during Reconstruction, a number of African Americans were appointed or elected to judgeships, including Jonathan J. Wright, who was appointed to the South Carolina Supreme Court in 1870.[33] Eric Foner has identified twelve men who became local judges in the South during this period, six of whom were elected to the office but only two of whom were elected before Bird in 1873.[34] In the North, however, where the population of African Americans was still very small, elected Black judges were exceedingly rare during the entire nineteenth century.[35] Bird was the first African American elected a judge in Illinois and may in fact have been the first such judge in any of the northern states.

This historic election shocked many White citizens of Cairo, who strenuously objected to the prospect of having a Black man on the bench who could pass judgment on a White man. Among those offended by the situation was virtually the entire Cairo police department. Shortly after Bird was seated on May 1, the city's police officers began a boycott of his courtroom, refusing to bring any of their prisoners before Judge Bird, taking all of them instead to the other, White magistrate, Fredoline Bross. During the previous decade, the town's two police magistrates had agreed to a policy in which they alternated days in court, so that all cases were brought to one magistrate every other day. Suddenly Bross was holding court every day.[36] A Democrat for whom Bird had campaigned during the election of 1872 as a member of the Citizens' Ticket, Bross apparently was not entirely sympathetic to the police department's actions but made no obvious objections to the situation. On May 9, Bird demanded a meeting with Bross to discuss the situation, and Mayor Wood ordered Police Chief William McHale to have his men return to the preelection practice and bring prisoners to Bird's court.

In this controversy, John Oberly, who had become increasingly friendly toward Bird in the Democratic *Bulletin* over the previous year, actively took Bird's side, in opposition to many in his own party. In a brief article on May 10, Oberly wrote, "Mr. Bird has rights, and we are glad he has the pluck to stand by them."[37] Mayor Wood's order that his police department take their prisoners to Bird brought harsh criticism from newspapers of other cities. The *Mound City Journal* argued, "We would rather see white people governed by whites, and justice dispensed among white people by white courts. Let those in Cairo who voted for Bird, and wish law dished out to them by him, enjoy the luxury; but to force the great mass of the white citizens of Cairo to resort to Mr. Bird's court, whether they would or not, is an unjust and arbitrary assumption of power which does not belong to the mayor of Cairo or any other city." Oberly, responding to the *Journal*, argued that Mayor Wood was simply requiring the police to continue a procedure that had been worked out by previous police magistrates and had not been changed by the current pair. He insisted that neither Wood nor the police had the authority to change it, nor could anyone exclude a duly elected official from their duties. Using argumentation that might have come from Bird himself, Oberly wrote,

> To decide that a police magistrate elected by the people should try no cases under the city ordinance, because he was black, is not within the authority vested in them by the city council. If Mayor Wood had appointed policemen who preferred Bird to Bross, and those policemen had agreed to take all city prisoners before Bird because Bross hasn't got curly hair or is a German or a Democrat, would not the "Journal" have denounced them as partial and prejudiced? Would not that paper have called upon Mayor Wood to interfere and compel his policemen to behave themselves? . . . The case under discussion is precisely this, except that the policemen happened to prefer Bross to Bird because Bird did have curly hair and had not a white face.[38]

Mayor Wood prevailed on this issue, and soon Bird was getting his share of the police docket, both Black and White.[39] On May 31, Oberly went to observe Bird's courtroom and published this brief account: "We yesterday saw, for the first time in our brief but brilliant life, a colored officeholder. We gazed upon Police Magistrate Bird in the performance of his duty. He presides with dignity, and runs the machine with ability."[40]

Oberly's support for Bird appears to have cemented a lasting friendship between the two men that can be seen in Oberly's consistently positive coverage of Bird, in spite of their vast differences in political and social beliefs. Bird's influence on him can probably be seen in the extent to which Oberly came to embrace African American political rights that placed him at the leftmost edge of the Democratic Party, sometimes to the detriment of his own political aspirations and putting him at odds with the sharply conservative majority of Democrats in southern Illinois. The differences between the editor and his regional colleagues exploded in 1874 when Oberly, elected to the Illinois House of Representatives in 1872, supported a bill in the legislature known as the Henry Act. Oberly joined the Republicans and a minority of Democrats in passing the "Act to Protect Colored Children in Their Rights to Attend

Public Schools," which forbade any interference by school officials or private citizens in Black children's attendance at public schools. This vote outraged most of the Democrats in southern Illinois, particularly those in the counties that composed the Eighteenth U.S. Congressional District, which included Alexander. Before his vote on the act, Oberly had been a favorite to win the Democratic nomination for U.S. Congress from the district. But when the Democratic congressional convention was held at Anna on September 3, 1874, no one even put Oberly's name forward. The conservative contingent, branding him a "hand-holding nigger man," was furious at what they saw as his betrayal of the party in voting for what they called the "mixed school law."[41] Following the election of William Hartzell as the candidate, a conservative delegate introduced a resolution denouncing the Henry Law as "inimical to the interests of the negro, and retrogrestive [*sic*] to white civilization." This was followed by another resolution attacking Oberly for having supported the act, having "thus forfeited the confidence of Democrats and ruined himself politically." Oberly, present but not a delegate to the convention, was given permission to defend himself and stood firm in his support of the law. Many of his former colleagues, however, never forgave him for his vote.[42]

Bird performed the duties of police magistrate from 1873 until 1879, when he resigned halfway through his second term. The types of cases he normally handled are illustrated through the *Bulletin*'s regular reporting on the police court—public drunkenness, prostitution, disorderly conduct, vagrancy, theft, assault, and other similar violations.[43] When prisoners were brought before him accused of a serious violent crime or significant theft, he weighed the evidence, and if he found it compelling, bound the defendant over to await a grand jury hearing. His salary for the part-time position was $25 per month, the same as that of Judge Bross.[44] Magistrates also received a percentage of the collected fines they imposed, but because most of the convicted prisoners did not have the money to pay their fines and instead served jail time for their offenses, this practice was not a major source of additional income.[45]

The published accounts of his court cases indicate that Bird was scrupulous in meting out justice to both Black and White defendants, and he quickly gained a reputation for fairness and humaneness. In cases where members of the two races were at odds, Bird was not afraid to convict the White defendant and exonerate the Black one, or vice versa.[46] Bird even presided over a potentially explosive case in which a White woman accused a Black man of raping her, and when the evidence showed that the man was innocent, Bird set him free.[47] In a January 1875 article analyzing the monthly statistics reports submitted to the City Council by the two judges, Oberly wryly described their differing judicial styles thusly: "In comparing the above reports of our two police magistrates, it will at once be seen that Bross is an unrelenting, hard-hearted man, while, on the contrary, it proves Bird to be a man who carries within his bosom a tender and loving heart."[48] Although Oberly ostensibly based his evaluation here on the analysis of a single monthly report, it seems from the published reports covering the years 1873–75 that his assessment that Bross was harsher in his judgments than Bird was probably accurate.[49] Bird's humaneness in dealing with defendants also seems confirmed by several of his cases described in the *Bulletin*. In a trial during July 1875, Bird fined a woman who had been in a fight five dollars and court costs. *The Bulletin* writes, "She was unable to pay in money, but she had three children, who in this case answered the same purpose as money, for his Honor, being of tender heart, thought it would be cruel to confine the mother in jail and let the little ones, who are unable to take care of themselves, go without anything to eat, and therefore discharged her, with some good advice, which she promised to follow."[50] In another case, he fined two women for fighting but allowed one who had a child a chance to raise the money without putting her immediately in jail.[51] Having a reputation for merciful treatment did not mean, however, that he was a pushover. For example, in May 1875, two African American prisoners asked for changes of venue from Bross to Bird, apparently hoping for more lenient treatment, but Bird convicted them both and imposed significant fines on them that probably would have equaled those imposed by Bross.[52]

The city of Cairo had a long-standing reputation as a violent and lawless town, a reputation based largely on the town's situation during the 1860s, but Cairo's crime rate in the 1870s may not have been quite as high as often portrayed.[53] Cases brought before the police magistrates were usually not particularly numerous. Bird might hold as many as five trials in one day, but there were other days in which the police made no arrests at all.[54] The *Bulletin* occasionally bemoaned the lack of interesting cases on which to report for its readers. In October 1875, Oberly wrote, "Judge Bird says our city is becoming extremely pious. He hasn't done any business in his court for three or four days."[55] And on January 28, 1876, "The monotony of our police courts just now is distressing. Judge Bross, in the absence of other business, divides his time between reading his law books and the Odd-Fellow's Digest, which he seems to be digesting pretty thoroughly. Judge Bird plays chess, and it takes a wide-awake player to beat him."[56] During most of the year, Bross and Bird held court on alternating days, but Bross was also a county court and probate judge and presided over those courts periodically. During those sessions, Bird usually covered all the business of the police courts.[57]

In the summer of 1875, a few of the policemen of Cairo, apparently still unhappy about taking White prisoners before a Black judge, discovered that the Cairo city ordinances allowed them to take prisoners to a justice of the peace for trial and began bringing White prisoners before Justice Alfred Comings. During the early 1870s, Comings had occasionally sat on the Police Court bench when one or both of the magistrates were out of town, but now he took cases when Bird was on the bench.[58] Bird complained about the situation, but there was little that he could do about it.[59] It appears, however, that most police officers still brought their prisoners to Bird, although Justice Comings, who maintained an antagonistic relationship toward Bird throughout the 1870s, continued to take cases.[60]

The William Campbell Case and the Limits of Black Influence in the Republican Party

In the summer of 1873, Bird became involved in a controversial murder case in Cairo. William C. Campbell, an African American deck hand on the steamship *Grand Tower*, was accused of the murder of Thomas Doyle, a White ship's mate in April. Campbell had hired onto the *Grand Tower* in Cairo for a run to Memphis and then back up the Mississippi to St. Louis. On the return trip from Memphis, the boat stopped again at Cairo, and Campbell and a friend, unhappy at their treatment on the journey, went to Doyle saying they did not intend to continue to St. Louis and asking for their pay. Doyle, described by defense witnesses as a violent and bigoted man, told the two that they would get no pay until the ship reached St. Louis, so the two decided to finish the voyage. But before the ship left Cairo, Doyle had a belligerent confrontation with Campbell, which culminated in his striking Campbell on the back with a coal shovel. Campbell left the ship after the incident without his pay. When the ship returned to Cairo about three weeks later, Campbell went to the dock with a long club looking for Doyle. In a confrontation, Campbell hit Doyle in the head with the club, and Doyle died of a fractured skull a few days later. Campbell was arrested and charged with first-degree murder. He did not dispute the fact the he had killed Doyle, but he claimed that he had only come to get his back pay from Doyle, that Doyle had pulled a revolver on him and that he had swung in self-defense.[61]

The trial was held before circuit court judge D. J. Baker on July 30 and 31, 1873, and it polarized the Black and White communities of Cairo. A major point of contention was the fact that the jury was all White, the jury pool having been assembled by the same police chief and officers who had boycotted Bird's court in May. The prosecution had no witnesses to the actual crime but presented it as a premeditated murder in revenge for Doyle's previous assault. The court-appointed defense team, led by Judge John H. Mulkey and attorney David Linegar (a solid pair of sympathetic attorneys), argued Campbell's version but also had no witnesses to the crime. They called several dock and ship workers who testified that Doyle was violent and dangerous, and particularly vicious toward Black workers. After sixteen hours of deliberations, the jury returned a verdict of guilty and sentenced Campbell to death by hanging. According to the *Bulletin*, this was the first death sentence handed down in the history of Alexander County.[62]

Mulkey and Linegar filed a motion in the circuit court for a new trial. The motion was debated on August 5 before Judge Baker, who had presided over the trial. Linegar made the argument that an all-White jury had been unfair in this case, but Baker denied the motion. The defense then filed an Arrest of Sentence motion, which was also overruled by the judge. On the next day, Baker sentenced Campbell to hang on August 29. The African American community was outraged by the situation, and soon a petition calling for an appeal of the sentence to the Illinois Supreme Court was being circulated.[63] When word of the trial reached Campbell's mother, who lived in Omaha, Nebraska, a petition was begun there as well.[64] On Monday, August 25, four days before the scheduled execution, Linegar traveled to Carlisle, Illinois, to meet with Illinois Supreme Court chief justice Sidney Breese in an attempt to convince him to delay the sentence. This, too, was unsuccessful. When Linegar returned to Cairo on Tuesday the 26th with the news that Judge Breese would not block the execution, Bird determined to seek a stay for thirty days from Governor Beveridge in order to allow the lawyers time to present Campbell's case to the full supreme court. That evening he took the train to Springfield hoping to speak to the governor, carrying with him the petitions from Cairo and Omaha, as well as supportive letters from Judge Mulkey and John

Oberly.[65] Upon arrival in Springfield, Bird learned that the governor was in Joliet, so he continued his journey to that city, reaching it on Thursday the 28th. It appears that he was not able to meet with Beveridge until Friday morning, the day of the hanging, when the two had a brief conversation on the train returning to Springfield. Bird got what he believed was an oral assurance from the governor that he would stay the sentence for thirty days so that he could look over the evidence and petitions. Bird got off the train in Dwight and sent a telegram to that effect to Oberly. But shortly afterward, it became clear that others had changed Beveridge's mind (or that he had never intended to intervene), when a telegram from the governor arrived at the sheriff's office, saying, "I decline to interfere in the case of William Campbell."[66]

Campbell was hanged that day, with hundreds of outraged but peaceful African American citizens standing outside the jail. Several White leaders in Cairo were also uncomfortable with the sentence including Oberly, who stated in the *Bulletin*, "We question the wisdom of the execution, and do not believe that the unfortunate man was guilty of premeditated murder."[67] Even the White sheriff of Cairo, Alexander H. Irvin, who had been appointed Campbell's executioner, apparently felt that the sentence was unwarranted.[68]

The failure of Bird's mission to Beveridge emphasizes the political calculations that White Republicans made at the state level in their relationship to African Americans. Although it seems probable that Beveridge was sympathetic to Campbell's plight and Bird's plea, his fear of political damage to his White support that might result from issuing the stay likely was too strong. Here he seems to have bowed to those who argued that granting a reprieve would make him appear to be supporting a Black man convicted of murdering a White man. David Linegar, although a White leader in the Republican Party, had been no more successful with his appeal to the supreme court judge Breese. While Republicans needed the African American vote in a few cities (including Cairo), the Black population of Illinois was still quite minuscule, and interfering with this execution was apparently felt to be too politically problematic to undertake.

Bird's Speech at Southern Illinois Normal University, 1874

The next year, Bird broke yet another significant racial barrier when the Board of Trustees of the new Southern Illinois Normal University (later Southern

Old Normal, the original building of Southern Illinois Normal
University, where the inaugural ceremonies of the university were
held July 1, 1874. Courtesy of Special Collections, Morris Library,
Southern Illinois University, Carbondale, UNPH 1.

Illinois University) invited him to speak at the ceremonies celebrating the university's official opening, on the topic "The Education of the African Race." This was the first time an African American had been asked to take part in a prestigious ceremonial academic event in Illinois. The other dignitaries on the program included Governor Beveridge; Robert Allyn, the new university's president; C. H. Fowler, president of Northwestern University; Richard Edwards, president of the Bloomington Normal School (substituting for Newton Bateman, the superintendent of the Illinois Department of Public Instruction, who was ill); William F. Harris, the superintendent of the public schools of St. Louis; and three religious leaders.[69]

Although the honor was tempered by the shocking behavior of the planning committee for the event described in the Introduction, Bird did not allow the situation to stop him from giving his speech on July 1, 1874.[70] The *Bulletin* printed a large excerpt and partial summary, providing the longest-surviving example of Bird's noncampaign oratory. It shows again his powerful use of history, literature, current affairs, and published statistics to build a carefully reasoned case for African American rights. He opened his speech by dramatically articulating the massive scope of the educational problem facing the nation's African American population and clearly setting out the specific causes of this dire situation:[71]

> Dr. Edwards in his very appropriate remarks this morning, stated that there was in this country over five millions native Americans above the age of 10 years who could neither read or write, and he was sorry to say, that over two millions of that number were whites. It is with feelings of deep sorrow that I must acknowledge that the remainder that goes to make up the five millions are colored, and yet when I reflect over the gloomy past, in which we have been shut up in utter darkness, where the radiating reflections of the sun of light and education did not beam upon us, I console myself with the idea, that we are not responsible for our present ignorant condition.
>
> The subject of education is one of such vast importance, that it should not be confined to race, clime or country. Neither should it be confined to those of royal birth, or the favored few who are born in the lap of luxury and ease; but should be founded on the enduring basis of justice and equality to the masses whether they be of patrician or plebeian birth . . .
>
> Confucius says that "ignorance is the night of the mind," but it is a night without the light of moon or star. Two hundred and forty-two years of our history in this country was as one long night of darkness and despair. We waited, hoped and prayed. Oftentimes in the gloomiest hour of our sorrow, we would cry, "Watchman, tell us of the night, what its signs of promise are." The answer would come back, falling on our ears with doubled force, "Perpetual slavery and ignorance is your doom forever."

After painting this grim picture of the past, Bird turned to the beginnings of progress that had come in recent years, praising both the work of African Americans and their White supporters who fought for the cause of education. He discussed reports on Black schools in several states that indicated that African American students showed equal levels of advancement with their White compatriots. He then pointed to the greatest threat to education in the southern states, the brutal White attacks on schools, teachers, and churches that made it impossible for children to receive an education, and he warned that "the educational interests of those people would certainly suffer so long as there was a public sentiment sanctioning such action."

Then he concluded his address:

> The establishment of the government was sealed with the blood of our marty[r]ed fathers in the streets of Boston, and at Bunker Hill, in the war of the revolution, and at New Orleans in 1812.
>
> Our years of unpaid labor enriched the south, and added to the material wealth of our common country. Our bravery and patriotism did much towards the preservation of the union, and the perpetuity of free American institutions during the late rebellion, and now that peace has been fully restored, and our country once more happily united, we ask you, in the name of justice and a common humanity, that you remove all obstacles out of the road of progress, throw wide open the doors of the common schools, and give us an opportunity to assist in shedding new lustre on this our great and rapidly growing country.

This was a bold speech for a Black man to give to what was probably an almost completely White, largely elite audience. It powerfully and deliberately laid forth the reasons why education was essential to the African American community and why it was incumbent upon the White majority to support the public educational institutions that would provide this opportunity. Bird skillfully included praise for those White people in the past who had supported African American education while aiming a sharp criticism of those who remained silent about the violence occurring in the South.

Bird gave this speech in the context of the recent passage in March of the controversial Henry Act that protected African American children's right to attend school. Passage of this law had produced a serious outcry against it from elements of the White population during the spring and summer, and it was not yet clear whether it would be enforced in many Illinois counties in the fall. Thus, Bird felt the need to reiterate the case for African American public education to his influential audience, because the actual success of the law had not yet been tested.[72]

John Bird and Cairo's African American School, 1872–1878

Although the surviving sources about John Bird in the 1870s rarely touch upon his extensive work in support of the city's public school for Black students, they still show that he was the primary representative of the African

American community in advocating for the improvement of the school and in working toward stronger Black control over it. He and the Black community joined forces with G. G. Alvord, a progressive superintendent of the Cairo schools, and Phoebe Taylor, the superintendent of Alexander County schools, after 1872 to create an exceptionally strong educational program for the school that flourished through the decade. The process by which the school officials made their key decisions on the Black school was never discussed in the *Bulletin*, and thus Bird's critical impact is relatively obscured for much of the 1870s. Undoubtedly, the majority of Bird's negotiations with the White leadership took place behind the scenes, in private meetings, rather than in a public context. However, an account of a controversy about the school that arose in the African American community in the spring of 1878 shows clearly that Bird had long been the community's primary figure in relation to the school.

By the early 1870s, the public education system in Cairo had become a high priority for its civic and business leaders. Most were convinced that, in spite of the economic downturn beginning in 1873, the city was still in a position to become one of the leading commercial hubs in the United States. In order to draw more industry, manufacturing, railroads, and culture, they believed that it was necessary for them to improve all aspects of the city, including infrastructure, law enforcement, and the educational system. They viewed the quality of the public schools as a vital component of their plan to present Cairo as a city on the move, and the African American community intended for the Black school to be part of that plan.[73]

As described above, the city had established its segregated public school for African American children in 1871 and appointed Phillip Tolford, a White teacher, to supervise it, over the objections of many in the Black community. Tensions between the community and the school board ran high during the first year or so, but slowly relations between the two groups began to improve. The education law of 1872 assured that the city would provide permanent financial support for the school and that all children could attend. There is no evidence that the 1874 Henry Law, which provided penalties for those attempting to keep Black children from gaining access to an education, was necessary in Cairo. Most citizens of the city apparently accepted the permanent existence of the school.

A key turning point in the board's attitude toward Black education was the arrival of two new school officials during this period—G. G. Alvord, whom the board appointed as superintendent of Cairo schools in July 1872, and Mrs. Phoebe Taylor, who became the first female superintendent of schools for Alexander County in November 1873.[74] Alvord came to Cairo with the intention of expanding the curriculum well beyond the "three R's" that had characterized the schools thus far. He gained the board's support to hire additional teachers to offer language courses in the high school, including Latin, Greek (briefly), and German as well as sciences, literature, and history. In addition, he convinced the board to allow him to teach students the new technologies of the day. He inaugurated courses on telegraphy in all the schools, including the Black school, and not just in theory. He had telegraph stations installed in each of the city's schools and wires run between them, so that students and teachers could communicate with one another directly in Morse code.[75] He also added the study of phonography— shorthand—to the curriculum, introducing it to students in the grammar schools, again including the Black school, and continuing it into high school.[76] Responding quickly to the Black community's concern over the educational staff at their school, Alvord hired two African American teachers for the 1872–73 academic year to work under Tolford, a move that was warmly supported by the community.[77] During the 1873–74 school year, Alvord added a fourth teacher to the school and extended its classes to the eighth grade from the original limit of fifth grade in 1871.[78]

Alvord's augmented curriculum created controversy among the citizens of Cairo, with many objecting to the additional costs and arguing that the public schools should stick to the basics.[79] But the school board and other city officials supported Alvord and refused to back down. An anonymous letter summarized the board's philosophy thusly: "Financial troubles have made us all more careful of our pennies, and we feel that our school expenses must be reduced in common with all the expenses of life. The members of the Board feel this, quite as keenly as you or I do, and you may be sure that they are just as anxious as any of us to see the school expenses decreased. At the same time they are determined that Cairo shall take her place in the foremost ranks as an educational centre."[80] Alvord's program paid off in good publicity for the city. The curriculum became widely known, and officials from other cities traveled to Cairo to take a look at it. In 1877, the *Bulletin* published a report from the Evansville, Indiana, *Daily Courier*, about a visit to the schools by an educational committee that included the city's mayor, superintendent of schools, and members of the school board. Deeply impressed by the teaching of telegraphy and phonography, as well as the advanced literature and composition courses offered in the high school, the committee's report stated, "Under the management of an able school board, and through the direction of an accomplished superintendent, the Cairo schools, in the introduction and practice of these sciences, have shown an enterprise and spirit consistent with the progress of the age—an example to be followed by other Western cities."[81]

Alvord was joined in his enthusiasm for upgrading the schools by Mrs. Taylor, who substantially improved the quality of the certification system for teachers in Alexander County after her election as county superintendent of schools in 1873. By 1874, all teachers in the county, including those teaching in the African American schools, were required to pass stringent tests for certification.[82] The teachers at the Black school in Cairo were paid the same as teachers in the White schools.[83] From 1874 to the end of the decade, the two superintendents and the school board presided over a period of remarkable excellence for all the public schools in Cairo including the school for African American students.

In the summer of 1874, the board undertook a major expansion and renovation of the building at Walnut and Nineteenth Streets that added a complete second floor with three new classrooms, thereby doubling its teaching area, and provided repairs and renovations to the first floor, along with some new furniture. This project, which cost $4,311, was made possible by a special school tax levy about 33 percent higher than the normal budgets of this period.[84] The next year, the board made additional improvements to the school, including the building of a new privy and a fence, as well as the purchase of the lot behind the school and the wiring of the school for telegraph service, all of which cost $947.08.[85] While the building was indeed structurally inferior to the White schools (it was wood frame, rather than brick, like most of the others), it was solid, clean, and reasonably well supplied, particularly in comparison to Black schools in most other Illinois towns.

In 1875, Taylor and Alvord recommended that the directors hire Miss Mary E. McBride to replace Phillip Tolford as principal of the African American school. McBride was a White teacher who had graduated in 1871 from the prestigious and innovative Oswego State Normal School in New York and had, in the intervening years, served as the lady principal at Wilberforce University, the important African American institution.[86] McBride sent a letter to the board informing them that she would not accept a salary of less than

$1,000 per year to come to Cairo, $300 more than the district's top teachers were making.[87] The board approved the salary on the condition that she would also oversee the annual teacher training course that all prospective teachers in the county were required to attend for certification, and she accepted. This hire illustrates the board's seriousness about the quality of the African American school. The salary, of course, caused controversy in Cairo, particularly since it was being paid to the principal of the African American school. Letters in the *Bulletin* opposing McBride criticized the board for wasting taxpayer money and also falsely accused McBride of teaching without proper certification. Although she was able to refute the latter charge and defend her value in regard to salary, the ugliness of the attacks against her led McBride to leave Cairo after one year and take the position of superintendent of schools in Van Buren, Arkansas.[88]

In hiring a replacement for McBride during the summer of 1876, the school board finally made a choice that Bird and his allies had pressed for since the beginning—they hired an African American as principal of the school, Professor Robert Alexander Pinn, who had attended Oberlin College from 1874 to 1876.[89] In addition, the board hired three new Black teachers for the other positions, thus placing the school, for the first time in its history, under the complete supervision of African American educators.[90] Shortly after Pinn's arrival, a small high school class was also established, which likely survived until Alvord's departure in 1881.[91]

Several articles in the *Bulletin* during 1877 described the "colored school" as a great success. Following a visit on February 20 to the school with a member of the board and others, John Oberly wrote, "Prof. Pinn ... [and] the colored teachers of the colored schools have made them much better than they ever were before, and we were pleased to observe that the pupils took a most lively interest in their studies and were making surprising progress in all of them."[92] On March 19, a special committee of the Taxpayers Association also toured the school and reported, "The colored schools are in a flourishing condition under the present corps of teachers, who are, as a whole, the most efficient they have ever had."[93] Another group visited the school during the examinations of the eighth-grade students and reported, "The classes in algebra, geography and arithmetic were examined thoroughly, and to all of the numerous questions put them by the white visitors present, they answered promptly and correctly in every instance. The school is one of the most orderly and attentive we have ever had the pleasure of visiting. . . . Prof. Pinn, the teacher, is a well educated and thorough gentleman, and takes great pride in his school. The high state of perfection to which this school has attained is due to his skill and energy as a teacher."[94] One could be skeptical about this high praise from White leaders who might want to feel good about their "colored school." But another classroom visit that year suggests that the local authorities were genuinely proud of the school. When Governor Shelby Cullom came to spend a day in Cairo that December, the city leaders took him to the African American school as part of his tour of the city, something they easily could have avoided if they had believed that it might have damaged the image they wished to present.[95]

All of this explains why, when a disgruntled group of parents started a campaign in May 1878 against the teachers at the school, the majority in the African American community strongly supported Mr. Pinn and his staff. The dissidents were led by Reuben Smith, whose son attended the school. Bird led the opposition to this group, defending the teachers and Phoebe Taylor, the superintendent of schools who had certified them. The details of the charges made by the dissident group are not described in the *Bulletin*, but the movement reached a key moment on May 16 when Smith wrote an open letter to Bird in which he challenged Bird's leadership in the community: "Mr. Bird—Sir: I take the liberty of writing you a few lines, understanding that the school was good enough. If you say that the teachers as they stand are competent to teach our children and train them properly, that the majority of people in this city say then you are a dishonest man. You need not suppose that you can represent the colored citizens of Cairo any longer, for they will not be dictated to by you any longer."[96] Smith and his supporters called an indignation meeting to voice their concerns on May 17, but when a larger group of people who supported the teachers arrived, the meeting was called off. Over the following weekend Bird vigorously opposed the Smith group at several community meetings, accusing Smith of fomenting this trouble because he held a grudge against the school board ever since he had been fired from his position as janitor of the Thirteenth Street School in 1871.[97] Smith responded to Bird in a letter to the *Bulletin*, published May 23, disputing that charge and arguing that Bird was trying to dictate "who Shall be Employed as teachers without the concent [sic] from the majoriety [sic] of the Patrons of the Schools."[98]

Bird replied in a rare letter to the *Bulletin*. In it, he argued that Smith was illiterate and had written neither of the letters to which he had signed his name. He thus was "wholly incompetent to judge of the qualification of teachers." He pointed out that Smith had not visited the schools since he had been fired seven years earlier and thus knew nothing of their management. He also noted that Smith's son was very irregular in his attendance, hinting that the son's problems with the teachers were the basis for Smith's opposition to them but that those problems were not attributable to the teachers. Bird sharply defended Phoebe Taylor and the teachers that she had certified for the school. Another major theme in Bird's letter was his denunciation of an unnamed White man who he charged was the orchestrator of Smith's whole movement: "It would be unwise and imprudent for me to attempt to fight against Mr. Smith's ignorance and venality, and doubly so, were I to array myself against a white man who, having sought and failed to obtain position through his white associates, stands concealed in darkness, blacker than midnight, and shoves his pen, made vile by impious hand, for the purpose of obtaining through the dissension of colored men, what he has failed to get, for lack of merit, from his own people." Bird concluded by proposing that "a committee, composed of the best educators in our city, be appointed to visit the colored schools for the purpose of having a fair and impartial investigation of the management of the schools and the competency of their teachers. I will consent for Mr. Smith and his white man Friday to select said committee, reserving to myself the privilege of being present during such investigation."[99]

There is no indication that Bird's committee proposal was taken up by Smith or anyone else. Rather, on June 3, the school board met to hear the complaints of Smith and other parents. Unfortunately, the article in the *Bulletin* is frustratingly short: "A meeting of the board of education was held yesterday to hear the complaints of Mr. R. Smith and others, against the colored teachers. The board made a patient and thorough investigation, and came to the conclusion that the complainants had no case. Even R. Smith admitted that he knew nothing himself against the teachers—that what he had to say against them was hearsay abuse. Of course, 'Rewbin' went out of court."[100]

Who was the White man Bird charged with orchestrating this entire attack on himself and the teachers of the Black school? Bird clearly assumed that many people knew exactly whom he was accusing, and an examination of the *Bulletin* leads to a probable suspect: Justice of the Peace Alfred Comings. On April 4, 1878, the *Bulletin* noted, "The opposition to the present management of our public schools is understood to be led by Mr. A.

Comings. Mr. Comings is an old school teacher, and in case a change in management should occur, it is said that he would be an applicant for the position now held by Prof. Alvord." On April 10, four days after a local election that included the choosing of all three members of the school board, the paper reported that Comings had prepared a petition to present to the board in support of his being named superintendent. However, the board asked Alvord to stay on, rather than choosing Comings.[101] Comings's situation is essentially identical to that of the White man described in Bird's letter. It is also clear from previous conflicts that there was little love lost between Bird and Comings. Thus, although Bird provided no evidence to support his charges about Comings's involvement with Smith, the *Bulletin*'s unrelated descriptions of Comings's activities certainly place him under suspicion.

The glory days of the African American school, however, were relatively short-lived and would begin to wane after the autumn of 1878, when a yellow fever epidemic hit Cairo and damaged its economy, leading the school board to cut the education budget by one third. Alvord remained superintendent of Cairo schools until the summer of 1881, and Mrs. Taylor lost an election to Mrs. L. C. Gibbs in November of 1882.[102]

Bird and the Republican Party, 1873–1878

Bird's election to the magistracy in 1873 further solidified his status as the head of the Black wing of Cairo's Republican Party and as a member of the local party's political leadership. His influence only increased as the decade proceeded. Repeatedly appointed as a member of several Republican central committees, as a delegate to both district conventions and the Republican state convention, as an election judge in the city, and as a keynote speaker at Republican rallies across the state, Bird became the visible symbol of the incorporation of African Americans into the political structure of the party in a way that few other Black Illinois politicians were. This impact can be seen already in the November 1873 election, when the African American voters again turned out in force, helping to put a number of Republicans into office, including John Gladney, Bird's colleague, who ran for and won the position of county constable of the North Cairo Precinct, thus becoming the city's second elected Black official. [103] Bird was one of the judges for this election, and during the following summer, he attended the state Republican convention in Springfield as one of Alexander County's three delegates. In August 1874, he and Gladney were appointed to the central committee of the Alexander County Republican Party and were named delegates both to the Republican Eighteenth District Congressional Convention (Bird for the second time) and to the convention that selected nominees for the state legislature.[104]

Bird's rise, however, coincided with the decline in the national Republican Party's popularity in the middle third of the decade. The 1874 midterm election proved to be a painful one for the Republican Party across the country, as the Democrats used the continuing economic depression, the scandals within the Grant administration, and the general weariness in the North concerning the federal engagement in southern Reconstruction to pull off a sweeping victory, gaining control over the U.S. House of Representatives for the first time since the 1850s, diminishing the Republican majority in the Senate, and taking over several governorships and state legislatures. The turbulence of this election in Cairo is apparent in the events surrounding the reelection campaign of Isaac Clements, the Republican congressman representing the Eighteenth District. Clements had been elected to the House in 1872, but in 1874, his seat was vulnerable. Charles Sumner's Civil Rights Bill, still being debated in Congress, was very controversial in southern Illinois and a problem for a Republican running in the region. With three largely White counties and two with substantial African American populations in his district, Clements tended to shift his view of the bill depending on his audience, questioning its constitutionality in the White counties while assuring his Black audiences in Alexander and Pulaski Counties that he fully supported it. His waffling on the issue became a major point of attack in the Democratic press and weakened his standing in the African American community. Cairo's Black leaders, including Bird and Gladney, still supported Clements, expecting him to keep his word to vote for the bill and pointing out that William Hartzell, the Democratic candidate, certainly would oppose it.[105]

Besides creating a dilemma for Clements, the Civil Rights Bill caused a major rift in Cairo's White Republican leadership during the campaign. David Linegar, one of the most important Radical Republicans in Alexander County, who had supported Bird for years and had been a champion of African American political rights, apparently could not accept the notion of social equality for Black citizens and in a dramatic speech in Cairo on October 26 denounced the bill as unnecessary, arguing that Black citizens now had their constitutional rights and did not need any further protection from the federal government.[106] Linegar made it clear that he was leaving the Republican Party, and indeed, over the next few years, he became a leader in Alexander County's New Departure Democratic faction.

Linegar's defection was a huge blow to the Republicans, and in reaction to it, the party leadership called upon John Bird to deliver a response to Linegar's speech on October 30 at the city courthouse. Both Republicans and Democrats speculated that Bird's speech would include a strong personal attack on Linegar. In a Republican dispatch to the Chicago *Inter Ocean*, an observer wrote, "He (Bird) will undoubtedly give him a worse skinning than he ever had before. The colored people hereabouts have always trusted Linegar as they never trusted any other man, and Bird, as their representative, who is able and willing, will give him a lashing that will last him as long as he lives."[107] But when Bird took to the podium before a crowd of some two hundred people, about half Black and half White, he said nothing at all about Linegar, but rather gave a detailed defense of the Civil Rights Bill and discussed other issues pertinent to the Black community. John Oberly, who had expected fireworks, was greatly disappointed and printed a very brief notice of the meeting in the *Bulletin*, which ended, "Owing to the lateness of the hour we cannot give a full report."[108] No report appeared the following day, either. Bird's speech that night, however, particularly illuminates an important aspect of Bird's character—it shows his reluctance to use easy ad hominem attacks in his public life and his insistence on presenting careful argumentation, rather than simple emotionalism, to persuade people of one's views.

Clements lost the election to Hartzell in a landslide on November 3, 1874. In Cairo, Hartzell won, 682 to 505, with 266 fewer voters participating in this election than in 1872, when Clements defeated his Democratic opponent 775 to 678. Since Hartzell received virtually the same vote as the 1872 Democratic candidate (678 in 1872), while Clements's vote declined by 270 (775 to 505), it appears that numerous Republicans, probably many of them African Americans, refused to vote for him, in spite of the efforts of Bird and his colleagues.[109]

This election heralded the approaching collapse of Reconstruction in the South. In a final action before giving up power, the lame duck Congress passed a significantly watered-down version of the Civil Rights Act, which President Grant signed on March 1, 1875. But even weakened, the act remained a serious attempt to create a more equal society, although in practice it was rarely enforced and eventually was declared unconstitutional by the U.S. Supreme Court in 1883.[110] The loss of the 1874 election caused the Republicans as a party to pull more substantially away from supporting federal enforcement of Reconstruction policies in the South in 1875. African American rights in the old Confederacy disappeared as an issue from subsequent northern Republican campaigns, and the year saw the aggressively violent "redemption" of Mississippi by the Democrats without any significant reaction from the Grant administration.[111] However, the Republican Party remained competitive in Cairo, and in the local election in April 1875, Bird was able to play a leading role in the successful campaign of Henry Winter, the Republican candidate for mayor.[112]

The presidential election of 1876 was the most turbulent one of the century. President Grant decided not to run for a third term, and with a number of contenders for the nomination, it took seven ballots for the Republicans to choose Rutherford B. Hayes, the governor of Ohio and a man with a record of support for the Black cause since antebellum days. His Democratic opponent, Samuel J. Tilden, the governor of New York, had a reputation as a reformer, a trait that appealed to many who were unhappy with the corruption in Grant's administration. He would bring the Democrats closer to the presidency than any time since the war.

In southern Illinois, Bird worked tirelessly during the summer and fall for the party. He attended the Republican state convention in May, was appointed the Alexander County member of the Eighteenth Congressional District Central Committee in June, and was a featured speaker at the African American celebration in Cairo of the Centennial Independence Day.[113] In the fall he traveled across the state speaking in support of Hayes, often accompanied by William Scott.[114] But although Hayes won the election in November, his administration proved to be disastrous for African Americans. With the election hinging on disputed returns from three states, the two parties eventually agreed that Hayes could assume the presidency if he promised to remove the remaining federal troops from the South. This brought the end of Reconstruction and an abandonment of the African Americans who lived in the former Confederacy.[115]

The Democrats in southern Illinois turned out in force for the election, and Cairo went for Tilden by a small margin (forty-three votes), as did Alexander County as a whole (1,280 to 1,219). This represented another example of the continual shift in power between the parties in the city and county, since in the previous presidential election, Grant had carried the county over Greeley 1,231 to 1,039. The Cairo Democrats also carried the vote for the state offices on the ballot, but the Republicans won the county offices by slim margins.[116]

Nothing about the Republican defeat of 1876, however, tarnished Bird's status in the party in Illinois. He would run for reelection to the police magistracy in 1877 and produce an even more stunning victory than his original election in 1873 (described below). In June 1878, the Alexander County Republican leaders again named him as delegate to both the Republican state and congressional conventions, the only person elected to both, and reappointed him to the County Central Committee for another two-year term.[117] But this year Bird also became a major subject of discussion in the regional convention selecting nominees for the state legislature. That convention was held in early July at Carbondale, and Bird's name came up as a potential nominee. No frontrunner had emerged for the State House of Representatives nomination, each of the three counties supporting its own local favorite. The thirteen-member Alexander County delegation, however, was divided between two local candidates: John Bird and Harmon Black, a young and ambitious White Republican of Cairo. At the convention, it became clear that the candidate from Jackson County, Judge C. H. Layman, had the votes to win the nomination, but his real desire was to be appointed the circuit court judge for the region. During the convention, members of the Jackson County delegation approached some of the pro-Bird delegates with a proposal that they would throw their support to Bird if the Alexander County Republicans would send a petition to Governor Cullom in support of Layman for the judgeship. Bird was not in Carbondale, and his supporters decided that the proposal was inappropriate, and so they declined the offer. Thus Layman became the candidate for the House seat. When word of the proposed deal was leaked to the *Bulletin*, Oberly portrayed it as an insult both to Bird and to the political process, praising Bird for not succumbing to the temptations of corruption.[118] Again the *Bulletin*, in an article designed to entice them toward the Democrats, voiced the legitimate frustration of Cairo's Black leaders that the White Republicans were not willing to bring African Americans into state-level positions of power. For Bird, Scott, Gladney, and others, this would become an increasing issue, but Bird nevertheless campaigned tirelessly for the party across Illinois throughout the summer and fall, before and after the Yellow Fever outbreak (discussed below).[119] His work was an important element in Congressman John R. Thomas's victory in November with the help of a strong vote in Cairo. The Republicans won all the local partisan contests, where four years earlier, in the midterm election of 1874, the Democrats had won.[120]

Following this new victory, substantially achieved with Black votes and organized under Bird's leadership, the African American community began pressing the White Republicans strongly to reward Bird with a prestigious patronage position in the legislature. In December 1878, his friends lobbied legislators to name him secretary of the state senate. The *Tribune* supported this idea, describing Bird as the "colored Republican leader of Lower Egypt. He is one of the most effective Republican orators of the State, and to him more than to any other one man Capt. Thomas owes his election. . . . He is a scholar and a gentleman." But he was not chosen. In January, he was the only African American among forty-six official candidates for state house positions and was pushed for doorkeeper of the house, but did not receive that job either. The reluctance of White Republicans to provide patronage positions to African Americans would strain relationships between themselves and the Black community and would soon explode in Cairo.[121]

Bird's Reelection Campaign and Masonic Elevation, 1877

The spring of 1877 brought Bird to the end of his four-year term as police magistrate, and he had to decide whether to run for reelection. In 1873, he had won the office in large part because the Democratic vote had split between three other candidates, but this year the Democrats did not intend to make the same mistake. In early March, Bird let it be known that he was thinking of running for reelection, although several friends urged him to seek a federal patronage job in the new Republican administration of Rutherford B. Hayes.[122] But on March 16 he officially entered the race for magistrate. The *Bulletin* assessed his candidacy positively: "Judge Bird has served as magistrate for four years, and has made an efficient officer. He has many warm friends, and in the contest just opening will be a formidable candidate."[123]

By April 6, three Democrats had entered the race, but in the absence of a "Citizens' Ticket," as in the early 1870s, the Democrats were determined to create a unified slate for city offices.[124] On April 7, party leaders met and nominated Richard Fitzgerald, the city jailor, as their candidate, and they forced

the other candidates to drop out of the race.[125] While the *Bulletin* supported
Fitzgerald, it never attacked Bird as a candidate. The Republicans did not field
an official slate, although party members ran for every office. The election was
held on April 17 and was a triumph for the Republicans and for Bird in particular. Four of the five open offices went to them. Bird defeated his single
challenger by thirty-nine votes, 680 to 641, a close but extraordinary victory
for an African American in a predominantly White city and a major endorsement of his performance as magistrate from both the White and Black communities of Cairo.[126] African Americans could have supplied no more that
400 to 425 of his 680 votes, and thus the White Republicans clearly rallied
behind him as well. One might consider this victory an even more remarkable achievement for Bird than his initial election.

Bird was not the only African American in Alexander County to run for
reelection in 1877. His friend and colleague John Gladney, who had become
the first Black county constable in 1873, ran again in the November election. He was joined by a second African American candidate for the same
position, Pink McAllister. There were five candidates for three positions in
that race. McAllister came in third and thus was elected, while Gladney
came in fourth. Also in this election Richard Taylor, an active member of
the Black Republicans, was elected justice of the peace.[127] Soon after the
election, it appears that positions as special sheriff's deputies came open for
both Gladney and Taylor.[128]

Shortly after Bird's reelection, Fredoline Bross, the city's other police magistrate, resigned from his position, leaving Bird the only judge on the bench.
Even though justice of the peace Alfred Comings moved into Bross's office
shortly afterward and took on some of the burden of Bross's departure, as he
had done before, the court reporting in the *Bulletin* indicates that after Bross
retired, Bird worked essentially full time in the position.[129] Eventually, the
city council decided not to replace Bross at all, leaving Bird as the city's only
police magistrate. While Comings continued to take on some cases when the
court got too congested, Bird handled the larger load from May 1877 until
his resignation in July 1879.[130]

Bird's reelection was not his only major achievement in 1877. His years of
involvement in the work of the Prince Hall Masons culminated that year in
his election as the Most Worshipful Grand Master of the Grand Masonic
Lodge of Illinois, the highest Masonic office in the state. Bird had been deeply
involved with the Masons in Cairo since 1867 and during the mid-1870s had

rapidly moved through the offices of the Grand Lodge. In October 1877, the election for the office of grand master for 1878 became a contest between Bird and John G. Jones, a prominent Chicago attorney and Republican activist. Bird won the election, held the position for a year, and made a strong impression on the members of the lodge. During his term in office, the Grand Lodge opened four new local lodges in Illinois and one in Milwaukee, the largest number established in a single year during the nineteenth century. In 1884, Jones, who was sometimes a political ally of Bird and sometimes an enemy, composed an article for the *Cleveland Gazette* describing the grand masters of the Illinois Lodge. Of Bird he wrote: "It can be truthfully said by all that he was the model Grand Master of Illinois, superior as a presiding officer to anyone who has ever wielded our gavel, ever ready and prompt and graceful, he was the master of the position, more eloquent than any of his associates in office."[131]

Bird and the Black Convention Movement in the Mid-1870s

While John Bird was very active in the Republican Party, he also became increasingly involved in the Black convention movement during the 1870s, although he did not begin to take a leadership role until the middle of the decade. Records survive of his attendance at the 1871 national convention in St. Louis (described above), as well as a sparsely attended state convention in Springfield in December 1873, but his real career in African American conventions began with his participation in the National Convention of Colored Men held April 5–7, 1876, in Nashville, Tennessee.[132] The convention was called by a number of southern Black leaders who were alarmed by the increasing collapse of the Reconstruction governments in the southern states. Already White, anti-Black Democrats had taken over several state legislatures and had forced Black Republicans out of office. Although the Ku Klux Klan had been suppressed by order of President Grant in the early 1870s, new paramilitary groups intent on intimidating Black voters had arisen. The delegates to the convention had been shocked by the violent Democratic takeover of Mississippi in the fall of 1875 and were disheartened at the national Republican leaders' lack of concern about the situation. The primary leaders at the conference included Pinckney B. S. Pinchback, the most prominent Louisiana politician, who had briefly served as governor of that state; Rev.

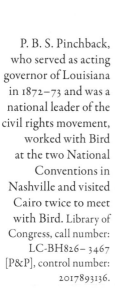

P. B. S. Pinchback, who served as acting governor of Louisiana in 1872–73 and was a national leader of the civil rights movement, worked with Bird at the two National Conventions in Nashville and visited Cairo twice to meet with Bird. Library of Congress, call number: LC-BH826– 3467 [P&P], control number: 2017893136.

Robert McCary of Indiana; Mifflin Gibbs of Arkansas; C. S. Smith of Alabama; and John Mercer Langston, now of Washington, D.C.[133] While Bird is not recorded as having addressed the assembly, he was placed on four of the eight committees formed during the conference—the Committees on Permanent Organization, Railroads, Resolutions, and Rules—more than any other individual.[134]

The delegates were deeply concerned about the violence in the South and the failure of the Grant administration to intervene, but their greater fear was that the Democratic Party might gain the presidency in the next election. There was discussion about whether African Americans should declare themselves independent of any party affiliation, but the majority insisted upon staying loyal to the Republicans. Delegates also debated whether or not the convention should take a conciliatory stance toward southern White society.

Engraving of the 1876 National Convention of Colored Men in Nashville, Tennessee, from *Frank Leslie's Illustrated Newspaper*, May 6, 1876, 145. The New York Public Library Digital Collections. https://digitalcollections .nypl.org/items/510d47db-c5c4-a3d9-e040-e00a18064a99.

The Committee on Resolutions, on which Bird sat, presented a set of resolutions to the conference that was fairly moderate. They called for compulsory education to be enacted in all the southern states, while strongly denouncing the violence against Black citizens, laying the blame for it directly on the Democratic Party. They reaffirmed African Americans' adherence to the national Republican Party but pointed out, "We have just reasons for complaint against those members who have proved recreant to the trusts committed to their keeping." The delegates disavowed any ill will toward ex-slaveholders and urged them to "protect all citizens against mobs, assassination and violence." They attacked efforts to establish "what is known as the color line, [which] present a condition of affairs to be deplored by all lovers of liberty and order," and denounced political corruption regardless of party. They concluded by thanking President Grant for "the services rendered in our behalf." Before the convention closed, four final resolutions were presented and passed, including one specifically by

Bird, "deprecating the demoralizing influence resulting from masses of colored people locating in large cities and towns where labor is scarce, and advising them to purchase farms."[135]

Nonpolitical Activities

Few sources from the 1870s provide information on Bird's private life and nonpolitical activities, but some articles shed a bit of light on his relations within the African American community in Cairo. For example, in February 1875, Bird gave a lecture titled "Music in Churches" at a meeting of the combined Black Sunday schools of the city.[136] In June, he was the keynote speaker at the African American Oddfellows celebration in Chicago and then gave the principal address at the annual state meeting of the Illinois Grand Lodge of Masons held in Mattoon.[137] On September 19, the Cairo AME church held the dedication of its newly constructed building, featuring a sermon by the prominent AME bishop Alexander Wayman of Baltimore and attended by a large crowd estimated at between six and seven hundred, of which some two hundred were White. After the sermon, Bird introduced Mayor Winter, who presented the church's Sunday school library with a collection of one hundred children's books.[138] Bird and others saw integrated meetings of this type, which occurred in numerous settings across Cairo, as a hopeful indicator of racial healing in the future. Others were less convinced. A brief comment in the *Bulletin* in 1875 shows that this issue was a common topic of discussion: "Judge Bird has been trying for a long time to convince John Gladney that the colored people will dwell in harmony with the whites in due time, though at present considerable animosity exists between the two races in certain localities. Gladney says he don't believe anything of the kind."[139]

Bird commonly addressed audiences about "co-operative societies." He spoke on the subject in March 1878 at the Young Men's Debating Club, an organization for African American youth in Cairo. The formation of co-ops in the Black community had been a subject of considerable interest even before the war and an important element of the antebellum middle-class agenda. It was viewed as a means to take a step toward economic independence from White society, where both Black sellers and buyers could reap benefits that had gone instead to White businesspersons. Although this is the earliest preserved reference to Bird speaking on the topic, it was certainly not his first.

The talk was well attended by many besides members of the debate club, including a sizable group of White citizens.[140]

The Yellow Fever Epidemic of 1878

Between 1876 and 1878, changes occurred at the *Cairo Bulletin*. John Oberly's increasing political activities during the Hayes-Tilden campaign had required him to leave the day-to-day work of the *Bulletin* in September 1876 and bring in his brother Cyrus S. Oberly as editor, while putting the paper up for sale. But the work was too much for Cyrus, and he left the paper in December, forcing Oberly to return as editor.[141] Unable to find a buyer, Oberly in June 1877 rented the paper to his two brothers-in-law, W. F. and Louis Schuckers, announcing that he was relinquishing all connection to the *Bulletin*. The job, however, also proved to be too much for the Schuckers, and on May 1, 1878, Oberly took back over as managing editor, appointing Thomas Nally, an experienced newspaperman, as editor.[142] On May 2, 1878, the paper's name became the *Daily Cairo Bulletin*, and there seems little doubt that much of the political writing was still Oberly's.

On August 10, John Bird officiated at the wedding of George Anderson, a young African American, and Frances Wilson, a young White woman. This may have been the first such wedding in Cairo.[143] But even as he was pronouncing Anderson and Wilson husband and wife, a natural disaster was taking shape in the South that would bring tragedy to Bird's family and terror and death to Cairo. These were the early days of the great yellow fever epidemic of 1878, the most deadly and widespread outbreak of that disease in American history. From its first appearance in New Orleans, it spread up the Mississippi River farther north than ever before, to Cairo for the first time and on to St. Louis. Between July and October, this mosquito-borne disease infected some one hundred twenty thousand people, killing about twenty thousand.

Bird's mother, Catherine, and stepfather, Augustus Green, were enveloped in the horror of the epidemic. Green had become a medical doctor during the mid-1860s and practiced medicine for years in the Washington, D.C., area, while continuing to serve as the single bishop of the Independent Methodist Episcopal Church (IME), his breakaway denomination. The IME never prospered, and finally in the summer of 1876, Green and most of his members were ready to give up. With the help of his son Alfred, Green appealed to the national leadership of the AME Church to absorb the congregations of the IME. The AME agreed to do so, but Green was expected to give up his bishop's title and return to the AME merely as an itinerant preacher. At age seventy-five, Green was willing to do so to live at peace with his church. He resigned his bishopric on October 1, 1876, and shortly thereafter, the church appointed him to be the pastor of the Chapel Church AME congregation of about two hundred members in Vicksburg, Mississippi, a town of about twelve thousand at the time. He and Catherine took about a month to travel to his new church, stopping along the way to visit their former congregations and see old friends in Zanesville and Cincinnati, Ohio. Augustus stayed in Cincinnati while Catherine took some time to visit John and his family in Cairo. They finally reached Vicksburg on November 16 and immediately jumped into the life of the small congregation, repairing its building and decorating it for the 1877 annual meeting of the Mississippi Conference of the AME Church.[144] Augustus was well received in Vicksburg, and he began actively corresponding with the *Christian Recorder* once again, writing both about activities in Mississippi and about the early days of his work in the church.[145]

Life was good for the Greens into the summer of 1878, when the yellow fever struck. In early August, the first cases began to emerge in Vicksburg. By August 22, a full-scale epidemic was ravaging the city. Although about one-third of the population fled Vicksburg at the first report of the illness, Augustus and Catherine stayed put. Green was both a minister and a doctor, and, refusing to leave the city, he (and presumably Catherine) began attending to patients.[146] As the sickness spread, the White leaders of the city put out a desperate call for doctors, and although Green was already taking care of the sick in the African American community, he volunteered to help with White patients as well. Between September 1 and 8, the number of cases in Vicksburg exploded from eight hundred to three thousand.[147] At the beginning of this horrendous week, Augustus contracted the disease, and on September 5 he died. Catherine stayed with him throughout the ordeal until she, too, was stricken, but she survived. On September 6, Bird received two telegrams, one from William Rockwood, president of the Vicksburg Board of Health, responding to a query from Bird: "If it is Dr. A. R. Green (colored) to whom you refer, he is dead—fell a martyr to the cause." The other was from Thomas W. Stringer saying, "Your mother is very sick. A. R. Green died last night." There was nothing that Bird could do for his mother, since Vicksburg was under quarantine at that point.[148]

However, he did not have much time to think about that, because six days later, for the first time in its history, Cairo found itself the victim of a yellow fever epidemic.[149] About one third (about three thousand) of the town's population fled from the city shortly after the first fatalities were announced, including, according to the *Cairo Evening Sun*, about three hundred African Americans.[150] We have no clear evidence as to whether the Birds left the city, but the *Sun*, the only Cairo newspaper that continued publishing during the epidemic, noted simply on October 26, 1878, that "Justice Bird has returned."[151] It isn't clear, though, if this is a reference to his family returning to Cairo after the plague or his return from a business trip. More than one hundred persons developed yellow fever in Cairo during September and October, with at least fifty-one fatalities. The city itself was quarantined and lost hundreds of thousands of dollars' worth of business, which significantly damaged its already weakened economy.[152] This would have serious repercussions on the school budget for the following several years, leading to a steady decline in the quality of Cairo's public education system, both Black and White, that brought an end to the "Golden Age" of the African American school.

CHAPTER FIVE

"Beware of Such Men"

Clash with the Republican Party, 1879–1880

A S THINGS BEGAN TO RETURN to normal in Cairo following the epidemic, an intraparty struggle among the Republicans of Alexander County began to take shape that would lead to a tumultuous situation during 1880, in which Bird's relationship with the party would be ripped almost beyond repair. For a decade, the Republican leadership had promised the African American community a share of appointed offices and a place on the ballot in local, state, and, more vaguely, even national elections. In Cairo, Bird, John Gladney, Pink McAllister and Richard Taylor had successfully faced the electorate during the 1870s. A few other African Americans had also been elected across Illinois, but fewer than most Black citizens felt were appropriate. In areas where African Americans were a significant voting group, such as southernmost Illinois, counties along the Mississippi River near St. Louis, and parts of Chicago, White leaders consistently discouraged the nominations of African Americans for office. Significant patronage jobs were also regularly denied to African Americans and often filled instead by members of immigrant groups the Republicans were courting—particularly Germans and Irish. The Black community was so solidly faithful to the Republicans that party leaders saw little reason to use patronage to keep their votes. And, of course, there were many blatantly racist Republicans who refused to support a Black candidate for any position the party might have to offer, elective or appointed. Bird had been a rare exception to this rule—he had been named to an honorific state-level position by the governor, but this had not been followed by state jobs or federal patronage positions for other African Americans. Bird had been put forward for state patronage posts in 1878–79, but received none of them. By 1879, the continued lack of support reached a crisis point, and many African Americans began to lose patience. Bird had remained solidly loyal to his party from the beginning of his political career, but now he expected more for his people, and he would become one of the leading voices of discontent in Illinois, refusing to back down over what he saw as an outrage. Twenty years after he had watched his stepfather, Augustus Green, stand firm against the leadership of the British Methodist Episcopal Church over a matter of integrity and principle, no matter how that response might damage his career, Bird now took a similar stance and refused to submit.

The Cairo Postmaster Affair

The trigger for this crisis was the federal reappointment of Colonel George W. McKeaig as postmaster of Cairo. McKeaig had been a lawyer in Shawneetown, Illinois, and had served as a colonel in command of the 120th Illinois Infantry during the war. He moved to Cairo in 1866, where he joined the law firm of Olney, McKeaig and Lansden.[1] He was appointed postmaster in Cairo in the summer of 1870 and reappointed (in the face of some discontent) in 1874.[2] Early on he had been a leading Radical Republican in Alexander County, and with a number of federal post office jobs that he could distribute among party members, he was also quite influential. The problem for the Black community was that he refused to appoint any African Americans to those jobs, in spite of their key position in the Alexander County Republican Party.

The city government in Cairo had opened a few jobs to African Americans during the early 1870s, giving business to local Black concerns and appointing Black workers to custodial positions in some of the schools (in spite of some opposition from the White community).[3] But state and federal appointments continued to be largely off-limits in the region, and McKeaig, controlling the primary federal positions in Cairo, was the most obvious obstacle. There are hints that Bird was already getting impatient with McKeaig by 1876, when Bird uncharacteristically failed to attend the Alexander County Republican convention that McKeaig led in June.[4]

When McKeaig's second term as postmaster was about to expire in 1878, Bird and many of his colleagues supported other candidates for the position who pledged to make African American appointments in the post office. But President Hayes (along with powerful Illinois Republicans at the federal level) saw McKeaig's service in the 1876 election as sufficient reason to reappoint

George W. McKeaig, Republican Cairo postmaster from 1870 to 1882, refused to hire Black workers for the post office, leading to a major confrontation with Bird in 1878–79. Courtesy of Special Collections, Morris Library, Southern Illinois University, Carbondale, Winifred Cox Papers MSS 289.

him.[5] Bird and a substantial number of Black Republicans refused to accept this. In early 1879, Bird took the lead in a campaign to remove McKeaig from office. As a part of this process, Bird, employing the techniques he and Henry O. Wagoner had used against the Democratic city officials in 1865, applied for an open position at the Cairo post office and was rejected by McKeaig on the grounds that Bird had worked against his reappointment. Then Bird named another qualified African American against whom McKeaig could have no political objection, but the postmaster refused to consider him, too.[6] The *Bulletin* once again supported Bird for the post office position:

> Mr. Bird is the ablest Republican in the district, and that the Democrats have not made inroads into the ranks of the two thousand colored voters of the district, is because Bird has been upon the constant lookout, fortifying the weak points, and defending with the skill of a veteran, the whole line. To this we can add that John J. Bird has, during the past six years, formed a more stuborn [*sic*] obstacle in the pathway to Democratic victory in this district, than any other Republican, or half dozen

Republicans, for that matter, that can be named. Of course Democrats owe him no good will for this, but the Republican party does, and ought to pay the debt. Some of our bourbonic friends may take offense at the remark, but that consideration shall not deter us from saying that had Mr. Bird been a Democrat, he would, ere this, have served a term in the Legislature, and be the present incumbent of an office, the emoluments of which would be adequate to his support.[7]

McKeaig's rejections cemented for most Black Republicans the conviction that he would never hire an African American. Bird then inaugurated a petition to President Hayes asking him to rescind his appointment of McKeaig. In March, Bird, Gladney, and Scott, along with several supportive White leaders, called a meeting of local Republicans to discuss a motion from the party itself to ask for the same thing. The courthouse was filled with supporters of the movement, but McKeaig and some allies also attended. At the meeting, Bird calmly charged McKeaig with consistent refusal to hire African Americans and described his own dealings with McKeaig concerning employment. The *Bulletin* provided part of Bird's speech:

> And I now tell Col. McKeaig to his face, that the man holding the official position that he holds, who tells the 2,000 colored Republicans of this congressional district, and the 800,000 of the United States, that the time has not yet come for colored men to hold office; and who shows by his stubborn refusal to give colored men positions to which in right and justice they are entitled—I tell him to his face that, as such a man, he is too great a load for the Republican party to carry, and the party must throw him off, or take the consequences! I tell him and all other Republicans whose duty it is to recognize the colored man as a political equal, as well in the distribution of offices, as otherwise, after thirteen years of devotion to the Republican party, clinging to it at all times and under all circumstance, that the time HAS arrived for them to hold office, and they will demand the right from this time forward and the Republican party will deny them at its peril. . . . I tell him he is a dead weight to his party, and entertaining the opinions he avows, his maintenance in office is a standing insult to colored voters.[8]

McKeaig responded by attacking Bird personally, arguing that he was angry at not being given the post office position and warning those in attendance against "wandering after Bird and Bill Scott, that they are abandoning their best friend to no good purpose." At no time did he suggest that he would be hiring Black employees for the Post Office. McKeaig was followed by short speeches from William Scott and a White speaker calling for McKeaig's ouster. A committee submitted a resolution stating that the reappointment of McKeaig had "created wide-spread dissentions in the ranks of the party throughout the entire district," that his conduct "has been such as to alienate and distract, rather than cement and harmonize the conflicting elements here," and resolving that "we citizens of Cairo and voters in this congressional district, in mass meeting assembled, do hereby urge and demand of the president, his removal." The resolution was "put to vote and carried, by an unmistakable majority of 'ayes.'"[9]

Shortly after this meeting, Bird departed for Washington, D.C., with the petition and resolution in hand to meet with party officials there. His plan was apparently to present his evidence and arguments to the Department of the Post Office and then move on to others if he could not get satisfaction there. Soon after he arrived, some high-level leaders of the party, most importantly Illinois senator John A. Logan, the head of the state's Republican Party, met with him and offered him a federal position "of trust and profit" if he would drop his opposition to McKeaig.[10] According to sources quoted in the *Bulletin*, "the offer was indignantly rejected—and that the Judge's would-be purchasers were told that there was not enough money in the federal treasury to buy him. Bird declares that the fight has become the fight of the 800,000 colored voters of the country—that his grievances and resentments are not involved, and that the only terms of compromise to which he can listen are such as cover the dismissal of McKeaig, and the recognition of the right of the colored race to equable portion of government patronage."[11]

Unable to get what he came for, Bird continued to seek audiences with other high members of the party. But McKeaig had considerable support from the Illinois delegation, and the national leadership saw little benefit to rescinding his appointment over this issue. Bird persevered until he finally got an appointment with President Hayes himself. The *Bulletin* reported the following from an interview with Bird:

> He [Bird] secured an interview with the president; laid before that dignitary the grievances of the Republican party of the Eighteenth Congressional district, and made such an impression upon his mind

that he called Judge Bird to a second interview—naming the time himself. Just what passed during that interview, we are not prepared to say. We only know that Judge Bird seems to be well satisfied with the result—that he is strongly impressed with the idea that the president will consider the claims of the Republican party—its unity and harmony, as paramount to the claims of any individual, and that, as a consequence, Col. McKeaig is, ultimately, bound to "step down and out."[12]

Bird returned to Cairo with a promise that an investigation would be made into the situation. And on June 19, 1879, special agents from the Washington Post Office Department arrived in Cairo to do just that.[13] This must have been an extraordinary moment for the African American community, a visible indication that the national party had taken its concerns seriously and that change was in the making. The investigation did have consequences, both for McKeaig and for Bird.

Within a few days of the agents' return to Washington, it was confirmed that McKeaig would keep his position as postmaster. But at the same time, the Post Office Department filled an open position of U.S. Mail agent on the Cairo and St. Louis Railroad, paying $900 per year, with John Bird, certainly over the objection of McKeaig.[14] Bird was not required to reconcile with or give up his criticism of McKeaig. Bird resigned from his position as police magistrate almost immediately, on July 1, and took on his new job, thereby becoming the first African American appointee to a federal position in Alexander County. Presumably Bird saw the job offered him by Senator Logan as having no impact on McKeaig and his supporters in Cairo, but he viewed the proposed position in Cairo as a rebuke of McKeaig's practices and thus appropriate to accept.

This position was a major change for Bird. It provided a much larger salary than the meager one he had earned as police magistrate. It is unclear whether Bird and his family had lived entirely on the latter salary, or whether he had also worked another job. But especially after Judge Bross resigned in 1877 and was not replaced, Bird had worked unprecedented hours on the bench without additional pay—"No man ever filled the position," the *Bulletin* wrote, "who can show a record of more than half the office hours that Judge Bird has made, yet the pay, outside the $300 from the city, has not averaged one-tenth of $3,000."[15]

Not surprisingly, Bird's new appointment created considerable agitation in parts of the White community in the region, both Republican and Democrat. Across the state, newspapers complained that the previous agent had been thrown out of the job so that it could be given to an unqualified Black man. The *Bulletin* disputed this, noting that Bird was appointed after the previous agent had died, and that "no man, white or black, belonging to the Republican party in Southern Illinois, is better qualified for the position of mail or route agent than John J. Bird. . . . If there is a Republican living whom the leading white republicans of Cairo would squelch, that man is John J. Bird. He was not made mail agent because the white Republicans like him and seek to help him; but because they fear him."[16] Although this description of Bird's relationship with the White Republicans of Cairo is clearly slanted by the Democratic leanings of the *Bulletin*, there is little doubt that it is correct in saying that he had little support from them in getting the job (McKeaig remained very influential, if wounded from this conflict), and that a key part of the motivation of the federal Post Office leadership in giving Bird the position had to do with the fear that he could turn many African Americans away from the Republican Party if he wanted to do so. In that way, his appointment was a victory for the African American community in southern Illinois, once again showing that when they were united, they could change things. During the 1880s, considerably more African Americans would be appointed to positions in the post offices, but Bird once again was the pioneer. His new position, however, did not diminish Bird's continuing pressure on the White Republican leadership to make good on its promises.

Increased Tensions at the National Level, 1879

During the spring of 1879, Bird was elected as one of two delegates from Illinois to the National Convention of Colored Men of the United States that was held in Nashville, Tennessee, on May 6–9.[17] Bird was joined by Ferdinand Lee Barnett, the young and rising lawyer and coeditor of the Chicago African American newspaper, the *Conservator*, who was making his first real appearance on the national stage at the conference.[18] Although the delegates focused mostly on the increasingly disastrous condition of African Americans in the South, a new but related issue that needed consideration had developed during the spring—the Kansas Fever, or Exoduster, movement, an explosive and substantial emigration out of Louisiana and Mississippi by African Americans who could no longer stand the violence and oppression in those states. The movement is often characterized as a quasi-millennialist movement, which arose as word spread that the federal government was going to provide free transportation for Black families to Kansas, along with land and houses. This was untrue, but many thousands nevertheless began to travel north to St. Louis and on into Kansas, which was freely open to Black migration.[19] White southerners vehemently opposed the movement, fearing the loss of their cheap workforce. Many Black leaders also opposed the idea of leaving the South, arguing that African Americans had strength in their numbers and economic importance and should stay to fight for their rights. But those who were leaving had little confidence in the White population and hoped to find a better life in the North.[20]

P. B. S. Pinchback of Louisiana was again the primary organizer of the Nashville conference, and he was joined by several other southern leaders.[21] While the southern states heavily predominated at the conference, a number of northern states sent delegations. Bird and Barnett played significant roles in the conference. Because the committees were to be composed of one delegate from every state, each wound up on three of the six committees— Bird on the Resolutions and Address, Education and Labor, and Resolutions Committees, and Barnett on the Permanent Organization, Colored Press, and Migration Committees. Shortly after the delegates convened, word arrived about a convention held in Vicksburg on May 5–6 that was organized by White planters and merchants seriously concerned about the African American exodus. Having invited a number of African Americans who also opposed migration, they developed a document that proposed a few reforms in the relations between land owners and their tenants, pledged that the planters would protect those who worked for them from violence, and voiced opposition to migration from the South. It also refused to acknowledge the actual causes of the exodus and the real fears of the Black community. Reaction was mixed among the delegates, but Bird submitted a resolution that denounced the Vicksburg Labor Convention and its address as an insidious sham, which ignored the main issues and was cynically designed to slow the exodus.[22] The resolution was debated, apparently garnering considerable support but also substantial opposition from those who saw the Vicksburg meeting as a positive step forward.[23] Eventually, the conference rejected Bird's resolution and instead produced a conciliatory statement on the subject urging dialogue between Whites and Blacks on its model.[24] This noncombative stance almost certainly reflects the influence of Pinchback and other more conservative leaders, who while they knew the Vicksburg Address's distortions of the situation presumably felt it was better not to offend the planters at the time. Of course, Bird's assessment proved to be correct. The promised reforms and protections quickly faded away.

The Democratic *Nashville Daily American* sharply attacked Bird over his resolution against the Vicksburg convention, arguing that as a northerner, Bird knew nothing of the actual situation in the South and that "the resolution of Bird is a substantial reiteration of [John A.] Logan's cheap political claptrap." The paper, which strongly defended the assertion that southern African Americans were not being terrorized or treated with systematic injustice, also attacked the northern delegates as a group, insisting that their goals were to slander the South about their treatment of African Americans and to lure Black emigrants to their districts to gain new Republican voters.[25] Bird responded to the *American* in two speeches at the conference, defending himself and his northern colleagues, pointing out that he got his information about southern conditions directly from southern newspapers, quoting as an example an editorial from the *New Orleans Times* of April 22: "The Negroes are leaving the State because there exists, among them a sense of insecurity— an apprehension that their civil and political rights are in danger—a belief that they cannot have justice. The truth compels us to admit that these apprehensions are not altogether unreasonable."[26]

The official documents released at the conclusion of the convention were powerful. The address, on whose committee Bird sat, laid bare in vivid language the terrible oppression African Americans in the South, and to a lesser extent in the North, endured. It called upon African Americans to redouble their efforts to seek education, to demand their constitutional rights and the enforcement of all laws passed for their protection. It also strongly endorsed the right of Black people to migrate.[27]

The report of the Committee on Education and Labor largely reflected the traditional ideas, supporting integrated schools but also insisting that in segregated schools the teachers should be Black.[28] The Committee on Migration's report stated in no uncertain terms that the primary cause of the exodus to Kansas was the violence against Black people and White intentions to curtail their rights. It supported African Americans' right to leave if they wished and laid the onus for stopping the Exoduster movement completely upon the White leaders of southern state governments, who must enforce the laws that provided African American rights and safety. No reference was made in it to the Vicksburg convention.[29] In sum, the conference voiced the anger of the delegates over the grim situation throughout the South and strongly endorsed the Kansas Fever Exodus as a legitimate response to the situation and as a warning that many more families would leave if southern Whites persisted in their practices. Bird certainly approved of all of these reports.

Back in Illinois, Bird's increasing dissatisfaction with the state Republican Party was evident in the fall of 1879, when he attended a state convention of African American men held in Springfield in mid-October. The primary purpose of the meeting was to present a unified message to the Illinois leadership that they could not retain African American political support without including African Americans in their appointments to state and federal jobs and as candidates for state office. In the address promulgated by this meeting, written by Bird, J. H. Washington of Galesburg, and J. H. Hollinger of Decatur, the convention bluntly stated what Bird had argued against McKeaig months before:

> Sixteen years of pupilage under a form of government like our own, with a people possessing the inherent qualities which are essential to their elevation and success, is sufficient evidence that the time has come for the colored men of this State to exhibit a determination to demand of those in control of the National and State Administrations, as well as the local officers, that recognition which we are, as a component part of the party, justly entitled to. . . . Our State administrations have done far less, in fact, nothing compensatory for the invaluable services rendered. We have stood at our posts as firm and as immovable as the immovable rock-rooted hills, defending and maintaining Republican principles with unquestioned unanimity, while our political recognition has been almost wholly ignored. . . . Believing these evils can be remedied within the bounds of our party organization, we are willing, or rather determined to make the effort. If we fail to accomplish the desired end, and dire consequences should befall our party in the future, the responsibility will rest where it justly belongs.[30]

The Election of 1880

The fall election of 1880 proved to be the crisis point in John Bird's political career. His conflict with the White Republican leadership reached its climax here, and key actions of his during the campaign also demonstrated the limits of his influence over African American Republicans. The events of this year would dramatically change the course of his life.

By the beginning of 1880, Bird's leadership of the dissatisfied faction of African American Republicans in southern Illinois was clear. He began to voice serious opposition not just to McKeaig again, but to the reelection of Republican congressman John R. Thomas, whom Bird had so strongly supported in the election of 1878. His opposition to Thomas was striking enough that it drew a comment from the *Chicago Tribune*: "In the latter city [Cairo] Judge Bird, the colored politician, has arrayed nearly all the colored voters against Thomas and Postmaster McKeaig, though the opposition is not considered sufficient to endanger Thomas' chances of reelection."[31] The reprinting of this note in the *Daily Cairo Bulletin* brought a letter the following day from Alexander G. Leonard, an African American who, although a staunch Republican, had been working for about a year in the newsroom of the *Bulletin*. In his letter, Leonard noted that Bird recently had confronted Thomas publicly about the latter's failure to advance the African American cause, and he warned, "If that gentleman [Thomas] expects any further honors at the hands of the negro or the party, there must be something done." Leonard's letter in turn provoked a startling threat from the *Cairo Evening Sun*, the leading Republican paper in Cairo. Referring to Leonard's letter, the *Sun* wrote, "Would it not be as well for the colored friends of the colored agent, Bird, to keep a little quiet about their opposition to these men?" The *Sun* had seen Bird as a troublemaker before, but this was a new level of antipathy coming from a mouthpiece of Bird's own party. The tension would not dissipate anytime soon.[32]

Relations continued to deteriorate between Bird and the White Republican establishment into the spring and summer. At the meeting of the Alexander County Republicans in May to select delegates for the convention choosing candidates for the state legislature, the two sides again came into conflict. As in 1878, the assembled African Americans argued that the delegation should support Bird for the state house of representatives, while most of the White Republicans again supported Harmon Black, the White candidate who had opposed Bird for the nomination in 1878. Black's supporters won the struggle at the meeting, but the African American delegates refused to accept the results and planned to put Bird into nomination anyway.[33] Bird was not in Cairo at the time of the Alexander County meeting, but when he returned in June, probably sensing that it was a losing battle and that by pressing for the nomination his enemies would characterize his entire campaign for greater African American opportunities in government as merely a plan to further his own career, he sent the chair of the legislative convention a letter withdrawing his name from consideration. At the convention in August, Bird, in fact, placed Black's name in nomination with, as the *Inter-Ocean* described it, "one of the neatest speeches in the campaign."[34]

In mid-April, a call was issued for another state convention of African American leaders to be held in Springfield, Illinois, on July 20, "for the purpose of concentrating our views upon some joint action as to how our claims may find a good representative in the issue now pending before the national campaign."[35] With all the tension between the party and its African American members, there was considerable apprehension among White Republicans and some African Americans that the convention was being called to try to divorce the Black community from the party.[36] Democrats saw it as an opportunity to siphon off some voters and sent representatives to the conference with the purpose of creating dissension.[37] On the appointed day, a solid assembly of 126 delegates convened in the chamber of the Illinois House of Representatives in Springfield. Although the primary organizer of the convention had been attorney John G. Jones of Chicago, Bird was the leading light throughout. On the opening day, he was chosen to chair the critical Address Committee and was named one of five vice presidents for a permanent committee intended to continue the work of the conference after it ended. To assure the Republican leadership that the convention did not consider itself to be in rebellion, the delegates approved a resolution supporting the party and denouncing the Democrats. That evening's program featured four speeches, including addresses by Governor Shelby Cullom and Illinois secretary of state George Harlow and concluding with a speech by John Bird, in which he gave a scathing denunciation of the Democratic Party and argued that the Republicans provided the only hope for African Americans in the South.[38]

On the second day of the conference, Bird submitted the address developed by his committee to the delegates, who adopted it unanimously. The address,

John G. Jones, a Chicago attorney, was a colleague of Bird's in the Black convention movement and in the Prince Hall Masons. Chicago History Museum, ICHi-0022362.

probably largely Bird's work, is a carefully constructed argument for African American inclusion in the structure of the Republican Party and a brilliant distillation of the fraught relationship between the party and its Black members. It is emphatic about African American support for the Republicans, but it also clearly states its dissatisfaction with the party's current practices:

"While this be true, we are of the opinion that its mission will not have been accomplished until it places the negro in this State—in all the States, alike—in a higher sphere of useful and honored citizenship." It goes on to provide a clear delineation of the philosophy underlying the plea for inclusion:

> We ask that recognition in the various departments of Government, which our numbers, intelligence and capacity entitle us. We ask it because we are, with you, laboring to maintain Republican supremacy

in this Government, believing it essential if we would have the Government of our fathers preserved and perpetuated. We ask it in the name of *Justice* and *Right*. We ask it because we recognize the fact that if what we ask is accorded us, it will place us as a people in a position, politically and otherwise, by which we can overcome the barriers to progress which meet us in every department of life.

The address concludes with both cajoling and a subtle threat:

Will the party of great and noble deeds; the party which conquered the greatest rebellion known in the annals of history; the party which emancipated four million of slaves, halt between duty and fear, or will it rise with boldness to the dignity of its true character as enunciated in its time honored principles, and make this act of complete justice the crowning work of its glorious existence? Believing these ends can be most readily attained within the ranks of our own party organization, we shall labor with increasing effort by urgent appeals and ceaseless agitation until the much desired result shall have been attained.[39]

Besides the address, the convention passed resolutions that demanded that teachers in Black schools in Illinois be required to pass the same qualification examinations that teachers of White students were expected to pass (as had been done in Cairo); that African Americans be encouraged to form local, nonpolitical organizations to advance their interests (Bird was placed on the committee assigned to create model constitutions and bylaws for such organizations); and that southern Black people emigrating from their home states be encouraged to settle in Illinois. Finally, the convention established a statewide Executive Committee, consisting of a member from each of the nineteen congressional districts, plus four at-large members, whose mandate, "to carry out the plan of organization," was intentionally vague so as not to offend the Republican leadership. Bird was named as the member from the Eighteenth District. The conference concluded with several speeches, but the final one, as on the previous evening, was given by Bird. In it, he urged his fellow citizens to take concerted action to secure their privileges. "There are three elements of strength . . . that are necessary to acquire success. We must have character, education and wealth, and we must also make ourselves proficient in whatever business we engage."[40]

The convention's address struck a very raw nerve with the White Republicans. The *Chicago Tribune*, the leading Republican paper in the city and the state, now controlled by the party's anti-Radical element, was outraged by it and published two editorials criticizing it on July 23, which both focused their anger specifically on Bird. Arguing that the Black delegates at the conference were "under the general direction of Mr. Bird, of Cairo," one author insisted that the "purpose of the Convention, plainly stated, was to urge upon the Republican party the claims of blacks to office." Deeply offended by the suggestion that Black Republicans had not been given a fair share of positions within the party, the writer insisted that they had received sufficient appointments from the Republicans and that they could move into higher leadership positions simply by demonstrating individual merit, just as Whites did. This angry editorial illustrates the striking defensiveness that White Republicans felt in the face of a more aggressive African American stance on the issue. Ignoring the document's arguments about the importance of Black incorporation into the party structure, the editorialist tried to isolate the leaders of the movement from the majority of Black voters: "We are inclined to believe that the mass of the colored voters, who, like the mass of White voters, expect to earn their living outside of politics, have no desire to make an issue with the Republican party over the distribution of offices on a race basis."[41]

The second editorial, which described the gathering as "Bird's office-seeking Convention in Springfield," echoes the arguments of the New Departure Democrats in insisting that African Americans in the South were responsible for the lack of Black office holders there: "If they are not now in possession of as many offices throughout the South as their votes should entitle them to hold, it is because the colored voters themselves have failed to exercise the courage, determination, and manhood necessary to the vindication of their rights." The author concludes with this startling description of the political situation in Republican Illinois: "In this and other Northern States, where they are on a perfect footing of equality with the whites in political affairs, their advancement to political position, high or low, depends upon individual merit and enterprise and not upon race, clan, or class cooperation such as Bird seeks to institute."[42]

While this reaction to the address likely represented the majority opinion of White Republicans across Illinois, African Americans applauded its publication.[43] In this divisive context, Bird now stood as the key representative of African Americans' desire for political equality in Illinois but had also exacerbated the anger the Republican establishment already had against him.

During the fall election campaign, Bird made a decision that caused all his previous conflicts with the party leadership to pale in comparison, a step that divided the African American community and gave his White enemies the ammunition they needed to sabotage the upward trajectory of his political influence. John Oberly had finally sold the *Cairo Bulletin* in 1879 and moved to Bloomington, Illinois, where he would establish the *Bloomington Bulletin* in 1881 and run it for several years.[44] By 1880, Oberly had redeveloped political support within the Democratic Party and received the nomination that year for Illinois secretary of state.[45] Bird's long friendship with Oberly, now a statewide candidate on the enemy's ticket, placed him in a complex position. During one of his speeches at the Springfield convention in July, Bird had rather dramatically praised "his highly esteemed friend J. H. Oberly" as an example of a good man in the Democratic Party, reminding his audience of Oberly's vote for the Henry Act that had "brought down on his head the wrath and indignation of his own party," and saying that he could trust Oberly individually, but not the party to which he belonged.[46] By early October, Bird decided to endorse Oberly for the office rather than Henry Dement, the Republican candidate—only Oberly, and no other Democrat—and he worked to convince other party members to do the same. His decision put him at war with large segments of the Republican Party, this time both White and Black.

On October 5, Bird was in Chicago to attend the Cook County Republican Convention, in part to talk with fellow Republicans in the city about supporting Oberly, and to address a meeting of Black citizens that evening. We have no information about Bird's overall success at the convention, but he raised considerable opposition to himself among several of the African American delegates there. At the evening gathering, that animosity exploded. During his address, Bird made reference to an incident that had occurred earlier in the day at the convention, when a Major Scott had nominated an African American, A. F. Bradley (probably Andrew Bradley, a Chicago newspaper editor), for county commissioner from the West Side. Bird asserted that when Scott had placed Bradley's name into nomination, others in the room hissed at Scott. Bird considered this to have been an open insult to the Black voters of Illinois. To Bird's surprise, much of the audience immediately jumped to the defense of the Cook County Republicans. Major Scott himself arose and denied that anyone had hissed at him and insisted that

Bradley had been defeated for the nomination in a system that treated all the candidates equally. Bird responded that he had been present and had heard the hissing himself. Then the real source of the hostility became clear. Someone yelled, "Who were you for?" and Bird replied that he had been there to support Oberly, who "was, although a democrat, a better representative of republican principles, so far as the negro's rights are concerned, than many men who claimed to be republicans."[47] This led to a huge outburst of shouting against Bird, and he was forced to leave the podium. After additional arguing, he was ejected from the meeting.[48] Word of Bird's support for Oberly spread quickly after the Chicago meeting and caused outrage among Republicans across the state. Republican papers viciously and incorrectly charged that Bird was supporting the entire Democratic slate and that he had been paid off by the Democrats.[49] Bird refused to back down from his position.

Bird (and Oberly) did receive support from some African American newspapers. The *Bulletin* quoted Chicago's *Republican Advocate* as saying of Bird, "He is an enthusiastic supporter of John H. Oberly for secretary of State and has excellent reasons for so doing. The Judge wields a large vote in this state, and as the honesty of his convictions can not be impeached, he will necessarily have a large following."[50]

On October 13, he traveled to Bloomington to attend the first meeting of the new State Executive Committee that had been organized at the Springfield convention, and in spite of the controversy, he was elected its president. Even more surprisingly, at the meeting he convinced all but three of the twenty committee members present to pass a resolution urging African American voters to support Oberly and to reject Dement, saying that the latter "has not had the courage to meet these questions with that boldness and impartiality which is so essential in party leaders." The resolution was printed as a circular and mailed to newspapers across the state under Bird's name, appearing in the *Bulletin* on October 21.[51] In Cairo, a number of Black Republicans gathered for a meeting at the courthouse on the evening of October 28 to discuss the situation and produced the following resolution: "Resolved, That we, the colored Republicans of Cairo, in convention, openly repudiate the action of the so-called Executive Committee, headed by John J. Bird, held at Bloomington, October 14, advising the colored people of the State to vote for the Hon. J. H. Oberly or any other Democrat, and we hereby pledge ourselves to support the Republican ticket without a scratch: and we further warn the colored people of the State to beware of such men." The *Chicago Tribune* and the *Inter Ocean* published the resolution, the former with an introduction indicating its support for the incensed Cairo Republicans.[52] The *Illinois State Journal* on November 1 printed a letter from John Stone, a member of the Executive Committee from Lincoln that denounced Bird's resolutions as "treasonable and damaging to the best interests of the colored people of this State." His argument is essentially the argument Bird had used for years in his own campaign speeches, that no Democrat deserved the vote of an African American because of the continued oppression of African Americans in the South.[53]

But Bird also had supporters in the Chicago African American community, where he was invited to speak on October 25 at a large mass meeting of Black Republicans, along with A. F. Bradley, whose treatment at the Cook County convention had so outraged Bird. The *Republican Advocate* in Chicago described Bird's speech as follows: "The former [Bird] endorsed the republican ticket, but declared that as John H. Oberly was a true friend of the colored man, he should support him for secretary of state, and advise the colored voters to do so." Bradley, in his speech, confirmed the story Bird told about his nomination and the hissing at Major Scott. At the conclusion of the meeting, "resolutions endorsing the sentiments of the speakers were passed by a large majority."[54]

The election was held on November 2, 1880, and, as expected, the Democrats lost in all of the state contests, including for secretary of state. It appears that Bird's endorsement in Cairo had a small but discernible effect. Of the slightly more than fifteen hundred voters who cast ballots, the vast majority of them, Republican and Democrat, appear to have cast the straight party ballot, with virtually identical numbers of votes for the presidential race and most state contests. However, Oberly received about forty votes from people who otherwise voted for the Republicans. Many of these were probably Black voters convinced by Bird, but this only amounted to about 7 to 10 percent of the Black ballots. Most of the community had voted the straight Republican ticket.[55] Statewide, Oberly did better than any other Democratic candidate except Lyman Trumbull, the gubernatorial candidate, but it is clear that he did not gain significant votes from the African American community anywhere.[56]

Bird almost certainly knew from the beginning that he had nothing to gain politically from his endorsement of Oberly. He also was likely aware that no state Democratic nominee had a chance of beating the Republicans in the election and that his support could never produce the number of African American votes to make a difference for Oberly. In the face of this knowledge, however, he took his stand for a man he trusted and admired, almost certainly knowing that this would cost him status in the party he loved.

Throughout the 1870s, John Bird had been the most prominent and respected African American in southern Illinois, honored as a leader in the Republican Party. He had been the Black community's primary paradigm of a trailblazer for African American advancement within the political system. He had been elected to city office and had been put forward seriously, if unsuccessfully, in 1878 and 1880 as a candidate for the Republican nomination for state representative. He had traveled Illinois speaking in support of the Republican ticket to enthusiastic Black and White audiences. He probably had had the deepest influence of any African American leader over the Black voters of southern Illinois. But after his confrontation with White party leaders over Colonel McKeaig and particularly his endorsement of Oberly, most of that status within the party disappeared. From the end of 1880 onward, no reference was made again concerning Bird as a potential candidate for state office, or even for county or city offices. The principled stands he had made in opposition to the Republican leadership had cost him any future advancement in the party. Although he had insisted that none of his disagreements with the leadership affected his loyalty to the party, his enemies took the Oberly incident in particular as an excuse to derail a rising star they felt for other reasons they needed to suppress. His stature within the party and the momentum that he had gained toward playing an even more substantial role in it were unique among the African American leaders in southern Illinois. Thus, with his fall here, his White opponents had no one else of similar status to fear. His popularity in the local African American community, where he had spent so much effort in keeping the voters loyal to the Republican cause, also suffered temporarily. But in spite of all this, Bird refused to abandon the party.

CHAPTER SIX

"One of the Most Intelligent Men in the State"

New Directions, 1881–1886

WHILE THE CONTROVERSIES OF 1879–80 brought an end to Bird's rise toward higher political office and damaged his direct influence on the White side of the Republican Party, they did not destroy his popularity within the Illinois African American community or leave him divorced from the party itself. During 1881–86, his final years living in Cairo, he maintained close ties with the state's Black Republican wing and supported the party as a whole during a complex period in the relationship between the party and the African American community. By late 1881, he had won another election in Cairo, this time as justice of the peace, and shortly thereafter had been reinstated into the local Republican leadership, participating in county, district, and state Republican conventions through his final years in Cairo. In 1884, he also finally broke down the local Republican resistance to hiring an African American inside the Cairo post office, when he became its first permanent Black employee.

However, the Republican decline in support for African American causes that had led to Bird's actions in 1879–80 continued through the 1880s and would climax with a complete abandonment in the latter half of the 1890s. Even when the Republicans won control of Congress and the presidency in 1880 and again in 1888 and some Republicans introduced bills to counteract the violence suppressing the Black vote in the South and aid education for African American children, they were unable to gain enough support within the party itself to get the measures passed. The Republican leadership focused rather on securing southern White votes by promoting economic policies toward the South that might attract businessmen and small farmers to the party.[1] In the face of these developments, many African Americans became disillusioned with the party, and the northern Black political leadership began to fracture further over the issue of how the community should respond to the situation.

Most African Americans, including Bird, saw no plausible choice besides continuing to support the party and agitate from within to bring the White leadership back to its earlier priorities. They continued to believe that the only way to secure African Americans' long-term well-being was through the passage and enforcement of civil rights legislation at the national and state levels. They also believed that, in spite of their deep dissatisfaction with them, the Republicans had been the only party to support the African American cause in the past and remained, in sharp contrast to the Democrats, the only hope for any continued progress.[2]

Others were more impatient, however, and argued that Black voters needed to declare an independence from the Republicans and seek candidates from any party who would support African American rights. During the 1880s, Democrats who gained control of state and local governments in New York, New Jersey, Pennsylvania, and Ohio sought to lure Black voters by making significant African American patronage appointments themselves and supporting some state legislation assuring civil rights, including bills integrating public schools (in New Jersey).[3] All the while, they attempted to divorce themselves from the violent White supremacist Democratic governments of the South, downplaying the severity of the actual situation in the region and pleading states' rights as their excuse for not intervening. This did not prove to be particularly successful in the 1880s, although individual White Democrats, such as Carter Harrison, mayor of Chicago from 1879 to 1893, gained substantial followings in the African American community.[4]

In Illinois, this difference in viewpoint led to a great deal of internecine strife and made it difficult for Black leaders to present a united front in both state and local politics. During the 1880s, Bird fought against the movement to break from the Republican Party, a movement led in southern Illinois by his longtime associate William Scott, and he repeatedly showed his value to the party at both the local and state levels. His loyalty to the party was a key aspect of his work within the state's continuing African American convention movement. These conventions were intended to advance a unified agenda for the Black community but during the 1880s often became the focal point for the controversy about the relationship between African Americans and the party. Bird, alongside such stalwarts as John W. E. Thomas and

J. W. W. Washington, played a significant role defending the party in this turbulent era while continuing to press it to support crucial Black causes, particularly concerning education for Black students, increased job opportunities, and a return of federal enforcement of basic civil rights in the South.[5]

He and many of his colleagues continued to press for the presence of Black men in positions of responsibility in local and state government as a visible sign of racial progress and the increased possibilities for influence on civil rights in the state. During these years, however, many African Americans came to see Black leaders' constant push for state and federal patronage positions as a distraction from the real issues facing the majority of Black citizens. Many viewed Black politicians as elitists, unconcerned about the problems of ordinary African Americans, and as looking after their own self-interests instead of those of the people. These criticisms, while certainly true of some, were unfair to others, including Bird, who seems consciously to have avoided even the appearance of profiting unduly from his political activities. Most leaders in the Black community believed that an African American presence in the political sphere was critical to the push for civil rights and thought that their efforts would lead to improvements in the lives of all African Americans.[6]

Besides his work with the statewide African American leadership, Bird found another way to influence the wider Black community. In 1882, he, William Scott, and Alexander Leonard founded an African American newspaper, the *Cairo Gazette*, which Bird edited during the first year of its existence. His belief in the importance of the Black press, certainly influenced by Augustus Green, his stepfather, who had published newspapers during John's youth, remained strong through the rest of his life. This first editing experience in Cairo, while short-lived, would directly lead to his work in 1887 as coeditor and editor of the much more widely known paper, the *State Capital*, once he moved to Springfield.

Bird's Return to Cairo Politics, 1881

The extent of Bird's loss of favor immediately following his Oberly endorsement became evident in the spring of 1881, when Bird decided to run for the city clerkship in Cairo, against the incumbent, Dennis J. Foley, who was a Democrat. He announced his candidacy on March 10, and although the

Bulletin did not endorse him (Foley was their candidate), it said of Bird, "That he is one of the best representative colored men in the city, honest, capable and energetic, can not be denied by any one, and there is every reason to believe that, if elected, he will serve the people faithfully and satisfactorily."[7] But many Republicans refused to support Bird for the position, and eventually several other candidates entered the field.[8] Bird had lost support not only among White Republican voters but also in the Black community. By April 9, a second African American, George W. Tanner, a teacher at the Cairo Black school and an active Republican, announced himself as candidate also for city clerk.[9] Tanner's candidacy was certainly a move in opposition to Bird by the more "stalwart" Black Republicans who no longer trusted him. There could have been little hope that Tanner would win the election—Bird still had support in the community—and Tanner's presence on the ballot would clearly split the Black vote, assuring that both would be defeated. On April 19, Bird came in fourth among seven candidates, with 277 votes compared with the unified Democratic vote of 632 for Foley and 155 votes for Tanner.[10] This must have been a crushing blow for Bird. But still, he had retained support in his community, having received almost twice the number of votes between himself and Tanner.

The fall election of 1881 for local offices shows, however, that by then Bird had regained the trust of many more Republicans in Cairo. During the early autumn, Bird and his family moved from their longtime home in the Third Ward on Twelfth Street to a house on Twenty-Second Street in the Fifth Ward.[11] In late October, Bird announced a run for the position of justice of the peace in his new home ward and won the election on November 5.[12] He was sworn in on December 1, 1881 and held the office until December 7, 1885.[13] The new position returned him to familiar legal territory—besides the job's regular duties, he now became the justice who took overload cases for the police magistrate, who at this point was Alfred Comings, Bird's longtime opponent, the former justice of the peace who had done the same thing when Bird was police magistrate in the 1870s.[14]

The Founding of the *Cairo Gazette*

As early as 1880, John Bird had determined to organize an African American newspaper in Cairo, but this did not happen until 1882. In the meantime, Martin Gladden and Alexander Leonard, two relatively recent arrivals to

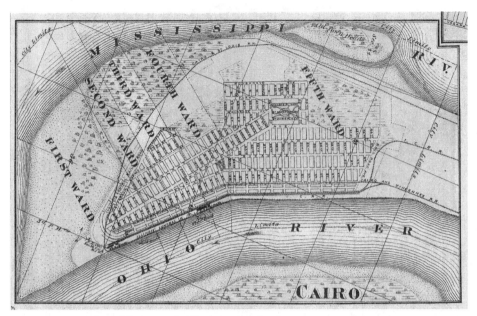

Map of Cairo, 1876. This map divides the city into its electoral
wards. Bird lived on Twelfth Street in the Third Ward through the 1870s,
then moved to Twenty-Second Street in the Fifth Ward in 1881. From
Atlas of the State of Illinois. Chicago: Union Atlas Co., 1876, 148.

Cairo, established the city's first Black newspaper, the *Three States*, in October 1881. Gladden had come to Cairo from Mobile, Alabama, in mid-1879,
during the Exoduster movement, as the representative of a group that was
seeking to relocate skilled African American artisans from Mobile to Illinois. Gladden focused his efforts primarily in the southern and central parts
of the state. In an interview in November 1879, he reported that he had
placed about thirty men and families into jobs and homes during his first few
months.[15] Gladden and the project became controversial by mid-1880 when
the *Bulletin* began publishing articles and letters charging that his real purpose in bringing the southern Black workers to Illinois was to increase the
number of Republican voters there. One article accused him of flooding Alexander County with Black men "of the most undesirable class, since they are
of low habits and many of them are brutal and dishonest." The writer insisted
that the immigrants were incapable of holding jobs and were a drain on society, and he described Gladden as "the worst enemy Cairo and Alexander
county ha[s] at the present time . . . and the sooner Cairo gets rid of him the

better for the county."[16] In early September, a pipe bomb was thrown into the house in which Gladden rented an upstairs room. In the aftermath, the *Bulletin* worked hard to argue that the bomb had probably been meant for the occupants on the first floor and not Gladden, apparently trying to deflect legitimate charges that its articles had incited the violence.[17] Gladden temporarily moved to Springfield in January 1881 but appears to have returned to Cairo during the summer.[18]

Alexander Leonard also apparently arrived in Cairo in 1879 and was hired by the *Daily Cairo Bulletin* to work as a compositor in the newsroom. From the beginning, he was active in Republican politics, in the Cairo Masonic lodge, and in the local AME church, interacting in all these contexts with John Bird.[19] Leonard was well regarded at the *Bulletin*, but on July 31, 1880, he had an argument with the foreman of the newsroom and resigned from the paper.[20] Interested in continuing his career in journalism, he learned that John Bird and William Scott were planning to establish an African American newspaper in Cairo. In January 1881, a brief opportunity arose for the three to buy the assets of the *Cairo News*, the last gasp of the *Evening Sun*, but they were unable to complete the purchase.[21] In the fall, however, Leonard joined Martin Gladden to buy the *News*' press and establish the *Three States*, a weekly whose premiere issue appeared on October 9, 1881.[22]

Gladden and Leonard soon began to disagree about the direction the *Three States* should take, and in February 1882 they dissolved their partnership, with Gladden keeping the paper and Leonard taking a position on a new local Baptist newspaper called the *Banner and Gleaner*.[23] But in March, another printing press came up for purchase in St. Louis, and Bird brought Leonard back as a partner to try a second time. After discussions with the owners of the press, it became clear that the two of them did not have enough money to complete the deal. Thus they turned again to William Scott, whom Bird had always held somewhat at arm's length but who was the wealthiest African American in Cairo, for financial assistance. Leonard, who was most knowledgeable about the technical aspects of the business, traveled to St. Louis in early April to complete the purchase and bring the equipment to Cairo.[24] On April 23, 1882, the first issue of the *Cairo Gazette* appeared. It began as a semiweekly newspaper and described itself as being "independent in politics," although it likely supported the Republican perspective during its first year of publication (it would become genuinely independent after Scott became its full owner in 1883). On April 27, the *Bulletin* published a brief notice about the paper's inauguration: "The second number of the 'Cairo Gazette,['] published by Messrs. Bird, Leonard and Scott, three of Cairo's representative colored men, has reached THE BULLETIN office. It is a six column folio, a very neat appearing paper and edited with ability by Judge J. J. Bird."[25] Scott apparently handled the business duties, while Leonard was in charge of the printing. The paper, under Bird's editorship, appears to have been an immediate success in Cairo and beyond. That success came in part at the expense of the *Three States*, which was severely weakened by the new competition. This led to a bitter rivalry between the two papers, which finally concluded with the demise of the *Three States* in February 1883.[26]

Intraparty Conflicts and Departures, 1882

African American Republicans in Cairo had split over Bird's endorsement of Oberly in 1880 and again the next year when George Tanner ran against Bird in the city clerk election. Another significant schism developed in the summer of 1882, when Representative John R. Thomas, the two-term congressman from the Eighteenth Congressional District (the Eighteenth had now become the Twentieth District), who was running for renomination, was challenged by a number of candidates. Leading among them was Charles N. Damron, a county judge for Johnson County, about forty miles north of Cairo. Damron's brother James was the state's attorney in Cairo, and the latter aggressively sought support for Charles among the city's Black citizens. He succeeded in bringing William Scott, Bird's *Gazette* colleague, and Martin Gladden of the *Three States* into the Damron camp. Bird and Alex Leonard sided with Thomas, who since 1880 had made some efforts to repair his relations with his African American constituents.[27] This contest immediately became a battle between the independent and establishment elements of the Black electorate in the district, leading to a tumultuous series of antagonistic encounters during the process of electing delegates to the nominating convention.

On June 17, 1882, local precinct meetings were held to choose delegates to the Alexander County convention. In Cairo, Damron supporters seized control of several of these gatherings, although Thomasites were in the majority, and named backers of Damron as delegates to the convention. The outraged Thomas supporters responded by electing their own slate.[28] At the county convention on June 22, both delegations arrived at the courthouse in Cairo, and after neither side could gain the upper hand, the two groups again split and elected rival slates for both the Republican state convention and the congressional nominating convention.[29] Through a series of astute and possibly underhanded maneuverings, the Damron camp was able to gain recognition as the legitimate Alexander County delegation at the state convention on June 28, which then made it easier for their delegation to be admitted to the Twentieth Congressional District convention as well.[30] At the latter on July 13, during the debate over which delegation should be seated, Milo Erwin of Williamson County spoke for the Damron side, and Bird presented the case for the Thomas delegation. When Bird finished, William Scott rose and viciously attacked Bird, asserting that Thomas had done Bird a personal favor and had thus bought Bird's support. Bird denied Scott's charges in a heated reply.[31] This public conflict contributed substantially to the deterioration of the relationship between Bird and Scott. Ironically, after this huge battle among the Alexander County Republicans, a battle that caused great damage to numerous relationships within the party, the Alexander County vote turned out to be irrelevant to the final outcome of the convention; Thomas easily won renomination.[32]

The success of the upstart Damron faction in Alexander County, however, had proved to be a great embarrassment to Thomas's Cairo delegation, which had included not just Bird and Leonard but such civic leaders as Mayor N.B. Thistlewood and business leaders like the Hallidays and Charles Galligher.[33] However, they could at least be gratified that Thomas won reelection in November and that in March 1883, State's Attorney James Damron, whose clever schemes during the campaign had so successfully thwarted the Thomasites, was indicted on bribery charges and ignominiously fled the state rather than face a trial.[34]

The relationship between Bird and Scott did not heal in the months following the congressional convention, and shortly after the fall election, the two definitively split. Bird left the editorship of the *Cairo Gazette* and presumably sold his share in the company to Scott in mid-November. Leonard appears to have become both editor and printer, while Scott continued as business manager.[35] Leonard's political leanings were more like Bird's than Scott's; he stayed only four months after Bird's departure, leaving the *Gazette* in March 1883. At that point, Scott took over the editorship of the paper and soon thereafter abandoned the Republican Party.[36]

Bird left another important position in the fall of 1882, when he resigned from the Board of Trustees at the Illinois Industrial University just three years into his second six-year term. It is uncertain what led him to make this decision, but there are indications that he found it increasingly difficult being the only African American on the board. From the time of his reappointment in March 1879 until he resigned, it appears that he attended only one meeting in Urbana, that of March 9, 1880, although he may have carried out his other duties until his departure.[37] The only surviving published explanation for his departure comes from a powerful defense of Bird that appeared in 1883 in John Oberly's newspaper, the *Bloomington Bulletin*, when the editor responded to an article printed in the Republican *Champaign Gazette* that harshly criticized Bird's tenure on the board. The *Gazette* had written, "Bird knew nothing about the duties of the position, seldom attended the board meetings, and was no credit to either himself, the University, or his race." Oberly heatedly responded:

> This does a great injustice to Judge Bird, the colored man who stood between the late colored convention and the Republican Party. He is one of the most intelligent men in the state. He knows all about his duties as trustee of the Industrial University, attended its meetings, and was a credit to himself, the Republican party, and his race. He was treated with great disrespect by the white members of the board because he was black, and was actually driven out of the board by Republican ostracism. He nevertheless remains faithful to the Republican party, for which he has done much service and from which he has received no kindness or reward.[38]

This represents the last example of Oberly's long-standing public support for John Bird, and it once again indicates the continued respect Oberly had for him. His explanation of Bird's resignation seems plausible and certainly fits into the context of Bird's complicated relationship with the party during this period. Those hard feelings against him over the Oberly affair may have subverted his dealings with some of the board members.

Bird's tenure on the Board of Trustees, while groundbreaking and well remembered in the Illinois African American community for decades, did not have an enduring impact on the White administration of the university.[39] Although it is probable that he attracted some African American students to IIU during his tenure there, after his resignation, the number of Black students arriving at the university remained small, and the institution would not see another African American board member until 1958.[40] But his appointment had raised expectations within the African American community that other appointments to significant state positions should be forthcoming, and it had already been the source of the Black leadership's demands for such positions. His experience at the university also had a powerful impact on him that led him to emphasize the importance of state institutions of higher education as an aspiration for young African Americans, an idea that he inserted into addresses and resolutions he put forward at Black conventions in the 1880s and 1890s.

Bird also undertook what proved to be his final campaign for public office during this period. In May 1883, he decided to run for alderman of Cairo's Fifth Ward in a special election against Charles Lancaster, a leading White Republican of Cairo.[41] It is unclear why Bird chose to do this, since this is the only time he ran explicitly against a party-endorsed candidate. It seems unlikely that he expected to win the election; his candidacy may suggest that Lancaster was not popular among the Black citizens of the Fifth Ward and that Bird ran to offer them a protest vote. He lost to Lancaster, 185 votes to 53.[42]

The 1883 State Black Convention

The battle between the Cairo independents and stalwarts over the nomination of Congressman Thomas in 1882 was a prelude to the much larger-scale conflict that took place at a State Convention of Colored Men held in Springfield on October 15–16, 1883. The call for the convention was signed mostly by leaders from the independent camp, although Bird was a signatory, and its plan was to convene a group of about four hundred delegates from every Illinois county.[43] Many Black stalwarts opposed the meeting, expecting the independents would dominate the proceedings and use their power to attack the party. When October 15 arrived, only fifty delegates from eight counties were present, with Cook County's eighteen and Alexander's twelve constituting 60 percent of the total. But the group was about evenly split between the two factions, and the party loyalists who attended were determined to blunt what they saw as the anti-Republican stance of the independents. William Scott, now prominent in the statewide independent movement, and John Bird, the loyalist, were two of Cairo's delegates.

After a stalemate between the two factions within the Committee on Organization over who should be the chair (Lloyd Wheeler or John Bird), the delegates decided to take nominations from the floor. John W. E. Thomas,

John W. E. Thomas of
Chicago was the first Black
member of the State Legislature
as well as Bird's colleague and
ally during the 1880s. Abraham
Lincoln Presidential Museum and
Library No. 29561.

the first African American member of the state legislature, the most prominent man at the convention, and a loyalist, was elected chair, with Bird as first
vice president and William Scott as second vice president. In his opening comments, Thomas argued that politics was not to be the focus of the conference and that its primary mission was to secure "greater freedom and the
better education of the colored race." But the independents had a clear political
agenda and were able to secure control over some key committees—Scott sat
on the Resolutions Committee and the Committee on State Organization,
where he could influence both what was discussed at the convention and also
its aftermath, by naming more independents than loyalists to the new central committee. Bird was not without influence, however. He chaired the Address Committee.[44]

The second day of the convention clearly illuminated the divisions between
the two factions. The delegates were united in unanimously approving the
resolutions and reports submitted by the Committees on Education, Labor,
and Civil Rights. As the 1880 convention had done, the Committee on State
Organization established a central committee intended to set up permanent
local organizations to promote the "educational, mechanical, labor, business
and political interests of the race." Bird moved to strike the word "political"

from the list, but the report was approved as it stood. The new executive committee was dominated by the independents, but the delegates added Bird to its membership to give it some balance. The final resolutions, approved without undue contention, leaned toward the independents' preferences but also reflected the anger of all the delegates over the Republican-dominated Supreme Court's ruling invalidating the Civil Rights Act of 1875 that had just been announced on the first day of the convention. They criticized the Republican Party for its poor record of nominating Black men for state and federal elective or patronage positions, encouraged Black citizens to vote only for candidates who supported African American causes, and approved of a speech by Frederick Douglass, in which he had expressed a measure of independence from the Republican Party.

But a huge controversy exploded when the resolutions committee presented a set of resolutions put forward by Scott and his supporters that essentially declared independence from the party. These resolutions had been formulated at a secret meeting of the independent delegates in Cairo before the convention, without the knowledge of the loyalists in town. They criticized the local situation in southern Illinois and climaxed with the following: "Resolved, That we denounce the bosses and managers of the republican party, in this congressional district, in the state, as well as those who manage and 'boss' the national republican party." These resolutions were outrageous to the stalwarts, including Bird, who must have been furious that they were described as having been adopted "in convention in the 20th congressional district," when that was hardly the case. The loyalists presented a motion to table the resolutions, and after a tumultuous debate and disputed vote, Thomas declared them tabled. Thus, the loyalists prevented the most blatant anti-Republican resolutions from being issued by the convention, at least a partial victory for them.[45]

The final item adopted by the conference was the address that came out of Bird's committee, no doubt largely written by Bird himself, because it focused on two subjects closely identified with him. The first was industrial education, a term that generally was used in the 1880s and 1890s to refer to trade schools for young men. The address, however, expanded its meaning to include higher education, specifically the Land Grant institutions. This was a first in addresses issued by African American conventions in Illinois. It praises the institutions as "colleges wherein the co-education of the races, and the co-education of the sexes are encouraged, promoted, and practiced. We

would, therefore, request and urge that the colored people of this state avail
themselves of the benefits of these liberal institutions." Here the influence of
Bird's years at Illinois Industrial University, the state's only Land Grant
school, made itself manifest, showing Bird's understanding of the critical importance of higher education in the long-term advancement of African
Americans in the United States. The language of this section also hints that
the Industrial University had Black students already. The second recommendation in the address, also dear to Bird's heart, was "to urge upon our people
the formation of co-operative organizations embracing every branch of legitimate business."[46]

The convention concluded that evening with speeches by independent Rev.
C. S. Smith and loyalist Bird. Little information is preserved about Bird's address, except that he focused more heavily on the issue of African American
education than on the failings of the Republican Party and the problem of
electoral office or patronage positions, the main subjects of Smith's speech.[47]
The convention concluded with the two factions very much divided. Neither
side had won a decisive victory, and the divisions within the African American community (and between Bird and Scott) would continue to widen and
weaken their political clout.[48]

The Decline of Cairo's African American School

In early 1883, Bird's family life underwent an important change when he and
his wife Annie sent their two sons, John W. and Egbert, aged seventeen
and fifteen, respectively, to live in St. Louis. The boys moved in with their
close family friends George and Elizabeth (McNany) Tanner.[49] Elizabeth had
lived with Annie's family at least from the time they were young teenagers in
the late 1840s, and Annie had always considered Elizabeth to be her older
sister.[50] Sometime about 1854, Elizabeth married George H. Tanner, and the
couple had a son, Egbert, about 1857 (presumably the Birds' Egbert was
named after him) and a daughter, Arena (clearly named for Annie's mother),
about 1859.[51] In 1861, when George apparently joined the war effort, Elizabeth
and the children moved to Windsor to stay with the Venerables once again
until George returned.[52] The Tanners moved to St. Louis in 1874, and George
opened a restaurant there.[53] In 1883, the Tanners had the opportunity to re-
ciprocate the Venerables' hospitality by taking in Annie's sons. St. Louis had
considerably more opportunities than Cairo, in terms of both education and

work. The boys had certainly exhausted the Cairo "colored" school's curriculum, which by 1883 only went to seventh grade.[54] The Tanners' daughter, Arena (nicknamed "Menie"), was a public school teacher and likely helped enroll Egbert into a high school program. Both boys took on jobs to help pay their way, John W. at a boot factory, Egbert as a porter.[55] But by early 1884, John W. seems to have moved out. He does not appear in the city directories between 1884 and 1887, although Egbert continued to live with the Tanners. John W.'s entry in the 1940 U.S. Census shows that he had received a college education sometime during his life, and it is possible that he got that education during this period.[56] Egbert may have continued his schooling, but by 1884 he had a steady job as an elevator operator. John W. reappears in the 1887 directory, once again living with the Tanners, now holding a job as a waiter, while Egbert was once again a porter.[57] Sometime in 1888 or early 1889, the two boys decided to strike out on their own and moved to Detroit.[58]

A decline in the fortunes of Cairo's Black school likely contributed to the Birds' sending their sons to St. Louis. This decline was part of a serious deterioration of the city's entire educational system in the early 1880s. By the end of the 1870s, many citizens were beginning to realize that their hope that Cairo would become one of the great economic hubs of the Midwest was not going to materialize.[59] The city's population had failed to grow at the pace of other river towns like Louisville or Cincinnati. Cairo had also grievously overinvested in railroads that had fallen into bankruptcy, leaving the city burdened with heavy debts, and it found itself unable to attract manufacturing at a level comparable to that of its competitors. All of this resulted in a slow exodus of Cairo's ablest economic leadership.[60] These circumstances conspired to bring about the demise of the public schools' brief period of excellence in the 1870s. In the 1878–79 school year, following the yellow fever epidemic, the board precipitously cut the annual education budget by one-third from about $15,000 per year during the heyday to about $10,000.[61] With a continuing rise in the number of students entering the schools, teachers found themselves in charge of many more students in their classes than they had had previously. In the lower grades, between eighty and one hundred students were crammed into a single classroom, under a single teacher.[62] During the 1879–80 school year, the board had hired twenty teachers for Cairo's four buildings, but for 1881–82, it cut the number of teachers to eighteen, dropping one of the five teachers at the African American school and one from the high school.[63] The next year, the board hired only seventeen teachers for the eleven hundred enrolled students (an average of sixty-five students per teacher) and began dividing the younger grades into half-day classes to deal with the overcrowding.[64] By 1883, the school system as a whole was under severe stress.

For the African American school, the crisis point hit early in the year. In February, the Ohio River suffered unprecedented flooding that affected many of the cities along the Ohio River. Cairo, with its high levees, was spared the worst of it, but several areas inside the levees were plagued with water seeping up out of the earth, including the grounds of the African American school.[65] For several days, the path to the school was impassable and the building itself, already in need of repair, was further damaged by the water and could not be opened. None of the White schools suffered from problems of this scope. Rev. Nelson Ricks, longtime minister of the Second Free Will Baptist Church of Cairo, found this situation intolerable and on March 8 gathered a group of students and parents to march to the White Thirteenth Street primary school and the high school to demand that repairs and improvements be made to the African American school, or that their children be admitted to the White schools. They also demanded more and better teachers and accessibility to high school grades.[66] Many of the parents began a boycott of the Black school, with a few students sometimes attempting to sit in at the White schools' classrooms.[67] If nothing were done, warned Reverend Ricks, the Black community would file a lawsuit against the school board.[68]

This, of course, caused a huge sensation across Cairo and the region.[69] On March 17, the school board responded punitively against the African American school, firing Mr. Baily, the fourth-grade teacher, ostensibly because "the attendance in his room is not large enough to justify the board in keeping him employed." This was certainly retaliation against Ricks and his group. It was followed by a threat to close down the whole school—certainly a hollow scare tactic, since that would have required the board to send the Black children to the White schools, the greatest fear of most White inhabitants in Cairo. Several of the parents whose students had been in Mr. Baily's class pooled their money and hired him to continue teaching their children privately.[70] As the city dragged its feet on the parents' demands, Reverend Ricks began to raise funds for the lawsuit. In the face of this potential legal action, the school board finally gave in and moved to make major repairs on the schoolhouse and the grounds. In July and August 1883, the school's foundation was raised two feet higher than before, and soil was brought to fill in the yard around the school and set the grading away from the building to allevi-ate the water problems.[71]

Oddly, in all the many articles written on these events in the *Bulletin*, Nelson Ricks is the only community leader ever mentioned as being involved—no references to or quotations from Bird, Scott, Gladney, or any other established leader are to be found. It is not clear why they seem to have been silent. It certainly was not because they disagreed with the basic issues. It is possible that the paper simplified its story by focusing only on the leader of the movement in order to turn Ricks into a boogeyman, as it had years before with Thomas Shores. It is also possible that, as was the case in 1867 when Shores used a similar confrontational style, the other leaders did not approve of Ricks's style of agitation. It is further possible that people like Bird worked behind the scenes to bring about an agreement, but it is likely that Ricks's activism was the primary element that eventually brought about the school repairs and improvements.

Bird and the Cairo Post Office, 1883–1884

In 1884, Bird finally achieved a long-sought victory in Cairo against the prejudices of the White members of his own party when, after years of intense pressure from the Black community, the city's Republican postmaster and the rest of the White party leadership at last decided to hire the first permanent African American employee in the Cairo Post Office—John Bird. Postmaster George McKeaig had been the focus of much strife in the party throughout the 1870s because of his refusal to hire a Black person in the Post Office, and Bird had been the leader of the agitation against McKeaig. Although Bird had been appointed as a mail agent for the Cairo and St. Louis Railroad in 1879, this job was not centered at the post office. It took a change in institutional leadership and additional pressure from the African American community to finally bring about the breakthrough.

Following the November 1882 election, attention once again turned to whether George McKeaig, who now had served three terms as Cairo's postmaster and whom Bird had so strongly opposed at the time of his previous reappointment in 1879, would keep the position for another term. McKeaig had done nothing during the previous four years to improve his standing in the African American community and apparently had lost support among White Republicans as well. Congressman Thomas thus supported

W. M. Murphy, the deputy collector of revenue in town, for the position, and he received the appointment instead, certainly a gratifying development for Bird and many others.[72] But initially it did not appear that Murphy was much of an improvement over McKeaig. Shortly after Murphy took over the position in March 1883, Alex Leonard, departing editor of the *Cairo Gazette*, applied for a job opening at the post office as a delivery clerk, a position for which he was clearly qualified, but was turned down by Murphy. Leonard not surprisingly expressed displeasure over his rejection in the *Gazette*, pointing out that it was part of the long-standing failure of the party to place Black workers in post office positions in Cairo. This provoked a vicious attack on Leonard from a Republican newspaper in Carbondale, *Barton's Free Press*, that laid bare the acute racism within the party in southern Illinois: "We believe we express the opinion of nine-tenths of the party when we say we are sick and tired of this 'Negro business.' Scarcely has there been an issue of the Cairo (colored) papers in which there has not been a clamor for office. And what is the claim set up? Simply that a man's skin is black and his hair kinky! We say the party is tired of this clamor and ought to rid itself of it."[73]

A few weeks later, a temporary, one-month position opened in the Illinois Central Railroad's mail service.[74] It seems that the local party leaders, probably stung by the controversy over Murphy's refusal to hire Leonard and feeling that the temporary nature of the position somewhat protected them from another *Barton*-style attack, decided to place an African American in the job. They did not choose the now-controversial Leonard but went with John Bird, who was not only the most (over)qualified African American in the county for the job but also had had previous experience as a mail agent on the Cairo and St. Louis Railroad from 1879 into the early 1880s. Bird's performance in the short-term position appears to have been successful and to have caused no substantial controversy, so that in January 1884, when a new permanent part-time position was created at the Cairo post office, Murphy and the rest of the Republican leadership—finally deciding that "the time had come"—appointed Bird to it.[75] Bird thus became the first permanent African American employee working in the Cairo post office.

The job was part of an expansion of services at the post office. The Postmaster General provided Cairo with ten outside mailboxes to be distributed around town, from which the mail was collected each day. Bird was responsible for gathering the mail and helping sort it at the post office. Although this was a new position and not one that had been "taken away" from a White man, the racist press did not refrain from attacking Bird's suitability for the job or the means by which they imagined he had obtained it. The *Mt. Carmel Register*, from a town about 150 miles north of Cairo, provided its readers with this extraordinary misrepresentation of Bird and the job: "Postmaster Murphy, of Cairo, is endeavoring to placate the irate coons of his city, and to do this Judge J. J. Bird has been appointed a letter-carrier in a portion of the city where there are no mail boxes, nor any letters to collect. The appointment is simply to provide a salary for a disgruntled coon, whose qualifications better fit him for a white-washer than a postoffice clerk."[76] By January 25, Bird had worked out his route across town to each mailbox so that an official pickup schedule could be posted. He gathered mail three times a day from each box, between 8 and 9 A M, 2 and 3 P M, and 8 and 9 P M.[77]

During these years, he continued to work as justice of the peace, but occasionally he also began to move to the other side of the bench to work with local trial lawyers. In June 1883, he joined the defense team on a case before Judge Otis Osborn's court. An African American couple, John Collins and Clarisa Bowers, had been arrested shortly after they married, authorities charging that Bowers was already married and thus was guilty of bigamy and that Collins therefore was guilty of adultery. Lawyer Justus Cunningham was appointed to the defense, but he asked the court for special permission to bring Bird and City Attorney William Hendricks onto his team. The trial of Clarisa Bowers was held on June 11, and the defense was able to show that there was no evidence that her previous husband was alive. The jury acquitted her, and her marriage to Collins was upheld by the court.[78]

Bird's Last Years in Cairo

During his final three years of residence in Cairo, Bird remained active in local party leadership, but it is clear that by early 1885, he was thinking of a future in Springfield, the capital. However, in spite of his extraordinary contribution to Republican success in southern Illinois, the state party leadership, probably because of his activism (especially in 1879–80), seemed to have little interest in rewarding him for his service with a state position in Springfield. This refusal kept him in Cairo through 1885 and 1886, but other factors would allow him and Annie to leave Cairo early in 1887 anyway.

It seems clear that by the mid-1880s, the local White Republican leadership was still happy to have Bird in a leadership role within the party. In 1884, he was named to both the state and congressional conventions once again, as well as an alternate to serve on the Alexander County Party Central Committee.[79] The Alexander County delegates to the state convention were instructed to support Bird as a delegate to the Republican National Convention, but Illinois once again appointed no African Americans to its delegation.[80] During the campaign, it appears that Bird, Gladney, and others were able to cripple the independent movement led by William Scott and successfully preserve the African American community's allegiance to the stalwart side of the Republican Party. Scott found himself with too little support in Alexander County even to field an independent slate of delegates for any of the conventions held in the spring and summer.[81] The 1884 election, however, proved disastrous for the Republicans nationally. Grover Cleveland won the presidency, becoming the first Democratic president since the 1850s, and the Democrats also took control of the U.S. House of Representatives. But in Illinois, Richard Oglesby, the Republican candidate for governor, won that race, although the state legislature became equally divided between the parties, causing many difficulties for his administration.[82]

John Bird's last two years in Cairo are less well documented than previous ones. No issues of the *Bulletin* survive from 1885 to 1904, and the only other preserved newspaper of the period, the *Cairo Citizen*, a new Republican weekly, did not begin publication until October 1, 1885. The *Citizen* was edited by George Fisher, a prominent civic leader and lawyer in Cairo. While nominally supportive of African American rights in his paper, Fisher seems to have been largely oblivious to Cairo's African American community, very rarely providing coverage of it. Bird does not appear in the paper until July 1886, just a few months before he left Cairo.[83] Generally, the paper only provided coverage of major events in the community, such as the untimely death of Martin Gladden in a boating accident in January 1886.[84] For the most part, in reading the *Citizen*, one could imagine Cairo as a virtually all-White town.

Following the election of 1884, several colleagues encouraged Bird to seek a patronage position from newly elected Governor Oglesby, and in February 1885 he applied. Several leading Republicans, including Lieutenant Governor John C. Smith, Congressman John Thomas, and respected Chicago attorney and former Cairoite Daniel W. Munn, expressed their willingness to speak to the governor or write to him on Bird's behalf.[85] Before composing his own letter, Bird asked his eldest stepbrother, Alfred M. Green, now a prominent minister and leader of the Republican Party in New Orleans, to write a reference letter. Bird enclosed Alfred's with his own letter of application though not indicating his relationship to Alfred ("I enclose you letter forwarded to me by a distinguished colored citizen of Louisiana"). His supporters were pressing for him to be named a commissioner at the State Penitentiary at Chester, but in his own letter, Bird wrote, "I deem it would be injudicious on my part, to aspire to a position so eagerly sought after by many prominent men in the state; and not desiring to embarrass your administration, I would simply request that you appoint me to some honorable position the compensation of which will justify and enable me to contribute in the future as in the past to the success of the 'Grand Old Republican Party.'"[86]

In spite of his qualifications and the support from his colleagues, Bird did not get a state appointment in 1885—but he was not alone. Oglesby exhibited little interest in naming any African Americans to state positions and made only one appointment the entire year, that of Dr. James H. Magee of Metropolis in the Office of the Chief Inspector of Grain in Chicago.[87] Thus Bird stayed in Cairo, working at the post office and concluding his term as justice of the peace.

While his record on patronage positions was poor, Oglesby did sign the extraordinary Civil Rights Bill of 1885, perhaps the high-water mark of African American civil liberties legislation in nineteenth-century Illinois. The bill was introduced in February by John W. E. Thomas as a reaction to the Supreme Court's 1883 overturning of the national Civil Rights Act of 1875. Although it did not seek to integrate schools or churches, it required that all public accommodations, from inns and restaurants to public conveyances and amusements, be open to people of all races. The bill passed the legislature in April and was signed by Oglesby in June. For many African Americans in Illinois, this law vindicated their long-suffering faith in the Republican Party, and it led to a relatively brief period of optimism that the long push toward equality was once again moving in a positive direction. However, the law was gradually undermined by court decisions that severely limited its scope, and soon it was largely unenforced.[88]

During the summer of 1885, Bird became involved in the opposition to another State Convention of Colored Men that had been called by the independent majority of the Executive Committee formed by the 1883 convention. As in 1883, many loyal Republicans saw this convention as another attempt to pull African Americans away from the Republican Party. The call

Letter from John Bird to Governor Richard J. Oglesby, February 11, 1885.
Having been proposed for a position at the Chester State Penitentiary
by several colleagues, Bird writes the governor to decline consideration
for that job but still asks for a state job. The underlining and parentheses
were supplied by Oglesby's secretary to indicate the most salient
sections of the letter. Illinois State Archives, Oglesby (3d term)
Correspondence, record series 101/020.

came under the names of Lloyd G. Wheeler, the chair, and R. M. Mitchell, secretary of the Executive Committee, without input from the loyalists, and Bird opposed it from the beginning. When Bird received a letter from Mitchell announcing the convention, he wrote Governor Oglesby to warn him about the gathering, noting that Wheeler had supported Democrat Carter Harrison for governor during the 1884 election.[89] Oglesby subsequently met with Mitchell, discussed the situation, and received assurances from Mitchell that he was a loyal Republican and that the convention would not attack the party. The governor then wrote back to Bird assuring him that he had everything under control.[90]

In Cairo, Bird, Gladney, and the party loyalists refused to send delegates to the convention, but William Scott called a meeting of the small independent group in the city and chose four delegates from among themselves.[91] Three days before the convention was to open, the Cairo loyalists called a meeting, chaired by Gladney, to denounce it, Scott, and his associates. Bird was apparently not present, but Martin Gladden gave a powerful speech against Scott.[92]

In other parts of the state, including Chicago, loyalists once again decided to attend the convention in order to oppose the plans of the independents, and unlike at the 1883 convention, they managed to gain full control and thwart the independents almost entirely.[93] As in 1883, John W. E. Thomas was elected the chair as a compromise between the two factions, and again, Thomas was able to steer the convention toward the loyalist side. He announced in his opening speech that he would rule any politically motivated resolutions out of order, and he kept his word.[94] Unlike in 1883, Thomas made sure that the key convention committees were controlled by party stalwarts, and when the new state executive committee was named, it was dominated by loyalists.[95]

During the summer of 1886, Bird once more was appointed as a delegate to the Twentieth District Republican Congressional Convention, which again renominated John R. Thomas for the office, and to the convention nominating a candidate for the Illinois senate.[96] This was Bird's final campaign in southern Illinois because circumstances in the fall would lead him to move from Cairo to the city that would be his final home—Springfield, Illinois.

CHAPTER SEVEN

"More Entitled to Recognition than Any Other One of His Race"

John Bird's Life in Springfield, 1887–1912

I N EARLY 1887, John Bird and his wife, Annie, left Cairo to settle in Springfield, Illinois, the state capital. It seems likely that the decision to move there was encouraged in large part by an opportunity for Bird to work as the coeditor of the *State Capital*, a new African American newspaper in the city. This type of position appealed to him and was one that he believed could have a significant impact on the African American community across the state and region. Springfield probably also attracted Bird as the center of state politics, a place where he might be able to pursue his political interests and perhaps have a greater influence within the state Republican Party than he had had in the smaller town of Cairo.

The move, however, proved to be a mixed bag for him. Bird's association with the *State Capital* was a major success. He and his coeditor, Sheadrick B. Turner, quickly developed the paper into what contemporary sources identified as the leading and most influential African American journal in Illinois, eclipsing even those in Chicago during the late 1880s and into the 1890s. Bird spent several years sometimes coediting or editing the *State Capital*, and when he left it in 1895, he founded and edited his own paper, the *Springfield Republican*, for a bit over a year.

On the other hand, Bird's relationship with the Republican Party in Springfield was less successful than he clearly hoped. He arrived in the city as an established and well-known African American leader and was accepted immediately into the local Black community. But his overall influence on local politics within the city was significantly diminished from what it had been in Cairo, where he had been the leader of a community that constituted over 30 percent of that city's population, had been the dominant figure for the Black Republican wing since its birth in the 1860s, and had played a major role in navigating the relations between Black and White Republicans in Alexander County. During his years in Cairo, Bird had focused much of his energy on bringing about tangible, significant improvements to the lives of the local African American community, and Cairo had regularly elected Black candidates to city offices since his groundbreaking election as police magistrate in 1873. Springfield, however, was quite different. It was a city politically dominated by the Democrats, and the African American community was not large enough to shift the balance of power in most elections (1,798 people in 1890, or 7.2 percent of the city's total population of 24,963, and 2,227, or 6.5 percent of 34,159 in 1900). Thus, it did not have the clout to pressure the local Republican Party to pay significant attention to the needs of its Black members, and Bird found himself unable to wield the kind of influence over his White counterparts there that he had exercised before.[1] However, while Democrats controlled local politics, Illinois as a whole voted Republican, and thus the latter party controlled the state political apparatus in Springfield, independently of the city. Because of this, local African Americans looked more to the state for support, and several party faithful received low-level patronage positions, mostly jobs as janitors or policemen at the State House during General Assembly sessions.

Bird expected more than such a position from the White leadership after his significant and continuing contributions to the party. From his arrival in Springfield until the mid-1890s, the Republicans regularly called upon him to campaign throughout Illinois, consistently addressing large gatherings, often alongside state party leaders. He also worked tirelessly in the ward politics of Springfield. But a state position commensurate with his talents and his investment in the party was never forthcoming. He applied time and again for a solid patronage job, with the support of several prominent Republicans, but ran headlong into the party's general disinterest in rewarding Black members for their loyalty. Only twice in his twenty-five years in Springfield did he receive appointments to posts that made use of some of his abilities, and both positions were temporary in nature. His financial situation forced him several times to accept a janitor's position in the State House to make ends meet. This circumstance provides one more vivid example of the widespread, tragic, and systematic waste of Black talent by the White Republican leadership.

Bird's residence in Springfield also coincided with the climax of the steady decline in the Republican Party's support for civil rights, which was characterized in the 1890s by its tolerance of the Jim Crow laws passed throughout the South and sometimes mimicked in the North during this period and the Supreme Court's notorious ruling in support of "separate but equal" segregation in 1896. These developments represented the loss of most of the political advances that Bird and his colleagues had worked so hard to achieve during the postwar era. It also led to the adoption among some Black leaders of a sharply depoliticized, anti-intellectual version of the old middle-class uplift ideology, most prominently advocated by Booker T. Washington. Arguing that African Americans should abandon their agitation for voting, civil, and social rights and reject the ideas of holding political office or seeking higher education for now, Washington and his mentor Samuel Armstrong of the Hampton Normal Institute in Virginia insisted that Black people should accept segregation and focus their energies instead on creating a nation of virtuous and thrifty citizens who, with the help of a basic industrial education, could learn to work successfully in agricultural or similar practical jobs, buy property, and gain acceptance in the White community through their rising economic power.[2] This ideology constituted a frontal attack on Bird's entire political and educational philosophy, and he rejected it. However, the country's White political leadership cheerfully accepted it, and thus by the mid-1890s, civil rights had become virtually a complete nonissue for the national Republican Party, which even decided to remove Black speakers from the campaign trail to make African Americans as invisible as possible to their White supporters. This effectively brought Bird's career as a significant Republican asset to an end.[3] In spite of all this, Bird continued to argue that African Americans' best hope of regaining their rights lay in supporting the Republican Party, and he and his colleagues refused to give up on their agitation for equal rights even in these darkest days. He never seems to have lost his long-standing faith in the ultimate power of the African American political leadership to turn the party around once again to its radical roots.

Faced with the increasingly grim political situation, Bird worked with others to encourage and strengthen a more unified, statewide African American political structure, both through his newspaper work and by his continued influence within Illinois's African American organizations. The latter work climaxed in 1895 after the violent attack on the Black community of Spring Valley, Illinois, when, for the first time in his career, he became involved in the creation of a truly nonpartisan African American organization that would agitate for Black causes without reference to political party. While he remained a stalwart Republican, he came to see the value of a larger unity in the Afro-American Protective League of Illinois that was intended to establish a more encompassing and self-reliant perspective for promoting African American welfare. As a member of the resolutions and address committees at the annual conventions and as an appointee to the league's executive committee, he played an important role in the direction of the league during its relatively brief period of unity.

While Bird was well regarded by most members of the African American elite of Springfield, in certain ways he did not fully belong to that group. Never financially secure once he and Annie moved there, he never accumulated the wealth to purchase a house. Rather, during most of his years in Springfield (Annie left him in 1889) he lived in the First Ward, in or on the border of the Badlands district, the poorest African American neighborhood in the city.[4] But his financial problems did not keep him from remaining beloved in the Black community. Even during the last decade of his life, when he was on the periphery of political activity, he was still asked to speak and participate in local events, and after his death in 1912, the community remembered him as one of the giants of his generation. Even the Illinois General Assembly acknowledged his importance by erecting the monument in Oak Ridge Cemetery that still marks his grave today.

Settling into Springfield, 1887–1888

The events that precipitated Bird's departure from Cairo occurred during the autumn of 1886. At the beginning of September, the Democratic administration of Grover Cleveland replaced W. M. Murphy, the Republican postmaster of Cairo, with a Democrat, Captain Tom Wilson. President Cleveland had laid out guidelines concerning the firing of Republican employees in federal jobs, discouraging wholesale removal, but allowing it when a Republican employee had been an "offensive partisan," who had actively campaigned against the Democratic Party in the 1884 election. Bird, of course, was vulnerable on that count, and thus when Wilson arrived, Bird lost his mail carrier job.[5] Now without steady employment, Bird looked again toward Springfield as a place of potential opportunity. In early January 1887, the *Cairo Citizen* noted that he and three other African Americans from

Cairo—Warren Wims, Richard Taylor, and Sidney Robinson—had gone to Springfield to seek a state position.[6] Bird's hope for a significant appointment, however, went unfulfilled, and what the party offered him was a position as janitor at the State House. About the same time, Sheadrick B. Turner, the Republican owner and editor of the newly founded African American newspaper in Springfield, the *State Capital*, invited Bird to work with him on the paper. Bird accepted both offers, and he and Annie moved to Springfield in early 1887.

The position as janitor at the State House proved problematic and embarrassing for Bird. His job was to clean the senate chamber at the regular salary of $2.00 per day for an expected 162-day term. The problem with the position was that at this time such janitorial posts had become a bloated and corrupt means for rewarding lower-level party faithful. The Republicans appointed dozens of janitors ostensibly to clean the State House, but without any concern as to whether there was real work for all the janitors to do. Bird was one of three janitors appointed just to clean the senate chamber. When the high payroll costs for senate employees came under public scrutiny shortly after the legislative term began, popular indignation forced the legislators in February to form a committee to investigate the large number of patronage jobs (janitors, policemen, and pages). During the committee's hearings, W. B. Lynn, the senate sergeant-at-arms, testified about the small amount of work done by some of the appointees, unsurprisingly picking three Black appointees, Bird; John M. Nuckols, another janitor; and a policeman, George Beard, as his examples. Lynn does not appear to have been an unbiased witness on this matter, but whatever the actual situation, the appearance of his name in such a negative public context must have been a significant embarrassment to Bird. The committee decided to cut the number of janitors, and Bird lost his job. However, the secretary of state's office also had a budget for hiring patronage employees, and Bird was simply transferred to another janitorial position in that department for the rest of the session.[7] This experience, however, soured him on taking another support job at the State House for the next eight years.

The relationship between Bird and S. B. Turner, on the other hand, proved to be a long and positive one. Sheadrick Bond Turner was born in Louisiana but had moved to Chicago as a young adult, where he ran a wood and coal business during the 1870s. In the early 1880s, he was hired by Henry Dement, the Illinois secretary of state, as a worker in his department, and in 1885, he

Sheadrick B. Turner was the founder
of the *State Capital* newspaper. Bird
coedited the paper with Turner and
sometimes solely edited from early
1887 to 1890. Bird returned to the
paper as editor in 1894–95 under a
new publisher. From Louis L.
Emmerson, *Blue Book of the State
of Illinois 1925–26*. Springfield: Illinois
State Journal, 1925, 125.

moved from Chicago to Springfield, where he took a patronage position on
the State House police force.[8] Toward the end of the next year, while still
working there, he inaugurated the *State Capital*, a weekly, on the side. Turner
brought Bird onto the staff shortly thereafter, first as "associate editor" and
by 1888, "editor."[9] The publication, a lively mixture of local, state, and national
news of interest to the African American community with a focus on political
issues, including a positive, but not uncritical, stance toward the Republican
Party and an editorial viewpoint that reflected many of Bird's ideas, quickly
became a substantial success.[10] I. Garland Penn, in his groundbreaking 1891
book on the African American press, described the *State Capital* as "the leading organ of the race, west of the Ohio river. It is the recognized organ of the
Afro-Americans of Illinois, and wields a potent influence in politics."[11] Turner
was very ambitious politically, and his activities often took him away from
the work of the paper. Sometime in 1888, he temporarily turned the newspaper's publication over to Robert O. Lee, a local lawyer, during which time Bird
served as sole editor. However, Turner apparently returned as coeditor with
Bird sometime in 1889, before Bird left the paper in 1890 for a state job.[12] The
aggressive Turner appears to have been reluctant to share credit for the success of the *State Capital* with Bird as he pursued his own political ambitions.

Bird makes no appearance in the discussion of the paper in Penn's book nor in later sketches of Turner's life.[13]

As soon as he arrived in Springfield, Bird enthusiastically jumped into Republican politics. The party leadership invited him to speak at local and state-level campaign events and meetings—he gave the keynote addresses at both Springfield's 1887 Emancipation Day ceremony at the State Capitol and Centralia's large celebration in 1888 and shared the podium at a large Springfield rally in June 1888 with Governor Oglesby and Secretary of State Yates.[14] He worked tirelessly for the 1888 ticket, speaking across the state, including at a rally back in Cairo for gubernatorial candidate Joseph Fifer.[15] He also involved himself with local, nonpolitical African American organizations in the city, talking, for instance, at a fundraising event for an African American boys' band and attending a "Young Ladies' Leap Year Party."[16]

Frustration in Politics, Disaster at Home, and a State Convention, 1889

In spite of Bird's intense work for the 1888 Republican campaign, the party's lack of interest in rewarding its Black leaders again became painfully clear the following year as Bird struggled to get an appointment to a stable state position. When Joseph Fifer won the election for governor in November 1888, African American leaders were generally optimistic that Fifer would distribute a few significant patronage positions within his administration to Black Republicans, and they had strong expectations that Bird would receive one of them. The press expected it, too. In January 1889, the *Register* noted that Bird "is hot on the trail of a Chester penitentiary commissionership, and is said to have the backing of Senator Cullom and a partial promise from Fifer that he shall have the place."[17] Indeed, Cullom, the former governor of Illinois, wrote a letter to Fifer in support of Bird on January 9, which stated, "I beg to suggest the name of John J. Bird as being worthy and deserving of such recognition. He is probably better qualified and more entitled to recognition by the Republican administration of our State than any other one of his race and I shall be very much gratified if matters can be so arranged as to give him some good position."[18] Another letter arrived from Robert Allyn, the president of Southern Illinois Normal University, saying in part, "My friend J. J. Bird, Esqr, formerly of Cairo now of Springfield is a gentleman of sense and knowledge, 'capable and honest,' I believe, and would in my opinion fill any one of a dozen positions, the holders of which will soon retire."[19]

Bird himself wrote to Fifer on January 6, 1889, making a strong appeal for a job. Feeling close enough to the governor after the campaign to address him as "Friend Fifer," he provided a résumé of his achievements and was not afraid to drop some powerful names as well:

> I trust you may see your way clear in my case. Requests come to me for information as to what Illinois will do for the Negro, from such men as the Hon. Fredrick [*sic*] Douglass, J. R. Lynch, Gov. Pinchback, Col. Robert Harlan and other intimate friends with whom I have been associated in public life for years. My reply has been invariably, "Illinois will do her duty."
>
> As to myself, I can say that I had the honor to serve the state for nine years by appointments from governors Beveridge and Cullom, as trustee of the Industrial College at Champaign—was each time confirmed by the senate, without opposition—and had the confidence and respect of the members of the board, faculty & students. My eleven years of service as Police Magistrate and Justice of the Peace in Cairo, is well known throughout the state.
>
> I have, since our enfranchisement delivered more speeches and made more sacrifices in the interest of our party, than any ten colored men in the state; and made the fight during the late campaign, under the most humilliating [*sic*] circumstances, and without compensation.[20]

But Fifer failed to appoint Bird (or any other African American), and he apparently did not respond to Bird's letter. On March 18, 1889, Bird wrote again, clearly in distress, feeling betrayed after such a public indication that the governor was going to act:

> Friend Fifer:—
> Chagrin, humiliation and suffering after a life-long sacrifice of time, feeble talent and money suggest to me the propriety of desiring to know whether I am to receive recognition at your hands. I have the consciousness to know from my varied experience that such recognition on your part under existing political conditions would strengthen our party, quiet the unsettled and restless condition among my own people, and

add new lustre to your well-deserved name and fame. As it now is, I am being subjected to political ridicule, and our party censured and condemned by our enemies, white and colored.

Definitive action by you will place me in a position to refute political slander, the better to provide for my personal welfare, and reply to the many and constant inquiries made.[21]

But again, Fifer made no appointment or response. Bird, however, did not give up. He asked other friends to write the governor on his behalf. During the rest of the year a steady stream of letters praising Bird arrived at the governor's office, climaxed in October, when John R. Lynch, former U.S. representative from Mississippi, one of the nation's best-known African American leaders, wrote a letter in support of Bird.[22] But even that letter did not move Fifer on Bird's behalf. By August, when Bird wrote Fifer a third letter, he no longer used the greeting "Friend Fifer," but "Dear Governor."[23] Bird ended the year with no job offer.

The year 1889 was a bad one for Bird in other respects as well. Most significantly, after twenty-five years of marriage, Annie left him and moved from Springfield to Detroit, where their two sons were now located. Perhaps John's constant absences over the years in service of the party, his jobs, and other organizations had irreparably damaged his family relationships. Whatever the cause, this was a permanent separation—in the 1890 *Detroit City Directory*, she listed herself as Annie V. Bird, widow of J. J. Bird. As this was manifestly untrue, it indicates that John was "dead" to her. She was listed as a widow from this point on in the city directories and in the 1900 census. John, on the other hand, still identified himself as married in the same census.[24] Besides this disaster, and perhaps related to it, Bird was under serious financial stress at this point, as indicated in his letters to Fifer quoted above. We gain a limited sense of his predicament from a cryptic reference in a September 27 letter to Fifer from J. V. Cheneworth, an AME minister and longtime friend of both Bird and Fifer. Cheneworth, writing without Bird's knowledge, strongly urged the governor to give Bird a position, remarking, unfortunately without context (Fifer presumably understood): "He has lost all of his possessions and has made some mistakes to which I hope you will excuse. Take hold of Bird by giving him some office that will pull him up the hill."[25] The cause of the loss of his belongings is unknown. Had they been seized for debt? Did his home suffer from a fire or other natural loss? Had Annie taken most of their common possessions with her? It is worth noting that when Annie died in 1903, she left an estate valued at $2,100, about $64,000 in 2020 dollars.[26] What were the "mistakes" Cheneworth refers to here? Might the collapse of his marriage have been one of them?

Whatever the case, after Annie's departure, Bird simply poured himself into his work. He was deeply involved in the 1889 State Convention of Colored Men, which met in Springfield in October. The convention was organized principally by three prominent Chicagoans, John G. Jones, Edward H. Morris, and Hannibal C. Carter, all Republican leaders.[27] Unlike at the previous state convention in 1885, few independents attended, so that support of the Republican Party was not an issue. Forty-five delegates participated, nineteen from Chicago, fourteen from Springfield, and the other twelve from smaller towns across the state (Bird's name appears with John Gladney's as a delegate from Cairo—probably to give a greater appearance of support from across the state). The convention appointed Morris as president, Sheadrick Turner as first vice president, and Bird as second vice president. The most important achievement of the convention was the establishment of the Colored Men's State League of Illinois, another attempt to form a permanent organization that could work year-round toward the improvement of conditions for African Americans in the state and agitate for federal intervention in the South. Earlier attempts to create such organizations had been unsuccessful. This one would last only until 1891, when it apparently merged into the state chapter of the national Afro-American League. Bird was at the center of the establishment of the State League. Morris was named its first president, while John G. Jones became first vice president and Bird the second vice president. Edward H. Wright, a Chicago attorney temporarily living in Springfield and a rising star among the African American Republicans, was named secretary.[28] Gladney and Turner were both placed on the executive committee. An Address Committee, consisting of Bird, Wright, and three others, was formed to produce the document that would articulate the primary issues of both the convention and the new league. In the address, the authors reiterated the foundational importance of education and the development of financial power within the African American community as long-term keys to equality. They set education as the league's first priority: the abolition of separate schooling, the employment of African American teachers in integrated schools, and encouragement of the Black community to take advantage of industrial education. The address again called for the

Edward H. Wright, colleague of Bird's at the *State Capital*, important player in the Illinois Black convention movement, and eventually a powerful Chicago politician. The New York Public Library Digital Collections. https://digitalcollections.nypl.org/items/510d47de-517c-a3d9-e040-e00a18064a99.

advancement of cooperative business enterprises in the African American community and extensively deplored the conditions of African Americans in the South, demanding that the federal government intervene. It concluded by urging the southern African Americans to move for their own protection to the new states that were opening up in the American Northwest.[29]

Bird, the Afro-American League, and the Bureau of Labor Statistics

Just three months after the foundation of the Colored Men's State League of Illinois, a number of African American leaders met in Chicago to found the Afro-American League, an organization determined to fight the increasing attacks on Black civil liberties on a national level. Largely the idea of T. Thomas Fortune of New York City, the most prominent African American newspaper editor of the day, its goal was to establish a network of state and local chapters that would work together toward ameliorating the violence in the South, bringing about equity in the school systems, and opposing the denial of accommodation in public facilities common across the country. The league also supported the establishment of African American businesses, cooperatives, banks, and trade schools for African American youth.[30] These goals were virtually identical to those of the Colored Men's State League of Illinois, but the new league was mostly organized by political independents. They called for all African Americans to disassociate from any political party and support only those individuals who "commit themselves to the best interests of Afro-American citizens."[31] In fact, the league's constitution forbade any officer of the league from holding either an elected or appointed political position. This immediately barred most of Illinois's African American leaders, particularly in Chicago and in Springfield, from playing a significant role in the league. Many members of the Colored Men's League refused to support the Afro-American League, although Edward Morris, its president, and S. B. Turner both endorsed it.[32] Republican loyalists and office holders in Chicago held a meeting days before the convention to denounce the proposed league.[33] Bird almost certainly opposed it as well, and there is no evidence that he attended the convention.

The Afro-American League was the first serious attempt to form a national civil rights organization, but it was ultimately unsuccessful and collapsed in 1893. There were several reasons for its failure. The estrangement between the league and the substantial, more party-oriented element of the community (including such national figures as Frederick Douglass, John Mercer Langston, and P. B. S. Pinchback) significantly damaged its ability to gain broad support among political leaders, and although the league softened its stance the next year to allow those involved in a political party to participate in its leadership, it was too late. Several major Republican leaders had already founded a rival organization, the American Citizen's Equal Rights Association, which also struggled to gain support. In addition, the concept of the league failed to capture the imagination of ordinary African Americans and create a viable base, a problem shared by the previous attempts to establish permanent structures. While it achieved a few legal victories during its short life, the lack of widespread support led to its quick demise.[34]

At about the same time that the Afro-American League was founded in early 1890, Fifer finally relented and gave Bird a substantial appointment, albeit temporary, as special agent of the Illinois Bureau of Labor Statistics.[35] Bird's duties were to gather information for one or more of the bureau's special investigations. In 1890, the bureau undertook two projects that required traveling special agents. The first was a comprehensive look into the earnings and work hours of coal miners in the state. Special agents traveled to the offices of mining companies to inspect the actual payroll records. The second project was an examination of judgments against debtors, liens on real estate and foreclosure, and land value records. This required agents to examine the court records at every county seat for those types of judgments.[36] Bird was

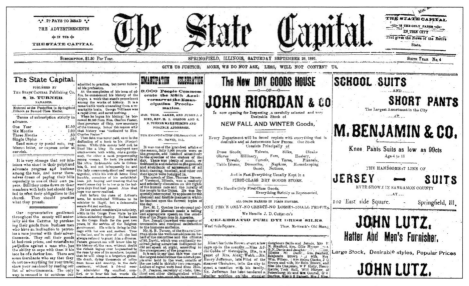

State Capital, September 26, 1891, p. 1. Although not editor for
the paper at this time, Bird was closely involved in its early ascent
to influence. He is mentioned in the subheadline of the article
"Emancipation Celebration" as one of the lead speakers. *Chronicling
America: Historic American Newspapers.* Library of Congress. https://
chroniclingamerica.loc.gov/lccn/sn84025827/1891-09-26/ed-1/seq-1/.

certainly assigned to one or both of the projects, and the *Cairo Citizen*'s article on his appointment indicated that his activity was concentrated in the
southern part of the state.[37] He left his position as coeditor of the *State Capital* and was replaced there by Edward H. Wright.[38] The *State Capital*, in a
nod to its former editor, optimistically called this appointment "an advanced
step and not only shows that the Governor is endeavoring to obliterate the
'color line,' but demonstrates that the head of departments under his administration are in accord with his policy."[39] This hardly reflects the facts of
Fifer's actions.

By June, Bird again was seeking a more permanent position at the Chester
Penitentiary. This time Congressman George W. Smith, who had succeeded
John Thomas in the Twentieth Congressional District, wrote a letter in sup-
port of Bird, saying in part, "Mr. Bird wields a large influence in Southern
Illinois and can be of great benefit to us in the entire state. He rendered valu-
able service in the last as well as preceeding [*sic*] campaigns and is always ready

and willing to work for the success of our party candidates."[40] But this, too, fell on deaf ears.

Bird's traveling position seems to have significantly reduced his participation in Republican politics in 1890. His only public event on which the Springfield newspapers reported was the regional Emancipation Day celebration at St. David, Illinois, in September at which he and S. B. Turner spoke.[41] His job with the bureau may have lasted into the summer of 1891 (the newspapers remain virtually silent about him until then),[42] but by August he was living in Springfield again, announcing in the *State Capital* that he was beginning a new occupation: "On or after September 1st, J. J. Bird will engage in the pension business." An ad in September stated, "He is prepared to prosecute claims for pensions and bounty."[43] His new office was located in the *State Capital* suite at 224½ South Fifth Street, which indicates that while Bird was not actively involved with the newspaper during this period, he still maintained a strong relationship with Turner.[44] This business proved to be modestly successful and long-running for Bird, and he continued to operate it at least until 1904.[45]

The Shifting Politics of the 1892 Campaign

The 1892 election campaign appears to have been the last one in which the Illinois Republican Party made heavy, statewide use of Bird and other African American campaigners. In May, he served as a delegate to the Republican state convention once again, this time representing Springfield.[46] On the 31st, he was a primary speaker (along with S. B. Turner) at a meeting held at Springfield's AME church, as part of an African American national day of prayer and fasting designed to call attention to the continuation of violent White supremacist activity in the South. His talk, "The Conditions, Cause and Remedy against Southern Outrages;" concluded with a sharp call for federal intervention in the South and for the education of the White population about the illegitimacy of prejudice against African Americans.[47] Between August and November, he was in Chicago, at least partially on campaign business (and perhaps to test the waters for a move there).[48] On September 22, he and Edward H. Morris gave keynote speeches at the Emancipation Day celebration in Galesburg, and in early October, he made a speaking tour across southern Illinois with the Republican congressional candidate Richard Yates and Charles Pavey, the candidate for state auditor, speaking at rallies in

Carbondale, Harrisburg, Du Quoin, and Galatia within the space of five days.[49] After this election, Bird's involvement in campaigning came to be restricted essentially to the local Springfield area.[50]

However, during the 1892 national campaign, African American frustration with the Republicans again reached a boiling point and produced a dramatic split in the Black political leadership that drew Bird into a dramatic role again defending a loyalty to the party. President Benjamin Harrison, who had actively campaigned in 1888 for the African American vote, had been a disappointment in office. Before the 1892 national Republican convention in June, a number of Black party members crafted a resolution calling on the Platform Committee to include a plank that would require the Republican candidate to enforce civil rights laws in all states. They also decided to form another national league, the National Colored Men's Protective Association, with George E. Taylor of Iowa as president, and planned an organizational meeting on September 22, 1892 in Indianapolis.[51]

When the Republican convention's Resolutions Committee coolly rejected the Association's resolution, however, Taylor angrily renounced his membership in the party but retained the presidency of what had been created as a Republican organization. He soon declared that the association's meeting in September would be "non-partisan," which indicated to most Black Republicans that it would be anti-Republican. Many members immediately resigned, and the Indianapolis meeting was sparsely attended almost entirely by Democrats and Independents. It produced an address attacking Harrison and the Republican Party and supporting free trade, that is, the Democratic party platform.[52] African American Republicans were outraged by the results of the convention and the fact that a Republican organization had been hijacked by Democrats.

In response, they decided to appropriate a Democratic organization, the National Colored Men's Tariff Reform League, founded during the summer at the Democratic National Convention to raise support among African Americans for free trade. At its convention on October 17–18, the vast majority of the one hundred delegates who attended, including John Bird, were faithful Republicans from across the country who proceeded to take charge from the Democratic organizers. Bird was elected third vice president of the convention and appointed to the Address Committee, along with C. J. Perry, editor of the *Philadelphia Weekly Tribune*; Perry Carson, a prominent African American leader from Washington D.C.; Edward H.

Morris of Chicago; and seven others. Bird and Carson also gave the primary speeches during the evening gathering on the 17th.[53] The address produced by the committee naturally supported protective tariffs and the Republican Party and attacked the Democrats. After the convention's adjournment, most of the delegates reassembled to form the framework for yet another national organization to compete with Taylor's. Bird was appointed to the new society's five-person Executive Committee.[54] Neither organization thrived, however, and although they seem to have reconciled shortly afterward and merged, the joint society apparently held only a single convention in Chicago in June 1893 before expiring.[55]

Bird's Return to Journalism, 1894–1897

Little information survives about Bird's activities in 1893, with the Springfield newspapers mentioning him only twice, in both cases concerning minor local political matters;[56] but 1894 saw his return to the *State Capital*, again as its editor. The newspaper had fallen into difficult financial times in 1893, and Turner sold it to a White man named Roberts from Evanston, Illinois. Roberts in turn sold it to two African Americans who already worked at the *Capital*—Otis B. Duncan, the newspaper's traveling agent, and Fred M. Waterfield, a compositor. Unfortunately, they had trouble meeting their payments to Roberts, and on January 31, 1894, they were forced to auction it off to pay their debt.[57] W. L. Yancey, who claimed to be a lawyer but apparently was a fraud, won the auction and took over the newspaper as owner and editor, but his tenure only lasted about two months, when he was forced to sell.[58] The new purchaser was R. L. Anthony, an African American recently arrived from Kentucky. He also bought another local African American newspaper called the *Daily Item*, merged them into a single paper called the *State Capital Item*, and issued it as a daily. He hired John Bird as managing editor for the new paper and Otis Duncan as its business manager.[59] Because of the daily schedule, this was certainly a full-time job for Bird, and one that brought him back to an occupation he enjoyed. The *State Capital Item*'s first issue was printed on April 10, 1894, but this version of the newspaper only lasted until December, when Anthony sold it to Captain Jordan S. Murray, a Springfield barber and saloon owner, who changed the name back to the original *State Capital*. He became its proprietor, while Bird continued on as editor and Duncan as business manager.[60] Bird was

Otis B. Duncan, Bird's colleague at the *State Capital*, later became the
highest-ranking Black officer in the U.S. Army during World War I. From Kelly
Miller, *History of the World War for Human Rights*. Washington, D.C.: Austin
Jenkins, 1919, after p. 272. NYPL catalog ID (B-number): b11722032.

still at the paper in May 1895, when the *Daily Review* of Decatur, Illinois,
described him as, "now the editor of *The State Capital*, the most prominent
colored newspaper in the state."[61] Murray returned its publication schedule
to a weekly format, assumed the editorial duties probably during the fall of
1895, and continued to edit the paper until it ceased publication about 1904.[62]

Bird clearly enjoyed newspaper work, so when he left the *State Capital* in
the fall of 1895, he decided to inaugurate his own, which he called the *Springfield Republican*, of which he was proprietor and editor. The first issue
appeared on November 30, and the paper was well received from the beginning. The Omaha *Enterprise* said, "It is newsy and well gotten up by its able
and well known editor, Judge J. J. Bird," and the *Illinois State Journal* described
it as "a very creditable production."[63] The paper's editorials were occasionally
quoted in other newspapers, including the *Journal*, the *Cleveland Gazette*, and

the *Enterprise*.[64] While it appears to have been well regarded, it apparently could not compete with the *State Capital*, which he had helped to establish as the city's leading Black newspaper. Bird seems to have shut the *Republican* down in late 1896 or early 1897.[65] No copies of the paper have survived.

Bird's Estranged Family in Detroit, 1891–1894

With Annie's departure from Springfield in 1889, Bird's family life effectively came to an end. It seems clear from the surviving evidence that John's two sons, John W. and Egbert, sided exclusively with their mother and that there was little or no interaction with their father after Annie left. The three of them lived in a house at 293 Catherine Street in Detroit, and in a stroke of independence, the sons began to spell their last name Byrd (Annie kept the original spelling until 1893).[66] Annie immediately involved herself in the local African American community to such an extent that the *Plaindealer*, a Detroit African American newspaper, several times reported on her activities, including her hosting of meetings of the Willing Workers, a women's charitable group, at her home, and on some extended trips she took to St. Louis to visit her "sister" Elizabeth Tanner.[67] The three were joined, also in 1889, by Annie's elderly mother, Arena, and her second husband, Patrick H. Inge.[68]

About the time that Annie arrived in Detroit, Egbert, her younger son, developed symptoms of tuberculosis. During 1890, his condition progressively deteriorated, and on January 26, 1891, he died at the age of twenty-two. According to the *Plaindealer*, "Mr. Albert Byrd (a mistake for Egbert), who has been suffering for some time with consumption died Monday at the residence of his mother on Catherine street and was buried from Bethel church Tuesday afternoon." The paper also noted that "Mrs. Tanner, of St. Louis, sister of Mrs. Byrd attended the funeral of her nephew Albert Byrd."[69] His father, however, did not attend. On the day of Egbert's burial, John wrote a heartbreaking letter to Governor Fifer: "Dear Governor, I am just in receipt of a telegram announcing the death of my youngest son, at Detroit, Mich. He will be buried Thursday. I am here, and unable to go without assistance. I especially request of you $50.00. I hope to be able to return it soon or in some other manner reward you."[70] No record exists indicating whether Fifer helped, but it seems unlikely, since a note on Bird's letter indicates that it was only answered on January 29, the day Bird thought the funeral would take place. The fact that he apparently was not informed that Egbert was failing, while Elizabeth Tanner presumably was present in Detroit before he died, once again suggests the degree of alienation between Annie and John.

The following year saw a joyous moment when on June 30, 1892 John W., now twenty-five years old, married twenty-two-year-old Laurette E. Wilson, a mixed-race woman born in Canada.[71] A description of the wedding in the *Plaindealer* indicates that John J. was not present for this occasion, either.[72] But tragedy again stalked the family, when Laurette died of kidney disease on January 7, 1894, after just a year and a half of marriage.[73] They had had no children. Her death must have been devastating to John W., because over thirty years passed before he married his second wife, Marion M. Mills, in 1925.[74] They had no children, either, and thus John and Annie never had grandchildren, their direct family line ending with John W.'s death in 1951.[75]

The Spring Valley Pogrom and the Founding of the Afro-American Protective League

The first half of the 1890s saw a sharp rise in the lynching of African Americans in the South, where at least 444 Black people were murdered by mob action between 1892 and 1894.[76] In 1893, this type of assault moved north, when two lynchings occurred in Illinois itself.[77] In light of this increasing threat against Black communities across the United States, the early 1890s also saw the reemergence of the idea of emigration to Africa as a solution to the problem.[78] It was a strong enough issue in Illinois that Bird was invited in May 1895 to take part in a debate in Decatur on the legitimacy of mass emigration in the current climate. He and his colleague Joseph Drake, a Springfield attorney, spoke in opposition to emigration, while the pair in support of it included Miss Laura White, a well-prepared school teacher, and Wilson Woodford, a young attorney who had seen firsthand the horrors of lynching in Decatur itself when Samuel Bush was murdered by a mob in 1893. Woodford was to have been Bush's lawyer after the latter had been accused of assaulting two white women, but Woodford had not even met his client before the mob killed him. In response, Woodford bravely published an open letter in the Decatur newspapers demanding the prosecution of those involved in the lynching.[79] At the conclusion of the debate, the judges voted that the Decatur team had won, reflecting the somber mood of the African American community about the overall situation in the country.[80]

The rising danger of racially motivated mob violence in the North was reinforced in early August 1895 when a horrific event shook the Illinois African American community to its core—a ferocious attack by a White mob against the entire African American population of the mining town of Spring Valley, a hundred miles west of Chicago, that had forced them all from their homes. The Spring Valley Race Riot, as it came to be known, shocked and enraged African Americans throughout the state, and indeed the nation, in a way that few racially violent events in the North had done.

The causes of the riot, better defined as an attempted pogrom, were complex.[81] The mines at Spring Valley were worked by African Americans, new immigrants from southern and eastern Europe, and native-born White citizens. Many of the African Americans originally had been hired by the mine owners as strikebreakers in 1894, a circumstance that had created hostility against them. On the night of Saturday, August 3, 1895, an Italian worker was shot during a robbery, and before dying, he identified his assailants as African Americans. The following morning a mob, mostly made up of Italians, marched to the Black neighborhood in Spring Valley and, as described in a report composed by a Chicago investigative committee led by Ferdinand L. Barnett, "began firing upon men, women, and children. Women and children screamed and fled terror stricken, while the men, equally helpless, were savagely driven into the woods. None were killed. The purpose of the mob appeared to be to drive the colored people away, using such force as was necessary. . . . The entire colored settlement fled to Seatonville, six miles away, except two or three invalids, who were allowed to remain until the next day."[82] All of this happened without interference from the city authorities.

From Sunday through Tuesday the mob ruled the town, announcing that the expelled families could remove their property from their houses but could never return thereafter. The mob leaders demanded that the city no longer allow African Americans to live in Spring Valley. They also declared a strike against the mine unless the company promised never to hire Black miners again, but the mine manager, S. M. Dalzell, refused to submit to the mob, closing the mine himself until the demand was rescinded. County and state authorities were slow to respond to the situation. County sheriff Atherton Clark, located in Princeton, some sixteen miles west of the troubled town, gave Spring Valley's mayor Martin Delmargo three days to get things under control before he intervened on Wednesday. Along with two representatives of Governor Altgeld, Clark finally arrived in town and made it clear that mob rule was over and that the African American inhabitants would be allowed to return home and work in the mines. They required Delmargo to recruit fifty-five police officers, including ten who were Black, to keep the peace.[83] On Friday, August 9, the African American refugees returned to their homes, the miners went back to work, and the violence was over.[84]

Although no one died, the reaction in the African American communities around Illinois to the situation was intense. Before 1895, there had been several cases of substantial racial violence in labor disputes, when White union strikers had attacked Black strikebreakers brought in from the outside. But Spring Valley was different. Here there was no strike, and the attack had been against a settled population.[85] This event shook the very foundations of Illinois's African American citizens' sense of security. In the first days of the mob action, rumors had spread of many deaths among the Black inhabitants of the town, and several in Chicago urged gathering weapons and marching to Spring Valley to protect and avenge their brothers and sisters. On Tuesday, August 6, state representative John C. Buckner of Chicago traveled to Springfield to press Governor Altgeld into action, then went on to Seatonville to evaluate the situation.[86] The Chicago African American community appointed a committee of three to travel on August 9 to Spring Valley to investigate and make recommendations for a response from the Chicago community. They interviewed the victims, city officials, and mining administrators and provided a substantial report on the attack and its causes. They praised the actions of Sheriff Clark, mine manager Dalzell, and Representative Buckner, while condemning Delmargo and the town authorities. They also criticized the Chicago Black community's slow and small financial response to the crisis and concluded by issuing three recommendations: (1) that the Chicago community push for "a vigorous prosecution of the rioters" and help victims file civil suits against the city to recover damages for their losses, (2) that it raise more funds to supply food and other necessities for the victims, and (3) that the African American citizens of Illinois develop a statewide organization to prepare them "to meet such an emergency as was here presented, wisely, promptly, and efficiently."[87]

The Chicago community took the recommendations seriously. Representative Buckner returned to Spring Valley on August 15–16 to help Charles Martin, who had been shot during the attack, file a legal complaint, and then to accompany Sheriff Clark, who had obtained thirty-six arrest warrants against the rioters, to make the arrests at the Number 3 mine shaft (it certainly did not hurt that the main rioters were Italian immigrants, not native Whites). Clark and Buckner brought twenty-five African American women and men along to help point out the perpetrators as they exited the mine.[88] The Chicago community sent two prominent White attorneys and Buckner back to Princeton in early September to support the victims during grand jury proceedings, which resulted in thirteen indictments against the rioters, and an indictment against Mayor Delmargo for neglect of duty.[89] When the trial began, the Black witnesses were put up in Princeton hotels, the cost covered by contributions from the Chicago community.[90] Buckner and one of the White lawyers from Chicago assisted the state's attorney, W. A. Johnson, at the trial.[91] The state called fourteen witnesses, mostly African Americans, who identified specific defendants as having attacked them personally.[92] The defense in turn called seventy-six witnesses who attempted to give alibis for the defendants. The jury deliberated overnight and on November 16 found all the defendants guilty of the most serious charge. Although the judge later vacated the convictions of five defendants, eight served prison sentences at the Joliet State Penitentiary. This seemed a triumph for the African American community, a remarkable demonstration to them that sometimes a measure of justice was possible in Illinois and a visible confirmation that African American involvement in this case had played a substantial role in assuring that result.[93] Unfortunately, this victory proved to be a rare one.

The Black community also acted upon the committee's third recommendation, to found an organization that would prepare African Americans for the possibility of another attack. A call was issued on August 16, signed by twenty-two leaders including Bird, for a conference to be held in Springfield to organize the new league.[94] The conference met on September 24, 1895, with a stellar group of 125 delegates from fifty-three counties attending. The seriousness of the occasion was emphasized in the fact that the delegates genuinely set aside their many political differences and formed an actual nonpartisan league, focusing specifically on the serious problems of Illinois's African Americans without reference to political party. Bird, who had spent the past fifteen years protecting the interests of the Republican Party at state convention after convention, now was part of the organizing leadership of this new league. He gave one of its five keynote addresses, but he was not elected to a position within the new organization's structure. Unlike so many of the previous state conventions, this one produced little conflict over resolutions, which included a call to organize mutual protection for all African

Americans and to use all legitimate means to secure equal rights, including desegregated schools in Illinois. The delegates denounced the Spring Valley outrages and called for the perpetrators to be prosecuted. In what edged fairly close to a partisan resolution, the convention called upon the Republican Party to appoint a new U.S. senator who was "as near the people as possible." The convention itself was described by the reporter from the *Journal* as "a model compared with former conventions. The delegates were the pick of the colored race of the state of Illinois and its promoters may justly feel proud of its successful termination."[95]

The new organization was named the Afro-American Protective League of Illinois, and its primary purpose was to "resist and stop every means of mob and lynch rule against our people, to demand a fair and impartial trial by judge and jury in all cases." The league's inaugural address, produced by its executive committee in October, was a powerful, strictly nonpartisan demand for equal rights and protections in the state. It placed the Spring Valley riot into the larger picture of prejudice in Illinois and stated that "this organization will ardently seek to find a practical solution of the civil, industrial, and economic problems that confront us today, not only in our state but throughout the entire country. . . . We hold that civil rights are not social privileges, and the right to earn bread by manual or skilled labor, in any capacity or community, should never be denied any honest, loyal, and patriotic citizen of Illinois."[96] The league was momentous because for a time it brought together the warring factions within the community into a unified organization. Bird became a leading figure in the league for much of its existence.

The second state convention of the Protective League, held in Rockford on July 8 and 9, 1896, was well attended and a success. For a second year, the leaders preserved a largely nonpartisan atmosphere in the meeting and managed to keep people of widely divergent political beliefs working together. When Democrat William Scott of Cairo introduced a resolution against Henry Hertz, the leading Republican for nomination for state treasurer, it was tabled. But in spite of his controversial motion, Scott was elected vice president of the organization for the next year beside loyal Republican Jordan Chavis as president.[97] Bird gave the keynote address of the first day, while in the final session of the second day, Ida B. Wells-Barnett of Chicago, the famed leader of the anti-lynching movement, spoke on lynch law and the Constitution.[98]

The Afro-American Protective League of Illinois began to fracture in 1897. The third annual convention was held in Chicago in August, but it proved to be dramatically divisive over issues of the league's leadership, not for ideological or partisan reasons. Several Chicago leaders, including John G. Jones, Edward Morris, and Sheadrick Turner, unhappy with the way the league was being run, took control of the convention and placed themselves in office, now for a three-year, rather than one-year, term. Many delegates supported the Chicago contingent, including John Bird, who became a member of the Executive Committee; Richard Blue of Bloomington, the new first vice president; and William Scott, who was elected second vice president. But a significant number of delegates refused to accept the new leadership, and after the convention, formed themselves into a rival faction under the 1896 league president, Jordan Chavis. Both groups continued to hold steadfastly to the original nonpartisan nature of the league.[99]

The Chavis faction held its own convention in Springfield on November 19–20, 1897, with seventy-five delegates in attendance. It elected a new slate of officers that, surprisingly, included John Bird, who was appointed to this group's executive committee, even though he had already been elected to the Chicago group's executive committee in August.[100] But this was not a defection on Bird's part. There is clear evidence that Bird had not given up his affiliation with the Chicago faction when he became part of the Chavis group's leadership. In January 1898, almost two months after the Springfield meeting, the Chicago group appointed Bird to be one of its delegates to the national Congress of White and Colored Americans held in Omaha in August.[101] It thus appears that he was accepted by both factions and was able to act somewhat as a bridge between them. The Springfield convention, like the Chicago one, remained consistently nonpartisan. Bird served on the Resolutions Committee, which presented statements against the reestablishment of segregated schools in Alton and other Illinois cities, as well as against lynching, while supporting the establishment of manual training schools, and other issues.[102]

By the middle of 1898, it was clear that the splits had badly damaged the league, and in September, the two major groups issued a joint call for a conference in Springfield on September 27–28 to attempt to reunify the organization.[103] But the meeting was not successful. Again, the problem centered on a disputed election. Two presidential candidates were put forward, Richard Blue of the Chicago faction and James H. Porter of Springfield, business manager of the new African American newspaper, the *Illinois Record*, of the Chavis group. The facts of the controversy are lost. Blue's supporters maintained that he had won the election, but that John G.

Jones, the chair of the convention, had declared Porter the winner anyway. The version of the split printed in Porter's paper ignored any voting controversies and laid the blame on the Blue faction's desire to support Republican governor John R. Tanner officially within the league. In this situation, Bird finally took sides and supported Blue. In a meeting of the Blue faction following the rupture, the group elected Blue as its president, and Bird once again as a member of the Executive Committee. John Gladney, Bird's old colleague, became first vice president and Robert M. Mitchell of Chicago was appointed attorney. The majority of the delegates from the two earlier factions, however, joined Porter's coalition.[104]

The Blue faction existed at least through 1899. Bird attended a meeting of its Executive Committee in Springfield on November 23, 1898, and the group held an annual convention in September 1899, in which Bird was chair of the Resolutions Committee.[105] The only resolution cited in the newspapers was one appreciating Governor John Tanner's role in mustering the African American Eighth Illinois Volunteer Regiment for duty in the Spanish-American War and for his insistence, in the face of great opposition, that all of its officers be African Americans as well. This was the first such regiment in U.S. Army history.[106] The resolution suggests that the Blue faction was beginning to shed its nonpartisan status.

The last clear reference to the Blue faction comes from a newspaper report that John Bird had declined an invitation to address a meeting of the league in Bloomington scheduled for November 19, 1899, because he had recently accepted a position in the office of the Illinois adjutant general. Bird wrote to Blue expressing his regrets but also his support for the league under Blue's leadership, In his letter, Bird concluded,

> Allow me to say that I fear our people have not, as yet, been properly aroused to the objects, purposes and importance of the organization. If there is a "race problem" to be solved, it must of necessity be on the lines indicated in the principles as set forth in the constitution of the Afro-American League of Illinois. Our national league constitution, nor none of the state league constitutions which have come under my observation, seem to meet the requirements of the hour, as does ours. The subjects of "industrial education" and "co-operative business enterprises" are a true and substantial basis upon which to rear lasting monuments to Afro-American genius and worth. We have not been educated up to a

proper conception of their value, because our would-be race leaders have been too narrow in their views, and extremely selfish in their ambition.[107]

Bird's emphases on his expansive view of "industrial education" and the importance of cooperative businesses were, of course, long-standing favorite subjects. The comment about the "would-be race leaders" was almost certainly directed toward Booker T. Washington and his limited ideas on Black aspirations. Bird's reference to "our national league" in the letter also indicates that the Blue faction, while smaller than the Porter faction, had become affiliated with the newly formed National Afro-American Council, the resurrection of the old Afro-American League of 1890.[108]

The Porter organization appears to have survived until 1901. In that year, the membership, once again under John G. Jones, definitively removed itself from the old nonpartisan protective league and affiliated with a newly formed National Republican League.[109] This state league was still in existence in October 1903, when the *Decatur Herald* took the league's annual convention in Springfield to task for criticizing Booker T. Washington.[110]

The Journey into the Nadir, 1896–1912

The new policy of the Republicans in 1894 of removing African Americans from their campaign rosters led to a significant diminution of Bird's party activities during the second half of the 1890s.[111] In 1896, his campaigning was almost entirely restricted to Springfield. Nonetheless, he used his newspaper, the *Springfield Republican*, to make up for the loss of his presence on the trail. Before the national convention, he was a vocal supporter of senator and former governor Shelby Cullom's campaign for the Republican nomination for president.[112] However, William McKinley's team outmaneuvered Cullom in Illinois, gaining the support of influential Republicans across the state, so that by the time the state district conventions were held in March and April, most delegates appointed to the national convention were instructed to vote for McKinley, not Cullom.[113] When McKinley secured the nomination in June, Bird supported him enthusiastically. In fact, African Americans had reason to be somewhat optimistic about the presidential ticket because the national convention, for the first time, had placed a plank in the platform explicitly condemning lynching and mob law.[114] Bird and many others saw this as a major and long-overdue step forward, and the platform was a substantial point of discussion in Bird's speeches throughout the campaign.[115] But McKinley, too, would prove to be a bitter disappointment.

For the rest of the decade, the party, while not providing him with a job, appointed Bird to several prestigious short-term duties. In 1897, the Sangamon County Republican Central Committee named him as a delegate to two judicial conventions, one in Decatur to choose a candidate for state supreme court judge from the third district, and the other in Pana to select a candidate for circuit court judge.[116] In June 1898, he was again a delegate to the Republican Seventeenth District Congressional Convention, and when President McKinley visited Springfield on October 15, Bird was part of the official reception committee that greeted the president.[117]

The mid-1890s, however, were difficult financially for Bird. He continued to operate his pension business, which by now had expanded into real estate and insurance, but with the decline and collapse of his newspaper, the *Springfield Republican*, he again found himself in need of a janitor's appointment in the State House during its session.[118] A newspaper report also shows that Bird still occasionally made use of his legal expertise. On July 13, 1898, he argued a case before the Board of Pardons seeking to exonerate Irwin Neal, an African American convicted of murder in 1888 and serving a twenty-year sentence. At the hearing, Bird submitted substantial evidence that showed that Neal's conviction was a miscarriage of justice, but none of that moved the board, and the appeal was denied.[119] In January 1899, he was an unsuccessful candidate for the State House position of superintendent of ventilation.[120] Later in the year, he received his brief, temporary appointment in the office of the adjutant general, Jasper N. Reece, in Springfield, but the details of the five-day assignment do not survive.[121]

Conditions for Illinois's African Americans citizens steadily declined during the first decade of the twentieth century. In Chicago, Blacks found themselves increasingly pushed into run-down, segregated neighborhoods, and job opportunities, never particularly good in the city, became even more restricted.[122] In Cairo, the African American community still maintained substantial political power in the local government during the first years of the 1900s, holding multiple seats on the city council, as well as other elected positions in both the city and the county. But in 1909, an emboldened White leadership pushed through a new voter registration law that required documented proof of length of residency that many Black residents did not have.

Then in 1913, they changed the form of Cairo's city government from its ward-based, mayoral and city council system to a city commission form in which all commissioners were elected at large, allowing the White majority to dominate the elections. This effectively eliminated African Americans from office in the city until 1980.[123]

Springfield underwent fewer dramatic downturns than either Chicago or Cairo, in part because its African American community had never seen the types of advances that had occurred in those two cities. Most Black Springfield families had long been isolated in two older neighborhoods and had generally been excluded from political power from the beginning. Its Black workforce, already shut off from manufacturing and transportation jobs, was largely stuck in the traditional types of jobs most Illinois African Americans had been forced to take, except that a larger-than-average percentage worked in the local coal mines or held modest patronage positions within the state government.[124] The latter were more plentiful because of Secretary of State James A. Rose, a Republican who held that office from 1896 until his death in 1912. A popular politician, he made more state positions available to African Americans than any previous Illinois politician and enjoyed substantial support in the Black community.[125] During the early 1900s, a small but busy Black business district developed on East Washington Street that for the first time brought a larger number of African Americans to the downtown area of the city. Before the summer of 1908, there was little indication that an unusual amount of deep-seated animosity existed in Springfield against the city's Black population.

The 1900 election is the last campaign for which there is evidence that Bird played a notable role. He began the year supporting Governor John Tanner in an ill-fated attempt to challenge incumbent U.S. senator Shelby Cullom for his seat. Cullom easily defeated Tanner in the contest, and Bird refocused his efforts primarily on supporting the party's candidate for governor, Richard Yates, with whom he had campaigned across southern Illinois in 1892.[126] Although he was the president of the African American Yates club in Springfield, the party restricted him to campaigning only in the local Black community.[127]

After 1900, John Bird's life in Springfield is attested only spottily in the sources. He no longer appears to have played leadership roles either in the Republican Party or in the statewide African American associations, although he still remained moderately active on the local political scene. He gave speeches at the St. John AME Church's Lyceum group in March 1902;

for the First Ward Republican club in January 1905 and February 1907; at the Republican city committee in January 1907; at a First Ward club that supported Richard Yates for governor in July 1908; and at a Sixth Ward club in February 1909.[128] In 1902, he wrote a letter to *the Illinois State Journal* in support of Governor Yates and Congressman Hopkins.[129] In February 1906, he attended a meeting in the First Ward that endorsed Otis B. Duncan, Bird's old colleague from the *State Capital* and now a major in the Illinois National Guard, as a candidate for city alderman and gave the primary address of the evening.[130] In 1907, showing a bit of his old activist flame, he spoke at a mass meeting that supported John W. Black, a reform candidate for Springfield mayor, opposing the Republican establishment's choice for the position.[131] He was still involved enough in politics in 1908 to be elected president of the African American Yates club, and in 1909 he led a meeting that supported the establishment of the Springfield Industrial and Training School for African American students.[132]

Little information survives about Bird's professional life during this decade. His pension business survived until 1904, and he served as a janitor at the State House three times between 1903 and 1907, although never for a full session, as he had before.[133] Except for a note in the 1907 Springfield city directory that he was working as a porter that year, there are no other details about how he made his living.[134]

Sometime during the 1890s, John's mother, Catherine B. Green, moved to Springfield from her longtime home in Vicksburg to be close to her son. In spite of her age, she became a well-known and beloved figure in the community. When she died on December 19, 1902, at age eighty-two, Bird bought her a grave in the "colored" section of Oak Ridge Cemetery, the prestigious burial ground that also held the tomb of Abraham Lincoln.[135] Less than a year later, on October 29, 1903, his estranged wife, Annie, died in Detroit and was buried in Woodmere Cemetery in that city. It seems unlikely that he attended her funeral.[136]

During the summer of 1908, a devastating event occurred in Springfield that brought an end to the hope that Spring Valley's riot had been a single, isolated aberration in Illinois. Sparked by a White woman's false claim that she had been raped by a Black man, the Springfield Race Riot led to the deaths of two African Americans and four Whites; about one hundred injured, eighty-three of them Black; the destruction of most of the African American businesses in the central part of the city, as well as forty Black residences;

and the looting or destruction of about $120,000 worth of property. In the aftermath of this massive attack, Springfield's government failed its African American citizens a second time. In spite of a grand jury issuing 117 indictments and a vigorous prosecution by State's Attorney Frank L. Hatch, the juries refused to convict the White rioters. Only two minor convictions resulted from the entire legal process. This stood in stark contrast to the trials and convictions of the indicted rioters at Spring Valley thirteen years previously. What little confidence African Americans had that there were enough White supporters of African American rights in Illinois to make a difference was shaken by the riot and its aftermath. In fact, this event was a major turning point in African American history. It unfortunately represented an early flashpoint of the horrific period that would see even more brutal and shocking anti-Black riots from the 1910s through the mid-1940s. At the same time, it sparked the movement that in 1909 led to the founding of the first truly successful national African American organization, the National Association for the Advancement of Colored People (NAACP).[137]

No information survives about Bird during and after the riot or how it affected him. On the first night of the riot, a small mob attacked and ransacked the house of Otis B. Duncan and his parents, located two houses down from where Bird had been living in 1907. Bird does not appear in the 1908 Springfield city directory, so it is unclear whether he was residing there at the time of the riot.[138] In any case, he must have been as traumatized as were most African Americans at the virulence of the hatred manifested in the violence in the heart of his own city. For people of Bird's generation, who had worked so long and hard toward improving race relations, the riot must have seemed proof that their hopes had been illusory. Bird would not live to see how the NAACP, founded in the riot's wake, would eventually play a key role in the great civil rights movements of the twentieth century.

Information about Bird's last three years also remains fragmentary. In 1910, he was working for Harvey T. Bowman, the publisher of the African American newspaper the *Advance Citizen*, and living in Bowman's residence at 1802 E. Cook Street during the early part of the year, but by April he had moved into the small boarding house of Henry and Anna Sallie at 726½ E. Washington Street, above the Sallies' secondhand goods shop at 726.[139] Sallie was a respected businessman and was active in the Republican Party. He had run a restaurant and a bicycle shop at his residence until they were both destroyed during the 1908 riot. When he and his wife, Anna, rebuilt, they

724–730 East Washington Street, Springfield, Illinois, just after the race riot of 1908. The second complete building from the right was 726, owned by Henry and Anna Sallie. After the riot, the Sallies rebuilt the interior and made part of the building a boarding house. This became Bird's final residence in 1910. He died in his room on June 1, 1912. Courtesy of Sangamon Valley Collection, Lincoln Library, Springfield. image 90–387B003.

had opened the secondhand shop and boarding house. This would be his final move.[140]

On August 3, 1910, he attended the state convention of the Negro Civic and Personal Liberty League of Illinois in Springfield, and delivered a speech titled "Our Duty as a Race." The next day, he gave what appears to have been his last major public address before about fifteen hundred people at an Emancipation Day celebration at Springfield's Mildred Park, titled "What We Can Do to Win." In its article on the latter, the *Register* referred to him as "Judge J. J. Bird, the negro historian."[141]

In 1911 Bird was appointed the custodian of the cloakroom for the House of Representatives for the Forty-Seventh General Assembly, a relatively prestigious position, and held the appointment again during its 1912 special session. On May 18, 1911, the house passed a resolution recognizing that Bird had worked numerous overtime hours during the session and granting him extra salary of $136 for his additional labor.[142] The special session in

1912 was held between March 26 and June 5, with a recess between May 23 and June 3.[143] Bird worked until the recess. During the break, three notable deaths occurred in Springfield. On the evening of May 28, Secretary of State James Rose fell ill unexpectedly, and he died at 3:30 the following afternoon.[144] Bird's old colleague and friend Dr. James H. Magee had worked for Rose as a messenger in the State Printer's Office for twelve years, and they had become friends. When news of Rose's death reached Magee, the *Illinois State Journal* reported, he "sat down, and, catching his side as if in pain, said: 'I don't see how I am going to get over this. He was my good friend.'" Magee died later that night.[145] Magee's death certainly hit Bird hard. Magee was one of his last colleagues from the generation that had come of age in the 1860s and 1870s.[146] On the evening of June 1, Henry Sallie, the owner of Bird's rooming house, became concerned that he had not seen Bird that day, and about 9:00 PM he looked into Bird's room and found him there dead.[147]

The muddled reporting of Bird's death that appeared in the two major papers of the city over the next few days clearly indicates that Bird had long since dropped below their radar. The headline of the June 2 *Register* article ran, "J. A. Bird Dies Very Suddenly." The writer of the story had no idea who he was, describing him only as "an elderly colored man ... [who] has been a janitor at the state house for a number of years." The *Illinois State Journal* did not even mention his death until it reported on the inquest that was held on June 4.[148] Bird was buried in the "colored section" of Oak Ridge Cemetery, in the same grave as his mother.[149]

On June 4, the day after the house returned to session, Representative Burnett M. Chipperfield of Fulton County introduced the following resolution, which was unanimously adopted:

> WHEREAS, John J. Bird, a valued employé of this House has, since the last adjournment, departed this life, and WHEREAS, It is our desire to leave upon the records of this Body a memorial of our appreciation of his devotion to duty and of his worth as a man; now, therefore, be it *Resolved, by the House of Representatives,* That we deplore the loss of this faithful employé, and we desire in this manner to express our appreciation of his long and efficient service and of his work as a worthy citizen who recognized that one of the highest tests was to quietly and faithfully discharge the duty which was his to perform.[150]

John J. Bird's tombstone, Oak Ridge Cemetery, Springfield,
Illinois. As indicated on the tombstone itself, the Illinois General
Assembly voted to erect the stone in Bird's honor after his death.
It was dedicated on June 9, 1912. Photo by author, 2020.

This rather patronizing resolution refers to nothing but his excellent job
performance in the State House. It is clear, however, that members of the
legislature soon became aware of Bird's former stature and achievements.
Before the General Assembly adjourned on the 5th, it voted to erect a fine
granite monument "to the memory of Judge J. Bird," over his grave.[151] The
dedication ceremony for the monument was held on Sunday, June 9, in Oak
Ridge Cemetery, and the *Register* reported that "a large number of people
[were] in attendance." The service was presided over by Quincy H. Bradley,
an African American who, like Bird, worked at the State House.[152] The program included the official presentation of the grave monument by two of
Springfield's state senators, Thomas E. Lyon, a Republican, and James F.
Morris, a Democrat.[153] Bird's friend and colleague Major Otis B. Duncan
spoke on behalf of the employees of the State House, and the Rev. A. L.
Stewart spoke on behalf of the citizens of Springfield. The Pleasant Grove
Baptist Church Choir and the State House Quartette both sang. Rev.

W. M. Collins eulogized Bird in a speech titled "Men for the Times," and elderly, but still active, William T. Scott, with whom John had worked and fought since the mid-1860s, and who now lived in Springfield, spoke on the "Public Service of Judge J. J. Bird."[154] The service concluded with the assembly singing "Blest Be the Tie That Binds" and with a benediction.[155]

While most of the White community had forgotten Bird, the African American community had not. No issues of Springfield's African American newspapers from early June have survived, but the *Advance Citizen* was still discussing Bird and Magee in its June 21, 1912 issue:

> Within a little over a week death has taken two of the best known Negro citizens and Republicans in Illinois—Dr. J. H. Magee and Judge J. J. Bird. Both in their time have done valuable work for the uplift of their people and have been loyal in the service to the G. O. P., and at the time of their calling away were holding places in the state department as representatives of their race. Dr. Magee's particular interest was always in the educational, religious and social betterment of his people, while Judge Bird to the place of a political Moses and historian. Both played well their part and ended a useful life spent for the betterment of their people and their country.[156]

The *Washington Bee* also reported Bird's death, noting with satisfaction the resolution of condolence passed by the legislature and reporting (probably a garbled account of the state's appropriation for the monument) that "more than $6,000 was subscribed for the erection of a monument to his memory."[157]

Epilogue

"Political Moses"

꧁

L IKE THE BIBLICAL MOSES, John Bird died with his people still in the wilderness. Forty years after his emergence as a symbol of racial progress and equality in Illinois, the nation that he loved so dearly had once again turned its back on its African American citizens. Less than four years before his death, a mob had attacked his neighborhood in Springfield and had spread death and destruction through its streets. The ideology that had permeated his worldview from his youth had proven inadequate in the face of intractable White prejudice and hostility, and his long-held optimism had likely dimmed by the time of his death. However, the surviving fragments of information about his final years suggest that he never entirely lost it. To be sure, the dawn spoken of in the old hymn had not arrived as he had hoped, but it seems from his continuing work until the end, that for him, the "glory-beaming" morning star still shone in the night as a beacon for the future.

In the decades following his death, Bird slowly suffered the fate that befell most of the pioneers of racial justice from his era—they, their struggles, and their victories were largely forgotten. The dramatic story of the postwar civil rights movements in the North was largely swamped by the immensity of the events in the South, and the latter narrative remained the primary focus of African American historical research through the twentieth century. Bird's achievements were remembered for several decades, however, in the African American community, so that as late as 1951, Roscoe C. Simmons, the noted Black columnist for the *Chicago Tribune*, still cited Bird's election as Illinois's first African American judge and his appointment to the board of the university as major milestones in Illinois's African American history.[1] But by the early 1960s, the few Black Illinoisans of the era who were popularly remembered were almost exclusively Chicagoans like John Jones, John W. E. Thomas, Ida B. Wells, and Ferdinand Barnett. Bird and his downstate contemporaries had faded from the narrative. The authors of a 1963 chronology of African American history in Illinois, unaware of Bird, anointed Albert B. George of Chicago as the state's first elected judge—in 1924, a half century after Bird.[2] From that point, the canon of those included in the story of Illinois's post–Civil War African American achievement was essentially set for the rest of the twentieth century, and Bird and most of his colleagues were not part of it. He did not appear in such essential works as the three-volume *Black Biography 1790–1950* in 1991, or in *African American Lives* in 2004.[3] But fragments of his story began to emerge in academic works beginning in 1968, with more significant elements coming to light since the 1990s, as scholars explored various aspects of the history of southern Illinois.[4]

John Bird may have been forgotten by later generations, but he had had a broad impact on his African American contemporaries across Illinois. His early leadership in Cairo and his role in the organization of its Black Republican wing had inspired many others to participate in the political process. His widely admired oratorical skills impacted both Black and White audiences in an extensive range of social contexts. His push to establish and improve Cairo's African American public school had shown his superb abilities to work with both White and Black leaders toward a goal that could benefit both communities. Governor Beveridge's appointment of Bird to the Illinois Industrial University in 1873 was precedent setting and opened the door for other African Americans to seek such state positions. His election and reelection as police magistrate in Cairo exposed the lie of Black inferiority to many White citizens in the city and became the inspiration for an African American presence in Cairo's political offices for nearly forty years. He had been a model of integrity and strength when he led the fight to expose the lack of racial justice in the Cairo post office, taking the cause to the highest levels in Washington and resisting Republican leaders' attempts to convince him to withdraw his complaints with federal job offers. While controversial, his decision in 1880 to support Democrat John Oberly for Illinois secretary of state also had shown his willingness to put what he believed were the best interests of his people before those of his party and himself. He had been a leader in the statewide African American convention movement and played a key role in the conventions' articulation of the primary issues of the Black community. He also had become a powerful voice across the state and the entire Midwest as editor of the *Cairo Gazette*, the *State Capital*, and the *Springfield Republican*, influencing African American public opinion on the full spectrum of political and social issues. Thus, for over thirty years John Bird had been a substantial voice in the African American community, and he affected many men and women across Illinois and beyond who admired and emulated him and who saw from his character that they, too, should work toward a better future.

This deep influence on individuals of his period can be seen in microcosm in an 1889 feature profile of William A. Price, a prominent Black attorney in southern Kansas, published in the Topeka newspaper the *American Citizen*. Price had had a long and successful career in Texas and Kansas, but he had spent the critical years between ages fourteen and twenty-one (1861 to 1868) in Cairo. In the article, looking back more than twenty years, he named two men from that city who had "inspired the young man with a desire to be something himself"—John Bird and William Scott.[5]

The middle-class political ideology for the advancement of the race that Bird had espoused and worked so hard to support in the late nineteenth century had indeed proven insufficient in its ability to sustain a successful drive toward equality. However, for all its weaknesses, defects, and pitfalls, several of its features, such as its insistence upon racial pride, on education, on an African American presence in the political sphere, on the use of the law for attaining equal rights, and on calling upon White America simply to live up to its supposed creed that all men are created equal, were the foundations on which most of the subsequent civil rights movements of the twentieth century were built.[6] Because of this, Bird's influence did not die with the arrival of the Nadir or with his death in 1912. It simply evolved—those men and women whom he had inspired during his lifetime in turn spent their lives working toward the justice for which he had called, and they in turn inspired the next generation, who took on the mantle and passed it on to their successors, all of them untiringly working toward the time when "darkness takes its flight."

> *Watchman, let thy wanderings cease;*
> *Hie thee to thy quiet home.*

NOTES

ABBREVIATIONS AND BIBLIOGRAPHY

INDEX

NOTES

Preface

1. Solberg, *University of Illinois 1867–1894*, 120.

Introduction

1. Beveridge was closely involved in the planning of the university. See Lentz, *Seventy Five Years*, 16–18.
2. CB, July 3, 1874, 4; July 7, 1874, 2. That the snub of Bird was likely intentional is suggested by the fact that the committee, located in Carbondale, also failed to invite a few notable locals, including the mayor and some of the aldermen, to the ceremonies, which also hardly seems accidental (cf. July 2, 4).
3. For general accounts of this period, see Du Bois, *Black Reconstruction in America*; E. Foner, *Reconstruction*; Holt, *Children of Fire*, 158–253; Beatty, *Revolution Gone Backward*; Gates, Jr., *Stony the Road*; Blum, *Reforging the White Republic*.
4. Manning, *Troubled Refuge*, 111–13; 127–32; A. M. Taylor, *Embattled Freedom*, 94–96; *Ninth Census 1870*, vol. 1, Table 1, 3–5; 108–21; Lansden, *History of the City of Cairo*, 208–10.
5. Bledstein and Johnston, *Middling Sorts*, 1–85; Blumin, *Emergence*. On the rise of the Black middle class during this era, see Bushman, *Refinement of America*, 434–40; Ball, *To Live an Antislavery Life*. On the wider picture of the New World African diaspora, see Rael, *Black Identity*, 12–27.
6. See esp. Rael's analysis, *Black Identity*, 118–56.
7. Ball, *To Live an Antislavery Life*, 10–61.
8. C. E. Walker, *Rock*, 26–51; N. M. Taylor, *Frontiers of Freedom*, 43–46; Jones and Allen, *Narrative*; Bailey, *Race Patriotism*, 1–17.
9. Manning, *Troubled Refuge*, 12–19; Bonner, *Remaking the Republic*, 162–63.
10. CR, October 4, 1862, 1; November 1, 1862, 1, see the letters of Henry M. Turner.
11. C. E. Walker, *Rock*, 46–70.
12. See Pimblott, *Faith in Black Power*, 35–36; and CR, March 26, 1864, 2.

13. Wheeler, "Together," 110–12.
14. Bird's role at the *State Capital* has been virtually unknown until now, since Turner, as owner of the newspaper and an ambitious politician, generally took credit for its success. Cf., Penn, *Afro-American Press*, 256–58.
15. Ball, *To Live an Antislavery Life*, 35–41.
16. Lacy, *Blue-Chip Black*, 8–17; 72–100. Lacy's study of the modern Black middle-class cultural strategies designed to help them succeed in White America describes the types of public identities formed by African Americans when interfacing with White society, in shopping, the workplace, buying a home, and other environments. Harrison, *Fight like a Tiger*, 2–3, has pointed out that this "tool kit" of specific modes of interaction that help create these "identities" have their roots in the Black social literature of the antebellum North and in the evolution of Black middle-class ideas in the postwar era. The goals of surviving as a minority in a racist White world, gaining respect from Whites by using their own social weapons against them, and being willing to confront authority figures at crucial times were all part of the playbook of Black leaders like Bird (Ball, *To Live an Antislavery Life*, 37–61). Bird was able to move within White society while also remaining deeply ensconced within his Black community and institutions. The ability to do this, what Lacy describes as "script switching," was somewhat less complex in the nineteenth century than in contemporary America, simply because there was much less societal mixture between Whites and Blacks in that period.
17. Lansden, *History of the City of Cairo*; Lantz, *Community*.
18. Wheeler, "Together in Egypt," 103–34; Hays, "Way Down"; Hays, "African American Struggle," 265–84; Mouser, *Black Gambler's World*; Pimblott, *Faith in Black Power*, 30–40; Ward, "Specter of Black Labor."
19. The *Cairo Bulletin* published under several titles over the years: *Cairo Evening Bulletin* (1868–70—hereafter CEB), *Cairo Daily Bulletin* (1870–72—CDB), *Cairo Bulletin* (1872–78—CB), *Daily Cairo Bulletin* (1878–84—DCB). No copies of the newspaper between 1885 and 1903 survive, but when issues resume January 1, 1904, the paper is again called the *Cairo Bulletin*. On Oberly, see WT, April 16, 1899, 3; Bateman, Selby, and Currey, *Historical Encyclopedia of Illinois*, 132–37.

1. "Prepared in Cincinnati, O"

1. Gibson, "Population," Tables 7 and 8.
2. *Cincinnati: A Guide*, 39–40.
3. Cist, *Sketches*, 46-48.

4. Cist, *Sketches*, 314–17.

5. Cist, *Cincinnati in 1841*, 34, 37; *Sketches* 44–46.

6. Horton and Flaherty, "Black Leadership," 80–84; Cheek and Cheek, "John Mercer Langston," 32–33.

7. Cheek and Cheek, "John Mercer Langston," 30–32.

8. For the boundaries of the First and Ninth Wards before 1851, see *Robinson & Jones' Cincinnati Directory for 1846*, 1. The city redivided the wards in 1851, converting the southern part of the Ninth Ward into the Thirteenth Ward. See Cist, *Sketches*, 14–17. On the importance of the area between Fourth and Eighth Streets, see H. L. Taylor and Dula, "Black Residential," 115–17.

9. Cheek and Cheek, "John Mercer Langston," 34–35.

10. N. M. Taylor, *Frontiers of Freedom*, 138–60.

11. *Seventh Census of the United States*, District No. 60, Schedule I—Free Inhabitants in the 9th Ward of Cincinnati, County of Hamilton, Ohio, November 6, 1850, 1039; *Williams' Cincinnati Directory*, 18, 20; ARUI, 776; Ohio, County Marriage Records, Montgomery County, 1838–1844, 190. On housing in the Ninth Ward, see Dabney, *Cincinnati's Colored Citizens*, 130.

12. The only existing information about John's sister is that she died in 1860 at the age of eight in Windsor, Canada, according to the *Census of Canada West 1861*, Essex County, Windsor, 42 (handwritten page number 29).

13. Shotwell, *History*, 447–55; Cheek and Cheek, "John Mercer Langston," 36–41; N. M. Taylor, *Frontiers of Freedom*, 161–65; Woodson, "Negroes," 17–20; Erickson, "Color Line," 92–95.

14. Erickson, "Color Line," 117–90; N. M. Taylor, *Frontiers of Freedom*, 161–67.

15. Erickson, "Color Line," 205–8; Shotwell, *History*, 455–57.

16. Shotwell, *History*, 455–57; N. M. Taylor, *Frontiers of Freedom*, 165–67; *First Annual Report*, 4–14.

17. The last contemporary reference to Bird is in *Williams' Cincinnati Directory*, 37, suggesting that he died shortly after the data for that edition had been collected.

18. Ohio, County Marriage Records, Hamilton County, 1789–2013: reference v B7, p. 218, no. 477; CR, April 4, 1855, 3. On Green at Allen Chapel AME Church, see Arnett, "Historical and Semi-Centennial Address," 24. Arnett's description of Green reads in part, "He did much good during his stay. He was one of the progressive men of his time."

19. Cf. *Census of Canada West 1861*.

20. Rebecca J. N. Green's name is preserved on the marriage certificate of her son, Richard A. Green, and Georgie Rice, October 19, 1880. Louisiana Compiled Marriage Index, 1718–1925, New Orleans, Louisiana, n.p.

21. Green and Venable, *Brief Account*, 6. See Flood and Hamilton, *Lives of Methodist Bishops*, 762, for a relatively inaccurate account of Green's life. Payne, *History*, 145.

22. Payne, *History*, 167–68.
23. Arnett, "Historical and Semi-Centennial Address," 21–22.
24. A. R. Green, *Discourse*, 9–10.
25. Payne, *History*, 219–20, and 278; Gardner, *Black Print Unbound*, 34–36.
26. The AME Church across the North was deeply involved in the Railroad, and all of the places that we know Green lived were major hubs (Pittsburgh, Cincinnati, Zanesville/Putnam). Cf. LaRoche, *Free Black Communities*, 130–40.
27. Coffin, *Reminiscences*, 323–27, 374–91. On the danger involved in helping fugitive slaves, see N. M. Taylor, *Frontiers of Freedom*, 146.
28. Payne, *History*, 220; on The Mystery, see Levine, *Martin R. Delany*, 25–40; and Ullman, *Martin R. Delany*, 45–88.
29. See Delany, *Condition, Elevation, Emigration*, 173–88; cf. also 9–10, 209–14; Griffith, *African Dream*, 30–81.
30. A. R. Green, *Discourse*, 11–20.
31. On Langston's transition from supporter to opponent of emigration, see Cheek and Cheek, *John Mercer Langston*, 231–33; Ullman, *Martin R. Delany*, 164–65.
32. *Proceedings of the Colored National Convention*, 26, 28, 29, 45, and 46. See the Report of the Colonization Committee in the *Proceedings* on 47–57; Luckett, "Protest, Advancement and Identity," 186.
33. PF, March 25, 1854, 4; October 14, 1854, 2.
34. *Proceedings of the National Emigration Convention*, 7–9, 12, 14; Ullman, *Martin R. Delany*, 154–71.
35. *Proceedings of the National Emigration Convention*, 33–70.
36. Ullman, *Martin R. Delany*, 177–83, 216–18.
37. PF, November 25, 1856, 2.
38. PF, April 15 and 22, 1854, both 2.
39. PF, January 13, 1855, 2. A description of a debate between Green and John. I. Gaines, the prominent Cincinnatian and opponent of emigration, appears in PF, February 17, 1855, 3.
40. Arnett, "Historical and Semi-Centennial Address," 24–25; CR, March 4, 1856, 1.
41. Schneider, *Y Bridge City*, 200–210. Schneider focuses almost entirely on the White side of the Railroad, but the description indicates the significance of the activity in Zanesville and neighboring Putnam. Cf. also Gerber, *Black Ohio*, 17.
42. PF, December 6, 1856, 2.
43. Cf. Erickson, "Color Line," 210–12; 249–51.
44. ARUI, 776.
45. PF, June 21, 1856, 2.

46. See Green and Venable, *Brief Account*, 3–4, 8.
47. See the *Census of Canada West 1861*, Essex County, City of Windsor, 42, which lists the children's ages as follows: Elizabeth, eighteen; John Bird, seventeen; William, sixteen; Richard, fifteen. James was in prison at the time of the census and is thus not named here. On James, see *Tenth Census of the United States*, Supervisor's District No. 17, Enumeration District No 69, Schedule 1—Inhabitants in Washington City, District of Columbia, June 2, 1880, 7. James A. D. Green's age is given as thirty-eight, which places his birthdate as 1842 and thus nineteen in 1861. See also Winks, *Blacks in Canada*, 396.
48. Only two issues have survived: May 10, 1860 and June 21, 1861.
49. The only surviving information about these two children is in the 1861 census column "Deaths in 1860," which asked only for the sex, age, and cause of death for each individual.
50. DFP, April 26, 1860, 1. It is difficult to trust any of the details of the trial from DFP. The paper was owned and edited by the notoriously bigoted Wilbur F. Storey, a Copperhead Democrat who vehemently opposed abolition, citizenship rights for African Americans, the Emancipation Proclamation, and the Lincoln Presidency. Storey developed an immediate dislike for Green because of his political activity in Windsor. See DFP, February 5, 11, 1860, both 1, for Storey's earliest venomous attacks on Green. During the next year and a half, until Storey left DFP to become editor of the *Chicago Times*, the paper attacked Green whenever possible, always on the front page (e.g., May 9, 1860, 1; September 18, 1860, 1; January 22, 27, 1861, both 1; June 16, 25, 1861, both 1; and August 2, 1861, 1). On Storey during these years, see Walsh, "Radically and Thoroughly Democratic," 193–225.
51. DFP, August 19, 1860, 1; October 11, 1860, 1; January 19, 1861, 1; February 3, 1861, 1. As with the previous trial, virtually none of the newspaper's accounts here can be considered reliable beyond their most basic elements.
52. *Census of Canada West 1861*, Essex County, Windsor, 42.
53. Descriptions of this controversy can be found in CR, in numerous articles, particularly during the early years of the conflict, 1861–63. Green published an exhaustive and defensive account of it from his perspective in Green and Venable, *Brief Account*. The final dissolution of the Independent Methodist Episcopal Church took place in June 1876 at the AME General Conference of that year. See C. S. Smith, *History*, 115–16; CR, June 8, 1876, 2; August 31, 1876, n.p.; September 21, 1876, 4; November 9, 1876, n.p.
54. CR, February 9, 1867, 1. Green's two older sons, Alfred and James, went into the ministry, but the younger sons did not choose that path. Richard became a physician, and John a politician. I have found no information about William.

55. These legal rights did not mean that Canadians were without prejudice against the African American immigrants. Racism was widespread in the towns where Black settlements existed. On this, see the extraordinary contemporary analysis of White prejudice in Samuel Gridley Howe, *Refugees from Slavery*, 37–55. Howe was a remarkable man, not only an abolitionist, but an advocate for the mentally and physically disabled. This report is fascinating, being in parts remarkably liberal in tone, while maintaining a striking racism at other points, particularly toward "mulattoes."

56. Green's activities in support of Rankin again drew the ire of Storey in Detroit. See DFP, June 29, 1861, 1, and July 3, 1861, 1. These stories, hugely distorted in the way they portray Green, show clearly, however, Green's leadership and influence in the Black community at the time.

57. DFP, August 1, 1861, 1.

58. Martin Delany had moved to Chatham in 1856, in spite of his uncertainty about the long-term safety of doing so (Ullman, *Martin R. Delany*, 183–94).

59. Annie's death certificate (as Annie Venerable Byrd) from Detroit gives her birth date as June 22, 1841, Transcript of Certificate of Death, Michigan Department of State, Detroit, 1903, Registered No. 4478. The Venerables also brought several other people with them from Pittsburgh who had lived in their Pittsburgh home in earlier years. In 1850, Samuel and Arena were caring for George, Elizabeth, and Margaret McNany, ages nineteen, sixteen, and eighteen, respectively (*Seventh Census of the United States*, Schedule I—Free Inhabitants of Pitt Township in the County of Allegheny, State of Pennsylvania, 1850, 22). In the *Census of Canada West 1861*, Windsor, County of Essex, District 2, 32, Elizabeth and Margaret were again living with them, but were both married and their husbands were elsewhere, perhaps serving in the war effort. Elizabeth, now Tanner, had two children, while Margaret, now Hawes, had none. Thus ten people lived in the Venerables' house in Windsor. Elizabeth and Annie, who was nine in 1850, were very close and always considered themselves sisters.

60. Samuel attended the State Convention of the Colored Freeman of Pennsylvania in 1841 held in Pittsburgh to protest the elimination of the African American right to vote in the Pennsylvania Constitution of 1838. Foner and Walker, *Proceedings*, 106–17. Cf. Ullman, *Martin R. Delany*, 35–44.

61. *Proceedings of the National Emigration Convention*, 14, 76–77.

62. The 1861 census provides his age as forty-nine and lists his occupation as "sailor." Cf. Howe, *Refugees from Slavery*, 75–77.

63. Green and Venable, *Brief Account*, 2.

64. Green and Venable, *Brief Account*, 18. Green mentions Arena three times in the book (see also 83 and 85), in each case pointing out her cleverness and

insight into the situation at hand. No other layperson, neither Catherine nor Samuel, appears in such a role in the book.

65. On the date of their marriage, see Annie's death certificate, which says she was twenty-three years old when she married, thus making August 1864 the most likely date, rather than the August 1865 date in ARUI, 776.

66. On Alfred, see Prince, *My Brother's Keeper*, 70; Bonner, *Remaking the Republic*, 154. His complete 1861 speech is found in Foner and Branham, *Lift Every Voice*, 357–59. See also A. M. Green, *Letters and Discussions*.

67. CR, August 19, 1880, 2; July 11, 1889, 3; January 13, 1898, 3.

68. CR, September 5, 1878, 1, describes a reunion of Alfred, James, and Richard. On Richard's medical career, see chapter 2. On the *Virginia Star*, see CR, July 12, 1877, 2; October 18, 1877, 2; February 7, 1878, 4; and September 5, 1878, 1; and Anderson, *Education of Blacks*, 62–64. After Augustus's death in September 1878, in Vicksburg, Mississippi, Richard moved to Vicksburg to take care of Catherine, his stepmother (CR, December 23, 1880, 2).

2. "A Cairoite to Some Extent"

1. Du Bois, *Black Reconstruction in America*, 57–83; Manning, *Troubled Refuge*, 6–15; Bonner, *Remaking the Republic*, 149–79; E. Foner, *Reconstruction*, 255–61; 444–49.

2. Reidy, "African American Struggle," 217–22; Wentzell, "Mercenaries and Adventurers," 57–67; Green and Venable, *Brief Account*, 106–7.

3. CR, January 30, 1864, 1, describes his stay in St. Louis. Two other letters from this trip appear in CR, February 20, 2; and February 27, 1, but are consumed with theological issues rather than descriptions of his travels.

4. Green and Venable, *Brief Account*, 132–33.

5. Elizabeth, Green's only daughter, had married James Neace of Windsor on March 17, 1864 (CR, April 23, 1864, 3). Their other son, James, may have stayed in Windsor, too, but he had moved to Washington by 1870 (BDW, 1870, 158). William's whereabouts are unknown. Green and Venable, *Brief Account*, 132–33.

6. Green and Venable, *Brief Account*, 139.

7. BDW 1867, 288 for Augustus, and 290 for Richard.

8. It is slightly possible that Bird made an earlier trip to Cairo during the summer of 1863—brief references in CT, August 23, 1888, 3, and January 31, 1889, 6, place him there—but it seems likely that the reporter had confused Bird with another person from Cairo. See the larger discussion of these references in chapter 7, n. 15.

9. Lansden, *History of the City of Cairo*, 30–62, 96–110.

10. Dickens, *American Notes*, chap. 12.

11. Lansden, *History of the City of Cairo*, 96–110, 209, and 220–21; Wheeler, "Together in Egypt," 107; Pimblott, *Faith in Black Power*, 26–30. On Cairo's prewar population, see A. Ward, "Spectre of Black Labor," 93–100.

12. Perrin, *History of Alexander*, 55: "Cairo was always 'diabolically Democratic,' at least until the 'man and brother' from the cotton-fields and jungles of the South parted company with the swamp alligators and toothsome possoms [*sic*] of that region and came upon the town like the black ants of his native Africa." Lansden, *History of the City of Cairo*, 128–37. On southern Illinois's secessionist tendencies, see Kionka, *Key Command*, 27–45.

13. Wheeler, "Together in Egypt," 106–8. Kionka provides a good description of the military aspects of Cairo's war years. On the Soldiers' Home, see Newberry, *Sanitary Commission*, 27–28, 220–21; 335–36 and 393. This report also mentions that forty thousand White refugees were helped by the Soldiers' Home during the war (394–95, 518); this number was mistakenly identified as the number of both Black and White refugees in Wheeler, "Together in Egypt," 107. The Sanitary Commission seems to have played little role in supporting the African American refugees in Cairo. I have found no official numbers for the "contrabands" who passed through during the war, but they do not appear to have exceeded more than ten thousand.

14. Hays, "Way Down," 131–38.

15. Manning, *Troubled Refuge*, 109–14; Hays, "Way Down," 171–88. Levi Coffin of Cincinnati visited the Cairo contraband camp in late 1862 at the same time that the Hadleys arrived to establish the school. In his *Reminiscences*, 619–25, he provides a description of the horrific conditions suffered by the refugees before the barracks were completed.

16. Manning, *Troubled Refuge*, 111–13; Hays, "Way Down," 187–88.

17. Schwalm, *Emancipation's Diaspora*, 72–77.

18. Hays, "Way Down," 188–93; Noyes, "Contraband Camp," 207–11.

19. Manning, *Troubled Refuge*, 125–30; Wheeler, "Together in Egypt," 107–8.

20. Wheeler, "Together in Egypt," 108–15; Lansden, *History of Cairo*, 209.

21. Sheard, "Notes," 1–2. This was the beginning of the church that in 1881 became Ward Chapel AME, see 6–7; Pimblott, *Faith in Black Power*, 35–36; CR, March 26, 1864, 2. On the Renfrows, see Hays, "Way Down," 58–59. Baptist congregations appeared in the city after the war.

22. Hays, "Way Down," 131–39; Trollope, *North America*, 112–13.

23. The small number of northern African Americans who settled in Cairo, in comparison to those of southern origin, is still visible in the 1880 U.S. Census, where southern-born Black inhabitants represent 39.2 percent of all the

household heads in Cairo, while northern-born Black residents represent only 1.7 percent. See Wheeler, "Together in Egypt," 109.

24. A writer from Cairo in 1864, with some hyperbole, put it thusly: "For it must be remembered, that, in no Free State in the Union, and in very few Slave States, have colored men received greater wrongs at the hands of the law or the people, than they have in this State." CR, July 16, 1864, 2.

25. Cf. Pimblott, *Faith in Black Power*, 239 n 46.

26. Heinzel, "Liberty Protected by Law," 57–72; 183–207; Ward, "Specter of Black Labor," 62–66, 118–19; Lusk, *Politics*, 333–35.

27. Heinzel, "Liberty Protected by Law," 317–23; Manning, *Troubled Refuge*, 10–13.

28. CR, July 16, 1864, 2.

29. CR, January 14, 1865, 2.

30. Garb, *Freedom's Ballot*, 40.

31. CR, March 4, 1865, 1. "Ruth," who began as an occasional writer of devotional articles to CR in 1862, became by 1865 a political activist and strong critic of most of the Black political and religious leadership in Illinois. See esp. May 20, 1865, 1; September 23, 1865, 1; December 15, 1866, 1.

32. Ward, "Specter of Black Labor," 145–47; Garb, *Freedom's Ballot*, 39–41.

33. CR, April 22, 1865, 1.

34. CR, April 29, 1865, 2.

35. CR, April 22, 1865, 1.

36. CR, May 20, 1865, 3. Sheard, "Notes," 2, places Jacobs's appointment in 1865, but he probably was sent in 1864, since he died on April 12, 1865, "after a protracted illness of consumption." All of Sheard's dates for the period between 1865 and 1877 are incorrect.

37. Records of the Assistant Commissioner, Images 439–42. See Hays, "Way Down," 191–92, who misdates the letter to 1863.This practice by shipowners continued into 1866, CR February 3, 1866, 1. On the closing of the office, see the Records of the Assistant Commissioner, Bureau Employment Book 1865, Samuel Gold Superintendent of Cairo, months of service, relieved December 1, 1865, M979 roll 51, image 956.

38. CR, January 6, 1866, 3.

39. CR, February 3, 1866, 1. On Young and Green, see Green and Venable, *Brief Account*, 11–15, 28–35, 135–37.

40. CR, August 2, 1862, 1; October 18, 1862, 1; May 30, 1863, 1; June 13, 1863, 2; November 21, 1863, 2; January 16, 1864, 1; March 12, 1864, 2; July 16, 1864, 1; October 14, 1865, 1; December 10, 1864, 1. On Strother and Wilberforce, CR, November 21, 1863, 2; January 16, 1864, 1; July 23, 1864, 1; On his writings concerning civil rights issues, CR, September 27, 1862, 1; October 4, 1862, 1; May 5,

1866, 1. Strother had supported Green in his opposition to Bishop Nazrey in letters to CR: February 15, 1862, 2; March 22, 1862, 2; April 5, 1862, 2; May 10, 1; and May 24, 1862, 1. This connection to his stepfather makes it possible that John knew the Strothers before they arrived in Cairo. On Fanny Strother and her schools, CR, February 1, 1862, 2; August 2, 1862, 1; December 10, 1864, 1; February 3, 1866, 1; March 10, 1866, 1; July 20, 1867, 1; October 27, 1866, 1; and October 24, 1868, 1. She also occasionally wrote letters to CR: February 25, 1865, 2.

41. CR, February 3, 1866, 1; March 10, 1866, 1; October 27, 1866, 1.

42. CR February 3, 1866, 1.

43. CR, March 10, 1866, 1. The importance of the church-related schools during and after the war in the South is described by Anderson, *Education of Blacks*, 5–20.

44. See the *Proceedings of the Illinois State Convention*, 2. The call gives Bird's name as John J. Byrd. He was actually back in Windsor by October 13, when he penned a brief letter to CR (published February 9, 1867, 1).

45. Bridges, "Equality Deferred," 86–95.

46. Trefousse, *Andrew Johnson*, 214–33, 250–66; Riddleberger, *1866*, 6–18, 86–104; Du Bois, *Black Reconstruction in America*, 269–310; Bergeron, *Andrew Johnson*, 125–28.

47. The proceedings of the convention were published as *The Southern Loyalists: The Tribune Tracts*. PET extensively covered the convention during the week of September 3–8, 1866, and CT reported on the tour of the Southern Loyalists from September 11, 1866, to October 12, 1866, 2.

48. CR, October 27, 1866, 1; CT, October 2, 4; October 3, 2 and 4.

49. CR, October 27, 1866, 1. CT was also outraged by the disruption of the meeting: October 6, 7, 1866, both 1; October 8, 1 and 2; October 9, 1 and 4.

50. CR, October 27, 1866, 1.

51. Hays, "Way Down," 134–45; CDB, February 18, 1871, 3.

52. CR, October 27, 1866, 1.

53. CR, March 10, 1866, 1. Cf. July 20, 1867, 1.

54. On the customhouse, see Lansden, *History of the City of Cairo*, 233–35. For the date of construction, see CR, July 20, 1867, 1.

55. Hays, "Way Down," 223–25; Ward, "Specter of Black Labor," 166–67.

56. CDD, April 18, 1867, 4. The account doesn't name Strother.

57. Andrews, *Masonic Abolitionists*, 71–81, 108–9. Andrews provides a good history of the Illinois Grand Lodge. On the Prince Hall Masons more generally, see Skocpol, Liazos, and Ganz, *What a Mighty*, 8–14, 61–94.

58. Morris, *Origins*, 4–12.

59. Pimblott, *Faith in Black Power*, 35–40.

60. James Rogers, superintendent of the Cairo contraband camp in 1863, described the religious meetings at the barracks as "both solemn and interesting." See Berlin et al., *Free at Last*, 197; CR, April 30, 1864, 1.

61. Sheard, "Notes," 2; CR, October 27, 1866, 1.

62. Hays, "Way Down," 328–32, significantly misinterpreted the roles of Cairo's early church leadership, inflating Shores's influence in the political scene, sharply misunderstanding the context of his congregation's demonstration at the White school building on October 12, 1867, missing Strother's activism, and misreading the reasons behind the broken relationship between Shores and Bradley, all discussed below. Hays's assertion that Bradley's congregation was made up largely of middle-class parishioners who didn't want to associate with the rural southern members of Shores's church is based on a misunderstanding of satiric language used by CEB in an article (August 4, 1869, 3) about Bradley's church holding a separate celebration of Emancipation Day, rather than joining other congregations at a combined event. The author of the article attributes this decision to Bradley's desire to keep his congregation away from "the common negroes," but this is patently the writer's regular use of racist satire, extremely common in the *Bulletin*'s reporting on both Shores and Bradley. The membership in both congregations was primarily made up of former southern refugees, and neither minister seems to have been formally educated. (*Ninth Census of the United States,* 1870, North Cairo Precinct, Alexander County, 95, lists Bradley as illiterate. On Shores' educational background, see the following section in this chapter.) Hays's ("Way Down," 243–45; 328–332) interpretation of Shores's march to the White public school in 1867 is also marred by a misunderstanding concerning Shores's very short-lived free school and the apparent reason for the march, discussed below. Pimblott, *Faith in Black Power*, 35–40, relied on Hays's interpretation and thus also provided a problematic view of the period.

63. On Shores's fights with Bradley, CEB, July 14, 1869, 2; August 2, 4, 10, 13, 16, 1869, all 3; September 14, 22, 25, 1869, all 3. On the times the two were removed from their churches, see CEB, May 5, 31, 1869, both 3; CDB, September 15, 1871, 4; October 6, 1872, 3; CB, September 17, 20, 1873, both 3; August 23, 1874, 4; June 11, 1876, 3 (Bradley); and CEB, November 26, 1870, 3; March 14, 1873, 4; June 22, 27, 1873, both 4 (Shores).

64. Pimblott, *Faith in Black Power*, 105–28. On modern social movement framing, see Benford and Snow, "Framing Processes," 611–39; Snow, Rochford, Jr., Worden, and Benford, "Frame Alignment," 464–81.

65. *Compendium of the Ninth Census: 1870*, pt. 1, 150–65; McCaul, *Black Struggle*, 45.

66. McCaul, *Black Struggle*, 44–72.

67. E.g., CEB, February 1, 1869, 1: "A law so repugnant to the people at large may, possibly, fall still-born. If it do not, however, it will lead to a demoralization and degradation of our common schools that will, and ought to, eventulate [*sic*] in their destruction." CDB, December 22, 1870, 3: "The day that negro children are forced into our public schools will inaugurate, in violence and bloodshed, the decline and downfall of the school system in Cairo. Our taxpayers, the friends and patrons of the school, will become enemies of the system, and work for its overthrow." Cf. also CDB, September 15, 1870, 1; December 24, 1870, 1.

68. CR, February 3, 1866, 1; October 27, 1866, 1; March 10, 1866, 1; CDD, December 21, 1866, 4; December 20, 1867, 4.

69. CR, October 27, 1866, 1.

70. CDD, September 22, 1867, 1, 4; On Bateman, see McCaul, *Black Struggle*, 111–17.

71. E.g., CEB, January 13, 1870, 4; April 1, 1870, 4; CDB, February 25, 1872, 4; June 27, 1873, 4; CB, June 10, 1876, 3; June 21, 1876, 3; July 9, 1876, 3; March 21, 1879, 4.

72. CDD, September 1, 11, 1867, both 4. Actually, the school was already open by October 3, cf. CDD, October 4, 1867, 1.

73. CDD, September 19, 1867, 4.

74. CDD, September 22, 1867, 1; *Tenth Census of the United States*, Supervisor's Dist. No. 8, Enumeration District No. 2, Schedule 1–City of Cairo, Alexander County, Illinois, 13; Will Record, *Alexander County Court House, Cairo, Ill.*, vol. A: 1880–1894, 394–95. On Shores's apparent ability to read, see CDD, July 6, 1867, 4.

75. CDD, September 26, 27, 28, 1867, all 1; October 1, 3, 4, 1867, all 1.

76. Cf. CDD, September 22, 24, 27, 29, 1867, all 4; October 1, 1867, 4.

77. CDD, September 26, 1867, 4; October 15, 1867, 4.

78. CDD, October 15, 1867, 4.

79. Shores's skepticism concerning public schools is in evidence in 1871, when he again opened a rival private school at the time that the Black public school was just opening. See CDB, October 12, 1871, 4. His school was still operating in 1878, CB, June 15, 1878, 4.

80. CDD, October 15, 17, 20, 1867, all 4.

81. CDD, October 20, 1867, 4.

82. CDD, October 20, 1867, 4; November 7, 1867, 4. If the school did open, it could not have lasted more than two years because Strother tried to organize a free school again in 1870, CEB, March 31, 1870, 4; April 9, 1870, 4.

83. ARUI, 776. The career details in the *Record* are imperfect, including wrong dates for some of his positions. It seems likely that Bird's longtime colleague,

William T. Scott, provided the imprecise bio to the university shortly after Bird's death, since he had furnished similar information for Bird's death certificate in 1912. Scott apparently used information he had gathered for a eulogy he gave in 1912 at Bird's memorial service in Oak Ridge Cemetery.

84. CR, October 24, 1868, 1; and CEB, March 31, 1870, 4. In 1869, the Strothers opened a small grocery store to help pay the bills. CEB, June 30, 1869, 3; July 15, 1869, 3; CDB, November 28, 1870, 1. They left Cairo in late 1870 or early 1871 to take over a congregation in Atchison, Kansas, where Thomas died September 7, 1872. LDT, September 9, 1872, 2.

85. CDD, December 18, 20, and 24, 1867, all 4; CEB, January 12, 13, 1869, both 4; June 16, 1869, 3. CEB sometimes gives Tolford's name as Tolburn, but there is no doubt that this refers to Tolford.

86. On Section 80 (originally 84) of the state education law, passed in 1855, see McCaul, *Black Struggle*, 29–31.

87. CEB, July 21, 1869, 3; November 6, 1869, 3. The Black Baptist contribution is mentioned in CEB, June 16, 1869, 3.

88. CEB, July 21, 1869, 3; August 10, 1869, 3. For the exact location of the school (Lots 21, 22, and 23 of Block 83), which became Cairo's first Black public school, see CEB, October 4, 1869, 1; March 9, 1870, 1; and the *Map of the City of Cairo* 1872.

89. McCaul, *Black Struggle*, 86–89; Du Bois, *Black Reconstruction in the United States*, 145–49; E. Foner, *Reconstruction*, 445–49.

90. CDD, July 6, 1867, 4.

91. Wheeler, "Together in Egypt," 112–15. The population and race statistics are from a local census taken by the Cairo city council in early 1865, cited in Lansden, *History of the City of Cairo*, 209; and *Compendium of the Ninth Census: 1870*, pt. 1, 108.

92. For indications of increased Republican interest in Black voters, although from the polemical perspective of a Democratic newspaper, see CDD, July 16, 1868, 2 and 4; July 30, 1868, 4; July 31, 1868, 4; August 6, 1868, 1. See Hays, "Way Down," 349.

93. CR, October 24, 1868, 1; CT, October 2, 1868, 1.

94. Mouser, *Black Gambler's World*, 4–27.

95. See the Illinois State Census 1865, County of Alexander, Town of Cairo (colored), July 3, 1865, 40. In the *Ninth Census of the United States*, 1870, North Cairo Precinct, 86, his name is misspelled as "Gladny," and his wife's name is given as Fannie. The *Twelfth Census of the United States*, 1900, Springfield, Ward 7, 14, gives his birth date as August 1844. On his Emancipation Day speech, CR, February 3, 1866, 1 (misspelled as Gladner). On his church work, CR, July 29, 1875, 7; August 9, 1877, 4; DCB, June 26, 1878, 4. For Gladney's

activities in the Republican Party, see CDB, September 6, 1871, 4; July 4, 1872, 4; CB, August 12, 1874, 4. On Gladney's work with the city, CDB, June 5, 1872, 4, August 8, 1872, 4, CB, May 30, 1873, 4. On his election as constable, CB, November 8, 1873, 3. On the Free Benevolent Sons of America, see *Private Laws*, 140–41.

96. Cf. Benford and Snow, "Framing Processes," 611–39; Snow, Rochford, Jr., Worden, and Benford, "Frame Alignment," 464–81.

97. On Munn, see *Biographical Encyclopedia*, 97–98. On Linegar, see *Biographical Encyclopedia*, 142; CEB, March 23, 1870, 3.

98. Bird is listed as a "Rail Road Man" in the *Ninth Census of the United States*, 1870, North Cairo District, 91. On Bird's address and occupation, see Oberly, *Cairo City Directory for 1872*, 19, and *Gardner and Gaines Cairo City Directory*, 47; and ISJ, February 19, 1874, 4. On the job of Pullman porter, see Tye, *Rising from the Rails*, 23–42.

99. McCaul, *Black Struggle*, 100–101, notes that only three African Americans were admitted to the bar by 1878: Lloyd G. Wheeler (1869); Richard A. Dawson (1870); and Ferdinand L. Barnett, Jr. (1878), all of Chicago. CEB, May 27, 1869, 3.

100. CEB, May 27, 1869, 3. John Olney was the local circuit court judge.

101. Cf. ISR, August 4, 1869, 1.

102. CEB, August 10, 1869, 3; cf. also August 4, 1869, 3.

103. On Oberly's opposition to the Fifteenth Amendment, CEB, January 22, 1869, 1; July 30, 1869, 1; April 1, 1870, 2.

3. "The Colored People Intend to Stay"

1. *Compendium of the Ninth Census: 1870*, pt. 1, Table 1, 3–5, 108–21; Carlson, "Black Migration," 37–46; Cha-Jua, *America's First Black Town*, 77–114.

2. Cf. CEB, March 4, 1870, 3, where Oberly argues that five-sixths of the jobs African Americans had were from businesses owned by Democrats. Also Hays, "Way Down," 198–99, 217; Ward, "Specter of Black Labor," 181–82; Lantz, *Community*, 34–36, 188–89n43, for the main business leaders in Cairo, mostly Democrats.

3. CEB, March 4, 7 and 10, 1870, all 3; CDB, July 27, 1870, 2. Shores threatened to boycott the Fifteenth Amendment celebration (CDB, April 11, 1870, 4) but did attend (CDB, April 13, 1870, 4).

4. CDB, March 30, 1870, 4; April 7, 1870, 4.

5. CDB, April 8, 1870, 4; CEB, January 3, 1870, 4; March 31, 1869, 1.

6. CDB, April 11, 12, 1870, both 4.

7. CEB, February 16, 1870, 3; March 18, 1870, 3.

8. CDB, April 12, 1870, 4; April 13, 1870, 2 and 4.

9. CDB, April 13, 1870, 2.

10. CDB, April 13, 1870, 2.

11. CDB, April 13, 1870, 2.

12. On the implications of this controversy, see Schwalm, *Emancipation's Diaspora*, 197–203; N. M. Taylor, *Frontiers of Freedom*, 173–74.

13. Davis, *We Will Be*, 72–84; McCaul, *Black Struggle*, 44–72. The Black communities of Decatur and Galesburg also specifically requested a separate Black school.

14. CDB, April 13, 1870, 2.

15. See McCaul, *Black Struggle*, 111–18.

16. CDB, January 29, 1871, 3.

17. CDB, January 29, 1971, 3; March 19, 1871, 3; April 4, 1871, 3.

18. CEB, February 1, 1869, 1; CDB, September 15, 1870, 1; December 22, 1870, 3. November 7, 1870, 1: "If it is your desire that ten thousand dollars a year be added to our taxes, for the purpose of educating the 500 negro children of Cairo, vote for Linegar and Wilcox, who will, if sent to the legislature, vote for laws to compel the school Directors to make such a levy."

19. CDB, August 24, 1971, 4; September 9, 1871, 4; August 6, 1872, 4; August 11, 1872, 3.

20. CDB, September 10, 1871, 4. See January 13, 1872, 4, which describes a movement to petition the school directors to stop paying the White teachers.

21. See CDB, September 12, 13, 1871, both 4.

22. CDB, September 13, 1871, 4. Cf. CDB, September 12, 1871, 4: "We do not profess to be the champion of the colored men of Cairo, but we are far from denying to them the right to labor for their daily bread, and we believe it should be the pleasure of every White man to lead them to industry and an enlightened understanding of their duties. In Cairo here, we have a colored population that will compare favorably with that of any other city in the country. We believe, indeed, that our resident colored men are, as a general rule, industrious and anxious to be considered quiet residents."

23. CDB, December 20, 1871, 4. These reports often spell Tolford's name as Talford.

24. CDB, December 9, 1871, 4.

25. CDB, December 20, 1871, 4. Oberly called for the firing of both Tolford and the teacher involved in CDB, December 22, 1871, 4.

26. See CDB, June 25, 1872, 4; August 31, 1873, 3; November 16, 1873, 2; April 5, 1874, 3; July 22, 1874, 4.

27. Cf. CDB, May 3, 1870, 4.

28. CDB, April 14, 1870, 2.

29. CDB, April 14, 23, 1870, both 2.
30. *Compendium of the Ninth Census 1870*, pt. I, 150.
31. CD, April 14, 1870, 2 and 3; CDB, April 16, 1870, 2.
32. CDB, May 6, 1870, 4. Bird spoke at another Fifteenth Amendment celebration on June 2 at Mound City (CDB, June 3, 1870, 4).
33. CD, May 12, 1870, 2.
34. CDB, May 21, 1870, 4; May 22, 1870, 2; May 31, 1870, 2.
35. CDB, June 16, 1870, 2; cf. CDB, April 15, 23, 1870, both 2.
36. CDB, November 28, 1870, 1.
37. The speech was printed in three parts, CR, January 28, 1871, 4; February 4, 11, 1871, both 4.
38. E.g., CEB, February 26, 1870, 3; March 4, 10, and 23, 1870, all 3; CDB, April 14, 15, 1870, both 2; August 22, 1870, 4; September 17, 1870, 1.
39. CDB, April 14, 1870, 2.
40. CDB, November 10, 1870, 1.
41. CDB, October 21, 1870, 1; November 9, 1870, 1 and 4; November 10, 11, 1870, both 4. Voter suppression at this time was not uncommon in the North; see Davis, *We Will Be*, 99–101.
42. CDB, November 9, 1870, 4.
43. CDB, September 6, 1871, 4.
44. CDB, February 8, 1871, 3. Oberly speculated that Bird might be a potential candidate for clerk, but it is not clear that this or the supposed "Colored Man's Party" was anything but Oberly's anti-Black imagination. It is highly unlikely that Bird was involved with any proposed split from the Republican Party. The article rather illustrates Oberly's continued use of fearmongering in suggesting that the Black leaders were scheming to take over the city government. In the article, Oberly referred to Scott as "the prominent colored Radical," while he characterized Bird as "a vindictive colored cuss, who has obtained some polish by contact with white men."
45. CDB, February 15, 23, 1871, both 3.
46. CDB, February 23, 1871, 3; February 24, 25, 1871, both 1.
47. Mouser, *Black Gambler's World*, 27, argued that Oberly and the others formed the Citizens' Party specifically to defeat Scott and the Black politicians. But the evidence does not sustain this interpretation. CDB, February 15, 1871, 3 shows that by then only Scott was running for a city office. There simply was no threat of a "Colored Man's Party" by the time the Citizens' Party was founded on February 22. In addition, a breakaway Black party would split the Republicans and thus assure a Democratic victory. On the "Grasshopper Party," see CDB, February 18, 1871, 3; February 23, 1871, 3; February 24, 25, 1871, both 1; September 23, 1871, 4.

48. CDB, March 5, 1871, 3.
49. CDB, April 26, 1871, 3.
50. CDB, June 7, 1871, 3.
51. CDB, October 19, 1871, 4.
52. CDB, November 7, 1871, 4.
53. CDB, November 8, 1871, 4.
54. CDB, August 26, 1871, 4.
55. DMD, September 23, 1871, 4; September 26, 1871, 2; September 27, 28, 1871, both 4.
56. CDB, February 24, 25, 27, 1872, all 4, describe two meetings of the Black community at which the merits of the local candidates were debated. See in February 25, 4, the excerpt of a response Bird gave to Scott's speech in support of Winston, which Oberly described as "a very skillful tit bit of elegant sarcasm."
57. CDB, March 2, 1872, 4.
58. Slap, *Doom of Reconstruction*, 126–63; E. Foner, *Reconstruction*, 499–511; Grossman, *Democratic Party*, 30–45.
59. CDB, April 26, 1872, 4; May 1, 1872, 4. As soon as he announced his support for Greeley, the *Bulletin* suddenly found their old boogeyman to be a model of integrity and courage in the face of supposed threats from the Black Grant Republicans, CDB, May 9, 1872, 4; July 18, 1872, 4; July 21, 1872, 2; July 26, 1872, 4; August 6, 20, 1872, both 2; September 5, 1872, 4.
60. CDB, May 28, 1872, 4; July 19, 1872, 4; August 25, 1872, 3; September 17, 1872, 4; September 19, 1872, 2; October 2, 1872, 4; November 7, 1872, 4.
61. DCB, April 17, 1880, 2 and 3; April 18, 21, 1880, both 4.
62. CDB, November 7, 1872, 4.
63. CDB, February 24, 1872, 4.
64. CDB, February 25, 1872, 4.
65. CDB, September 5, 1872, 4.

4. "The Morning Seems to Dawn"

1. *Compendium of the Tenth Census*, pt. 1, 382–85; Wheeler, "Together in Egypt," 111–15.
2. Cf. CDB, February 24, 25, 1872, both 4; May 9, 18, 1872, both 4; June 21, 1872, 4; December 28, 1872, 4; CB, September 19, 1875, 3; December 29, 1875, 3; October 25, 1876, 3; DCB, January 4, 1880, 4. For additional instances of integrated facilities, see Wheeler, "Together in Egypt," 130n16.
3. *Compendium of the Tenth Census*, pt. 1, 382.

4. E. Foner, *Reconstruction*, 512–34; Beatty, *Revolution Gone Backward*, 8–30; Du Bois, *Black Reconstruction in America*, 690–700.

5. Cf. Garb, *Freedom's Ballot*, 43–45; Joens, *From Slave*, 11–24; Cha-Jua, *America's First Black Town*, 105–20.

6. Bernstein, "American Labor," 59–83; E. Foner, *Reconstruction*, 512–34; Hays, "Way Down," 299–307; Schwalm, *Emancipation's Diaspora*, 137–43.

7. Grossman, *Democratic Party*, 45–59; 98–106; E. Foner, *Reconstruction*, 505–8.

8. Solberg, *University of Illinois 1867–1894*, 80–83. See BTIIU, *First Report*, 1868, 5 for the establishing law, and 11 for a list of the first set of trustees. By the election of 1872 there were nineteen congressional districts in Illinois. See the list of the thirty-eight board members for March 1873 in *Illinois Industrial University Catalogue and Circular 1873*, 4. For the ages of the board members of this period, see the biographical sketches in SCAR, 969–82. On Gregory, see Solberg, *University of Illinois 1867–1894*, 84–117.

9. Howard, *Mostly Good*, 156–61.

10. JS, 1873, 264–65. The misspelling appeared in Philo J. Beveridge's letter to George H. Harlow, March 4, 1873 (Beveridge Correspondence, ISA, record series 101/017) and thus carried over to JS. It was also misspelled in BTIIU from 1873 to 1880. Why these reports continued to misspell Bird's name for seven years is unclear, since the handwritten notes taken by the secretary at the board meetings (University of Illinois Archives, record series 1/1/6, boxes 1 and 2) regularly spelled his name correctly after his first meeting. Thus someone carefully "corrected" his name every year for the published version of the board's transactions.

11. Cf. Lusk, *Politics*, 341.

12. I have found no reference to any other African American with a similar appointment during the 1870s. Peter Clark of Cincinnati was the first Black appointee to the board of trustees of a state university in Ohio, in 1884, when he became a trustee of Ohio State University (Grossman, *Democratic Party*, 84). Cf. Solberg, *University of Illinois 1867–1894*, 120.

13. BTIIU, *Sixth Report*, 1874, 69, 104, 109–10 and 112.

14. JS, 1874, 70. On Brown and Slade, see SCAR, 970 and 980.

15. CB, July 8, 1873, 4; IO, July 2, 1873, 1.

16. JS, 1874, 260–61.

17. ISJ, February 19, 1874, 4. Also see CCG, March 4, 1874, 6; CT, February 19, 1874, 8.

18. BTIIU, *Sixth Report*, 1873, 154–55.

19. JS, 1879, 385, 389–90.

20. Solberg, *University of Illinois 1867–1894*, 115–32.

21. CCG, September 13, 20, 1876, both 1; CT, September 14, 1876, 1.

22. Solberg, *University of Illinois 1867–1894*, 119, 145–66.

23. BTIIU, *Tenth Report*, 1881, 177, 190, 228; *Eleventh Report*, 1882, 245; *Sixteenth Report*, 1892, 120, 121, 122, passim; *Eighteenth Report*, 1896, 149.

24. "University of Illinois Negro Students," 2, University of Illinois Archives, box 2/9/16.

25. ISR, October 17, 1883, 3; Brown, "Initial Admission," 233–36.

26. CDB, March 29, 30, 1872, both 4; April 3, 1872, 4.

27. CDB, August 18, 1872, 3.

28. For the development of the candidacies for police magistrate, see CB, March 16, 1873, 4; April 1, 6, 12, 13, 1873, all 4.

29. CB, April 13, 1873, 4.

30. CB, April 17, 19, 1873, both 4. Black population figures for Wards 1 through 4 were published in CB, March 1, 1873, 4. On statewide reporting, see, e.g., ISJ, April 17, 1873, 1; CT, April 17, 1873, 8.

31. Secretary of State (Index Division): Executive Section, Register of Justices of the Peace and Police Magistrates, 1873, 8, (ISA, record series 103/077); CB, May 1, 1873, 4; Oberly, *Cairo City Directory*, 103; *Gardner and Gaines Cairo City Directory*, 47.

32. CB, May 2, 1873, 4.

33. E. Foner, *Freedom's Lawmakers*, 236.

34. William Lewis, Jr., was elected a judge in the remarkable, largely Black community of Davis Bend, Mississippi, in 1865 and served for two years. George H. Lee was elected to the inferior court for Charleston County, South Carolina, in 1872. Judges appointed to their positions include Cleveland Moulton, a city court judge in Mobile, Alabama, in 1869; James M. Simms, a judge of the Superior Court of Chatham County, Georgia, in 1870; Macon B. Allen, who became a municipal judge in South Carolina in 1873 (E. Foner, *Freedom's Lawmakers*, 133, 130, 156, 196 and 5; cf. also Smith, *Emancipation*, 194–95). Mifflin Gibbs (84–85) was elected city judge in Little Rock, Arkansas, in November 1873, for a two-year term and is often erroneously identified as the first elected Black judge in the United States (e.g., Simmons, *Men of Mark*, 410). Foner's list is not comprehensive, but the relative rarity of elected judges in the South suggested by his small number is probably correct.

35. The few examples I have found were appointments rather than elections to a judgeship: for example, Robert Morris, Sr., was commissioned as a magistrate for Essex County, Massachusetts, in 1851; George Lewis Ruffin was appointed a municipal judge in Charlestown, Massachusetts, in 1883, which made him "the first negro to obtain a judicial office higher than magistrate in the North." Perry B. Jackson became the first municipal judge in Ohio only in 1942. See Smith, *Emancipation*, 416.

36. This issue is discussed in two articles in CB, June 5, 1873, 2.

37. CB, May 10, 1873, 4. Oberly also insisted, not entirely convincingly, that Bross was innocent of any impropriety concerning this situation.

38. CB, June 5, 1873, 2.

39. CB, June 5, 1873, 4.

40. CB, June 1, 1873, 4.

41. McCaul, *Black Struggle*, 118–22. This was a common but fraudulent charge used by Democrats against the Henry Act, which said nothing about integration of schools in Illinois.

42. CB, September 5, 1874, 2, gives the official minutes of the meeting, which omit any sense of the conflict over the Henry Law. Oberly provided his version of the story in CB, September 6, 1874, 2. That he was under fire well before the convention is clear in CT, August 19, 1874, 8, in an article evaluating the situation in the eighteenth congressional district: "True, there is nothing certain as yet in regard to the nominations. The only men now talked of for Congress are Oberly, of Alexander, and Wasburn, of Williamson. Wasburn has fewer sins to answer for, but promises none of the working ability that Oberly does. Oberly's record in the General Assembly would damage him very much, especially his vote in favor of mixed school[s]." In CB, August 22, 1874, 2, Oberly defended his vote on the act, noting that he had suffered several attacks from various Democratic leaders and newspapers. This issue was still being used against him two years later, CB, October 14, 21, 1876, both 2. See McCaul, *Black Struggle*, 122.

43. See, e.g., CB, June 3, 1873, 4; March 21, 1875, 3; November 7, 1875, 3; April 27, 1877, 3; December 12, 1877, 3.

44. See, e.g., the salary figures in CB, August 8, 1873, 4.

45. See, e.g., CB, May 6, 1875, 3, the reports submitted by the two magistrates for the months of March and April, 1875: Bross had assessed fines totaling $233, but only $5 was actually paid; Bird assessed $169, of which $36 had been collected. See the list of Bird's prisoners who did not pay their fines between June 1, 1873 and June 1, 1875 in CB, July 13, 1875, 2. Fines received for the fiscal year ending April 30, 1875 were Bross: $1,465 and Bird: $991 (CB, June 2, 1875, 3).

46. See the case of Reuben Smith (African American) and Frank Hencamp (White) in CB, March 21, 1875, 3, where Bird convicted Hencamp for hitting Smith with a stone during an argument, even though Hencamp claimed that Smith had attempted to strike him first.

47. DCB, November 29, 1878, 4.

48. CB, January 8, 1875, 3.

49. Cf. CB, April 9, 1875, 3; May 6, 1875, 3.

50. CB, July 8, 1875, 3.

51. CB, September 18, 1875, 3.

52. CB, May 28, 1875, 3.

53. Lantz, *Community*, 68–71, discusses the negative effects of Cairo's extensive areas of saloons, illegal gambling, and prostitution, which did foster crime in the city. He notes that city officials normally allowed these establishments to operate largely unimpeded by the police, who arrested mostly the drunk and disorderly and ordered only occasional raids, primarily for appearances' sake (apparently focusing on Black establishments more often than on those owned by Whites). The city charged annual license fees for saloons, and these became the cornerstone of Cairo's annual operating budget.

54. CB, March 21, 25, 1875, both 3.

55. CB, October 24, 1875, 3; March 6, 1875, 3; April 29, 1875, 3; October 7, 9, 1875, both 3; December 12, 1875, 3.

56. CB, January 28, 1876, 3.

57. CB, September 22, 1875, 3; November 7, 10, 1875, both 3.

58. See, e.g., CB, June 23, 1875, 3.

59. CB, July 21, 1875, 3.

60. See CB, July 8, 1875, 3. Cf. CB, February 20, 1878, 3, where police officers refused to accept the validity of a trial by Comings, because Bird was the judge on duty that day.

61. CB, July 30, 31, 1873, 4; August 1, 1873, 4.

62. CB, August 1, 1873, 4.

63. CB, August 6, 7, 12, 13, 1873, all 4.

64. CB, August 31, 1873, 3.

65. CB, August 27, 1873, 3.

66. CB, August 30, 31, 1873, both 3.

67. CB, August 31, 1873, 2. In the article, Oberly also expressed opposition to the death penalty in general. Cf. also Oberly's ironic comment about Governor Beveridge and Campbell in CB, September 2, 1873, 3.

68. CB, August 30, 1873, 2.

69. CB, July 3, 1874, 4.

70. CB, July 7, 1874, 2. Oberly expressed what appears to be genuine outrage over this treatment, although he was also happy to characterize it as an example of Republicans' hypocrisy: "It is true Mr. Bird is a negro. His face is black. He does not deny that he belongs to the proscribed race. His attention has been often called to the fact, and he has become a firm believer of the assertion that he has no rights a white man is bound to respect. But, colored and proscribed as Bird is, he is also a man of ability, and a pleasant orator who always talks in a forcible and sensible manner."

71. CB, July 3, 1874, 4.

72. McCaul, *Black Struggle*, 118–25. The law subsequently survived several attempts to weaken it or repeal it. See Bird's letter denouncing two such attempts, CB, January 21, 1875, 3.

73. Lantz, *Community*, 28–40.

74. CDB, July 31, 1872, 4; CB November 6, 1873, 2; cf., October 15, 1873, 2.

75. CB, June 21, 1874, 4, and July 7, 1874, 2; July 30, 1875, 3; August 7, 1875, 3; August 19, 1875, 2; April 6, 20, 1876, both 2, April 30, 1876, 3. Most descriptions of the school curriculum are found in complaints against it.

76. See CB, October 30, 1875, 3: "Mrs. Ella Granger has introduced phonography into the high school, and also into the colored grammar school of this city. Those of the pupils in both departments who have taken hold of the study, seem to be greatly pleased with it, and manifest much interest in it."

77. See CR, May 15, 1873, 2, for a description of the first public examinations of the students at the "colored school." Alvord and members of the board attended part of the ceremonies, and Rev. William Jackson and Bird were the primary speakers of the day.

78. CB, July 22, 1874, 4.

79. See CB, June 21, 1874, 4; April 20, 1876, 2; April 29, 1876, 3; April 30, 1876, 3; December 5, 1877, 3. Opponents to Alvord's program included, for a while, John Oberly, CB, July 7, 1874, 2, but Oberly eventually changed his mind, CB, February 21, 1877, 3.

80. CB, April 27, 1876, 3.

81. CB, February 22, 1877, 3.

82. CB, April 22, 1876, 3; September 7, 1879, 4.

83. See CB, April 8, 1877, 3, for a general listing of teacher salaries. The four Black teachers are not distinguished here, but even if they were given the lowest pay grade here ($240), they were joined by four White teachers. Robert Pinn, the principal of the school from 1876, almost certainly was paid more than the minimum.

84. CB, July 22, 1874, 4.

85. CB, July 30, 1875 3.

86. CB, April 27, 1876, 3. On McBride at Oswego, see Pope, *History*, 287. On the impact of the Oswego Normal School on American education, see Hollis, *Contribution*, 15–38. Of note is the school's emphasis on education for the poor.

87. These figures are the basis for an attack on McBride in a letter by Mrs. A. Harrell in CB, May 9, 1876, 3.

88. See McBride's response to Harrell in CB, May 13, 1876, 3. For other attacks, cf. April 28, 1876, 2; April 30, 1876, 3. On McBride's departure, CB, August 29, 1876, 3. See Pope, *History*, 287.

89. On Pinn at Oberlin, see Oberlin's list of African American students at Oberlin College Archives, "Minority Student Records: Addendum to the 'Catalogue and Record of Colored Students,'" http://www2.oberlin.edu/archive/oresources/minority/addendum_record.html.

90. CB, February 21, 1877, 3; March 21, 1877, 3.

91. DCB, November 15, 1879, 4; June 5, 1881, 4.

92. CB, February 21, 1877, 3.

93. CB, March 21, 1877, 3.

94. CB, March 29, 1877, 3.

95. CB, December 5, 6, 1877, both 3. At the main reception for Cullom that evening, Bird led a delegation of local African American leaders to meet with the governor and gave a short address on behalf of the town's Black citizens.

96. DCB, May 22, 1878, 4.

97. CDB, August 24, 1871, 4; September 14, 1871, 4.

98. DCB, May 23, 1878, 4.

99. DCB, May 24, 1878, 4. A blistering attack on Smith by J. T. Allen, an African American citizen of Cairo, was published in CDB, September 19, 1871, 4, in which Allen also accused Smith of being under the influence of certain White leaders.

100. DCB, June 4, 1878, 4.

101. CB, April 4, 5, 7, 10, 1878, all 3.

102. DCB, June 5, 1881, 4; November 11, 1882, 4.

103. CB, November 5, 8, 1873, both 3.

104. ISJ, June 17, 1874, 4; CT, June 9, 1874, 5; CB, August 12, 1874, 4. William Scott, still unable to break into the party leadership, once again was named an alternate to the latter conventions.

105. CB, October 12, 22, 1874, both 2; November 1, 1874, 2.

106. CB, October 28, 1874, 1.

107. IO, October 30, 1874 1; CB, October 28, 1874, 4; October 29, 1874, 2.

108. CB, October 30, 1874, 4.

109. See CB, November 4, 1874, 1; November 6, 1874, 4; and November 7, 1872, 4.

110. Du Bois, *Black Reconstruction in America*, 591–94; E. Foner, *Reconstruction*, 519–27, 549–54.

111. Du Bois, *Black Reconstruction in America*, 681–93; E. Foner, *Reconstruction*, 557–63.

112. CB, July 21, 1875, 3; April 20, 1875, 2; April 21, 1875, 3.

113. CB, May 24, 1876, 3; June 25, 28, 1876, both 3; July 6, 1876, 3.

114. CB, July 18, 20, 23, 28, 1876, all 3; August 3, 1876, 3. September 6, 10, 14, 16, 30, 1876, all 3; October 8, 1876, 2; October 12, 14, 25, 1876, all 3; November 3, 1876, 3; CT, September 14, 1876, 1.

115. E. Foner, *Reconstruction*, 575–83; Du Bois, *Black Reconstruction in America*, 691–94.
116. CB, November 11, 1876, 2. For the 1872 returns, see CB, November 3, 1876, 3.
117. DCB, June 23, 28, 1878, both 2. Gladney and Scott also were delegates to the congressional convention.
118. DCB, July 16, 1878, 2, 4; July 17, 1878, 4; July 20, 27, 1878, both 2; cf. June 30, 1878, 2.
119. DCB, July 16, 1878, 2; cf. July 25, 1878, 2. On Bird's campaigning, see, e.g., DCB, August 3, 1878, 4; November 3, 1880, 4.
120. CT, December 14, 1878, 2; DCB, November 7, 9, 1878, both 4.
121. CT, December 14, 1878, 2; ISR, December 19, 1878, 2; January 5, 1879, 2; DCB, December 19, 1878, 4.
122. CB, March 3, 10, 1877, both 3.
123. CB, March 16, 1877, 3.
124. CB, March 21, 1877, 3; April 6, 1877, 3.
125. CB, April 8, 1877, 3.
126. CB, April 18, 1877, 3.
127. CB, November 8, 10, 1877, both 3.
128. See DCB, June 10, 1877, 3; August 10, 1878, 4; January 10, 1879, 4.
129. CB, May 17, 1877, 3; June 5, 1877, 2; June 7, 10, 1877, both 3.
130. DCB, July 19, 1878, 1; July 1, 1879, 4.
131. Andrews, *Masonic Abolitionists*, 109–10; CB, October 18, 1877, 3; CG, January 5, 1884, 1. See his annual report to the lodge in *Condensed Report of the Twelfth Annual Communication*, 44–48. In succeeding years, Bird had a long dispute with the Grand Lodge over whether he owed them $106 from his term as Grand Master. At the October 1884 annual meeting, the leadership held a trial in Bird's absence and with no real defense provided in his place, at which they found him guilty and expelled him from the Masons (*Proceedings of the Eighteenth Annual Communication*, 21–27, 37–39). However, Bird was back in the full graces of the lodge at least by the annual meeting of October 1887, where he acted as the grand marshal in the installation ceremonies of the new lodge officers for the coming year (*Proceedings of the Twenty-First Annual Communication*, 47). His tombstone bears the Masonic emblem, indicating that he spent the rest of his life in the organization.
132. For 1871, see above, chap. 3, n52. ISJ, December 3, 1873, 4. CB, November 23, 1873, 3. Cf. NR, December 10, 1873, 4 (the Illinois delegation chosen at the convention did not attend the national convention in Washington). Bird also addressed a Convention of Colored Men of Southern Illinois in Du Quoin in May 1876 (CB, February 9, 1876, 3).

133. CB, February 20, 1876, 3. Accounts of each day's proceedings appear in the *Nashville Daily American* (later the *Nashville Tennessean*), April 5–9, 1876, all 4, with editorials on 2. The latter are largely friendly but dismissive of the convention's significance.

134. NDA, April 6, 1876, 4.

135. NDA, April 8, 1876, 4; CB, April 11, 1876, 3. Pinchback would visit Cairo twice early in 1878, on his way to and from Chicago, where he spoke at a celebration of the anniversary of the Fifteenth Amendment, both times meeting with Bird and his colleagues. On April 30, his second visit, Pinchback toured the public schools before giving a well-attended address in the evening at the Atheneum. The *Bulletin* reported that the large audience included both Blacks and Whites and that the speech was well received (CB, March 27, 1878, 3; March 30, 3; May 1, 3).

136. CB, February 9, 1875, 3.

137. CB, June 18, 1875, 3. Bird was also involved in the Free Benevolent Sons of America: CDB, July 28, 1871, 4.

138. CB, September 21, 1875, 3.

139. CB, November 6, 1875, 3.

140. CB, March 23, 1878, 3.

141. CB, September 6, 24, 1876, both 2. Cyrus's name disappears after December 27, 1876.

142. CB, June 1, 1877, 2; April 24, 1878, 3.

143. DCB, August 11, 1878, 4.

144. C. S. Smith, *History*, 115–16; Flood and Hamilton, *Lives of Methodist Bishops*, 765–66; CR, June 8, 1876, 2; August 31, 1876, n.p.; September 21, 1876, 2 and 4; January 11, 1877, 7; February 1, 1877, 2; July 12, 1877, 4.

145. E.g., CR, January 4, 1877, 6; March 1, 1877, 6; March 8, 1877, 3.

146. On the epidemic in Mississippi, see Nuwer, *Plague among the Magnolias*.

147. On this week in Vicksburg, see Bloom, *Mississippi Valley's*, 115–16. Cf. also Nuwer, *Plague among the Magnolias*, 73–74.

148. DCB, September 7, 1878, 4; CES, September 6, 1878, 1; Bloom, *Mississippi Valley's*, 116. Green was one of fourteen doctors out of thirty-eight in Vicksburg who died while treating patients during the epidemic. Although segregated in a separate paragraph from the other martyred doctors, the surviving physicians paid a modest tribute to Green in a letter published in the *Vicksburg Herald*: "Dr. A. R. Green, a colored man, did good work for many days, and then was numbered with the dead." Quoted in Power, *Epidemic of 1878*, 144–46.

149. Ironically, on the same page that contains the report of the telegrams to Bird, DCB published an article insisting that fear of a yellow fever plague in Cairo is

totally unfounded. Five days later, on September 12, Thomas Nally, the editor of the *Bulletin*, and Isaac Mulkey, one of its typesetters, were the first two citizens to die in the epidemic in Cairo. The paper suspended its operations from September 13 until November 1, and Oberly and his family left town. DCB, November 3, 1878, 4.

150. CES, September 14, 1878, 4; DCB, November 2, 1878, 4.

151. CES was the leading Republican paper in town. Only a few issues of it have survived, primarily a set of the papers published during the epidemic of 1878. These copies are probably the set given to John Lansden by the *Sun*'s editor shortly after the epidemic and were still in his possession in 1910 when he wrote his history of Cairo (Lansden, *History of the City of Cairo*, 124).

152. Lansden, *History of the City of Cairo*, 122–26; CES, November 11, 1878, 1, and DCB, November 2, 12, 1878, both 4, the latter of which places the death toll at fifty-eight.

5. "Beware of Such Men"

1. On McKeaig's life, see CC, April 29, 1897.

2. See CB, August 21, 1874, 2.

3. In 1871, the city had hired four African American workers, while the school board had hired two Black janitors, CDB, September 13, 1871, 4. John Gladney had a contract during the early 1870s hauling garbage and lumber for the city, CDB, May 9, 1872, 4; July 13, 1872, 4; June 22, 1873, 4.

4. CB, June 25, 1876, 3.

5. DCB, January 24, 1879, 4; February 4, 1879, 4.

6. DCB, March 11, 1879, 4.

7. DCB, March 2, 1879, 4.

8. DCB, March 11, 1879, 4.

9. DCB, March 11, 1879, 4; March 7, 1879, 4.

10. DCB, March 25, 1879, 4; July 28, 1880, 4.

11. DCB, March 25, 1879, 4.

12. DCB, April 17, 1879, 4.

13. DCB, June 19, 1879, 4.

14. DCB, July 2, 1879, 4; ORPO, 1879: 31; cf. McKeaig's comments in DCB, March 12, 1879, 4.

15. DCB, July 1, 1879, 4.

16. DCB, August 5, 1879, 4. More general White Republican opposition to the appointment of Black Republicans to office is seen in DCB, March 12, 1879, 4.

17. DCB, April 24, 1879, 4. On the conference, see *Proceedings of the National Conference*.

18. On Barnett, see Finkelman, *Encyclopedia of African American History*, 1:137–38.

19. On the Exoduster movement, see Painter, *Exodusters*; Jack, *St. Louis*.

20. On the reasons for the movement, see Painter, *Exodusters*, 187–94; Jack, 1–25.

21. *Proceedings of the National Conference*, 5–6.

22. Painter, *Exodusters*, 216–20; *Proceedings of the National Conference*, 19–20.

23. NDA, May 9, 1879, 1. See *Proceedings of the National Conference*, 32–33.

24. *Proceedings of the National Conference*, 95–96.

25. Two articles in NDA, May 9, 1879, 2; May 10, 1879, 2.

26. *Proceedings of the National Conference*, 35, 38.

27. *Proceedings of the National Conference*, 94–96.

28. *Proceedings of the National Conference*, 65–67.

29. *Proceedings of the National Conference*, 100–105.

30. DCB, October 21, 1879, 2; ISJ, October 17, 1879, 3. The *Bulletin's* editor, now Mose B. Harrell, Oberly's former nemesis, used the address to bash the Republicans. Harrell's editorship from November 1878 to April 1880 (DCB, November 9, 1878, 2; April 20, 1880, 2; April 21, 1880, 4) moved the paper toward a more racist position, but he was kept somewhat in check by its publisher E. A. Burnett, a longtime associate of Oberly's who had bought the newspaper from Oberly. The continuing support for Bird in the paper during this period is certainly due to Burnett.

31. CT, January 28, 1880, 2; DCB, January 30, 1880, 4.

32. DCB, January 31, 1880, 4; *Sun* quoted in February 1, 1880, 4. Cf. DCB, July 28, 1880, 4.

33. DCB, May 29, 1880, 4; June 6, 1880, 4. The *Bulletin's* new editor, Ernest H. Thielecke, continued to "support" Bird just to attack the Republicans. DCB was not above misrepresenting Bird's political career to do so (July 20, 1880, 4; November 2, 1880, 4).

34. DCB, June 25, 1880, 4; July 13, 1880, 4; IO, August 6, 1880, 1.

35. DDRep, April 21, 1880, 3.

36. IO, July 9, 1880, 6.

37. Cf. MG, July 23, 1880, 5; CT, July 22, 1880, 2; ISJ, July 21, 1880, 2.

38. ISJ, July 21, 1880, 5; July 22, 1880, 3; CT, July 21, 1880, 1, 4.

39. ISJ, July 22, 1880, 3; CT, July 22, 1880, 2.

40. ISJ, July 22, 1880, 3.

41. CT, July 23, 1880, 4.

42. CT, July 23, 1880, 4.

43. DCB, July 28, 1880, 4.
44. DCB, March 15, 1879, 4.
45. ISR, June 11, 1880, 1. Cf. DCB, June 10, 1880, 1; June 11, 1880, 4.
46. DCB, July 27, 1880, 4.
47. CT, October 6, 1880, 6; DCB, October 30, 1880, 4. On Bradley, see CCons, November 18, 1882, 1; and Belles, "Black Press in Illinois," 348.
48. This is the version of the meeting found in CT, October 6, 1880, 6. IO's account, October 6, 1880, 3, is startlingly different and does not mention the negative reaction to Bird's speech or Oberly. IO appears to have been more sympathetic to Black members of the party and was apparently less interested in describing such controversies.
49. See the responses to a series of articles printed in the *Cairo Evening News*, a Republican paper, in DCB, October 17, 19, 1880, both 4; October 20, 1880, 1. The *News* insisted that Bird was "working for the success of the Democratic state ticket, notwithstanding his statement to the contrary." ISJ, November 1, 1880, 4, accused Oberly of offering Bird a clerkship for his support.
50. DCB, October 12, 1880, 4.
51. DCB, October 21, 1880, 4.
52. CT, October 29, 1880, 3; IO, October 29, 1880, 3. See also DCB, October 30, 1880, 4, which reported (perhaps not convincingly) that the Cairo meeting had few attendees.
53. ISJ, November 1, 1880, 2. On page 4, the ISJ editor repudiated Bird as well.
54. RA is quoted in DCB, October 30, 1880, 2.
55. DCB, November 3, 4, 1880, both 1; November 5, 1880, 4.
56. CT, November 20, 1880, 2 and 7; IO, November 24, 1880, 4.

6. "One of the Most Intelligent Men in the State"

1. The legislative activities of Republican leaders like Senators Henry Blair and George Hoar, as well as Representatives James O'Hara and Henry Cabot Lodge, were one of the reasons African Americans remained hopeful about the party. Jenkins and Peck, *Congress*, 210–59.
2. Beatty, *Revolution Gone Backward*, 31–44; Grossman, *Democratic Party*, 60–63.
3. Grossman, *Democratic Party*, 63–98; Beatty, *Revolution Gone Backward*, 61–91; Garb, *Freedom's Ballot*, 68–75.
4. Materson, *For the Freedom*, 50–55; Grossman, *Democratic Party*, 60–106.
5. Joens, *From Slave*, 112–15.
6. On this issue, see Painter, *Exodusters*, 13–34, who provides a pessimistic (somewhat distorted) view of the political leadership of this period. This

understanding is vigorously opposed by Beatty, *Revolution Gone Backward*, x–xi, and Davis, *We Will Be*, 27–31. Cf. Gaines, *Uplifting the Race*, 41–43; and the descriptions of Black leadership in the 1860s in Litwack, *Been in the Storm*, 524–27.

7. DCB, March 11, 1881, 4.

8. DCB, April 17, 1881, 4.

9. DCB, April 9, 1881, 1

10. DCB, April 26, 1881, 1.

11. Bird was still in the Third Ward in September 1881 (DCB, September 30, 1881, 1). His Fifth Ward address is in *Chas. O. Ebel*, 74.

12. There is a gap in the surviving issues of DCB between October 30 and November 26, 1881, so the details of the election are lost. On the date of the election, cf. DCB, October 14, 1881, 4.

13. Register of Justices of the Peace and Police Magistrates, Alexander County, 1873–85, 9, ISA, record series 103/077.

14. DCB, June 29, 1882, 4; July 11, 1882, 4; January 12, 1883, 4; June 1, 12, 1883, both 4; July 13, 1883, 4; August 2, 12, 1883, both 4; September 23, 1883, 4.

15. DCB, November 15, 1879, 4.

16. DCB, May 23, 1880, 4. See also March 2, 1880, 4; June 4, 1880, 4, where the editor stokes fear that the recently arrived African Americans, presumably those brought by Gladden, are planning massive voter fraud in the fall election.

17. DCB, September 8, 9, and 11, 1880, all 4.

18. DCB, January 22, 1881, 4; June 4, 1881, 4.

19. DCB, December 27, 1879, 4; July 18, 1880, 4; June 10, 1880, 4.

20. DCB, August 3, 1880, 4; July 10, 1879, 3; March 31, 1883, 4.

21. DCB, January 15, 1881, 4.

22. DCB, September 28, 1881, 4; October 9, 1881, 4.

23. DCB, February 10, 1882, 4.

24. DCB, March 26, 1882, 4, identifies Bird and Leonard as the original two partners of the proposed newspaper. But by April 4, Scott had joined the publishing firm; DCB, April 4, 9, 1882, both 4.

25. DCB, April 27, 1882, 4; September 30, 1882, 4; Penn, *Afro-American Press*, 128. There seems to be confusion about the *Cairo Gazette* among journalism historians. Belles, "Black Press in Illinois," 346, listed a *Weekly Gazette* among African American newspapers, with the dates 1862–81, under the editorship of William Scott. This is a ghost. Two newspapers called the *Gazette* existed in Cairo before 1882, but both were White newspapers (1856–64 and 1871–76). See Perrin, *History of Alexander*, 131, 138. J. E. K. Walker, "Promised Land," 13, merged material about the actual *Gazette* of the 1880s into a description of these older newspapers, while several other sources, making the same mistake,

now erroneously name the *Cairo Gazette* as the first African American newspaper in Illinois.

26. DCB, February 4, 11, 13, 1883, all 4. No issues of the *Cairo Gazette* or the *Three States* survive. Our knowledge of their contentious relationship comes only from comments in DCB, April 30, 1882, 4, June 2, 1882, 4; September 1, 1882, 4.

27. On Charles, see DCB, October 27, 1880, 1; April 26, 1882, 4; June 16, 1882, 4; On James, see November 7, 1880, 4; August 29, 1880, 4; October 10, 13, 1880, both 4; June 21, 1882, 4. On Thomas's improved status among African Americans, note July 16, 1882, 4, indicating that Thomas had appointed a few Black postmasters in some small towns and Scott's critique of Thomas's patronage appointments.

28. DCB, June 18, 20, 21, 1882, all 4.

29. DCB, June 23, 25, 1882, both 4; June 27, 1882, 1, 4.

30. See DCB, June 29, 30, 1882, both 4; BP, June 29, 1882, 1.

31. CT, July 14, 1882, 2; July 15, 6. Scott is mistakenly called "Jim Scott" throughout the account.

32. DCB, July 14, 15, 16, 19, 1882, all 4.

33. ISJ, August 10, 1882, 4.

34. DCB, November 11, 1882, 4; March 2, 30, 31, 1883, all 4; May 10, 1883, 4; August 17, 1883, 4.

35. DCB, November 16, 1882, 4; cf. WB, January 27, 1883, 2, which assumes Leonard was the editor.

36. DCB, March 20, 1883, 4; December 7, 1883, 3. For a while, Scott made the *Gazette* a daily paper, one of the first African American dailies, but the pace and cost proved unsustainable. By September 1885, the paper had reverted back to a weekly format, in which it continued until its demise in the early 1890s. Cf. CG, September 19, 1885, 1; CDG, November 30, 1892, 1.

37. BTIIU, *Tenth Report*, 1881, 220–33. See references to Bird (misspelled Byrd) on 220 and 230.

38. CDG, December 11, 1883, 1; DCB, December 19, 1883, 3.

39. The appointment is still mentioned by Black columnist Roscoe Simmons in CT, January 21, 1951, 175.

40. CT, June 26, 1958, 18 (the paper, unaware of Bird, calls Richard Harewood, the new trustee, "the first Negro to be nominated by either party for a state-wide office in Illinois"); November 22, 1985, 46. The university was very slow to support African American students; see Williamson, "Snail-like Progress," 116–18.

41. On Lancaster, cf. DCB, May 5, 1880, 3; September 30, 1881, 1.

42. DCB, May 15, 16, 1883, both 4. The Fifth Ward was smaller than the other wards but had the highest percentage of Blacks (43%); see Wheeler, "Together in Egypt," 114.

43. DCB, May 16, 1883, 4.

44. ISJ, October 16, 1883, 7, and ISR, October 16, 1883, 3. On the convention and Thomas's role in it, see Joens, *From Slave*, 85–92.

45. For the second day, see ISR, October 17, 1883, 3. The October 17 issue of ISJ is lost. The Democratic ISR downplayed the overall unity of the convention and focused on the Cairo resolutions, portraying the independents as heroes fighting corruption among the Republicans. See ISJ's response, October 18, 1883, 4. See also Joens, *From Slave*, 89–91; Mouser, *Black Gambler's World*, 50–54.

46. ISR, October 17, 1883, 3. On co-ops, also see DCB, June 26, 1879, 1; July 29, 1883, 4.

47. ISR, October 17, 1883, 3; ISJ, October 18, 1883, 4.

48. ISR, November 24, 1883; CC, August 26, 1886, 4; August 30, 1888, 4.

49. John W. and Egbert appear in GSLD, 1883, 148, living at 1406 Morgan, the Tanners' address, 1074. This George Tanner should not be confused with the Tanner who taught in the Cairo Black school and who opposed Bird politically within the city.

50. *Seventh Census of the United States*, Schedule 1—Free Inhabitants in Penn Township, Pennsylvania, July 20, 1850, 22. Annie identified Elizabeth as her sister in the *Detroit Plaindealer*, September 5, 1890, 4, and January 30, 1891, 5.

51. An Elizabeth Tanner is listed as a delegate from Allegheny County along with Samuel and Arena Venerable to the National Emigration Convention of 1854 (*Proceedings of the National Emigration Convention of Colored People Held at Cleveland, Ohio 1854*, 16). If this is our Elizabeth, then she was married before August of that year.

52. *Census of Canada West 1861*, Windsor, County of Essex, District 2, 1861, 32.

53. George and his restaurant first appear in GSLD, 1874, 872. The restaurant appears also in GSLD, 1877, 1196; 1878, 1160; and 1880, 1302.

54. DCB, March 10, 1883, 4.

55. GSLD, 1883, 148.

56. *Sixteenth Census of the United States*, Population Schedule, Wayne County, Michigan, Detroit City, Ward 6, S.D. 13, E. D. No. 84–295, Sheet No 47A, April 6, 1940. John W. spelled his last name Byrd in Detroit.

57. GSLD, 1884, 153; 1885, 157; 1887, 156.

58. DCD, 1889, 350.

59. Cf. CB, June 1, 1877, 3.

60. Lantz, *Community*, 36–48, 101–5.

61. In the 1873–74 school year, the budget for the schools was $20,266, which included the $4,311 for expanding the African American school—thus $15,995 for regular operations (see CB, July 22, 1874, 4). The 1874–75 budget was $16,840 (CB, July 30, 1875, 3). In both years, the amount paid in teacher salaries was just

about $13,000. The 1878–79 budget shrank to $9,646, with $7,836 paid for teacher salaries (DCB, July 6, 1879, 4).

62. See DCB, January 31, 1879, 4, which argued that there was a great need for an additional school building and an increased budget. It gives a brief history of the annual tax assessments between 1866 and 1879.

63. Five African American teachers taught at the Black school during the 1878–79 academic year (CES, September 24, 1878, 1). The teachers for 1879–80 and 1881–82 are listed in DCB, January 11, 1880, 4; DCB, July 21, 1881, 4.

64. Perrin, *History of Alexander*, 194.

65. On the long-term problem of seep water in Cairo, see Lantz, *Community*, 132–39.

66. The clearest expression of Reverend Ricks's demands is found in DCB, March 11, 1883, 4. A description of the schools in DCB, March 10, 1883, 4, shows that classes in the Black school went only up to seventh grade by that time. There had been a high school class in the school during the late 1870s; cf. DCB, November 15, 1879, 4.

67. See DCB, March 9, 10, 13, 14, 15, 18, 20, and 22, 1883, all 4. See also Hays, "African American Struggle," 282–84; and Wheeler, "Together in Egypt," 125–26.

68. DCB, March 10, 11, 18 and 27, 1883, all 4; and April 6, 7, 1883, both 3.

69. Rittenhouse, *Maud*, 175.

70. DCB, March 20, 27, 1883, both 4.

71. DCB, July 21, 1883, 4; August 16, 17, 1883, both 4.

72. DCB, November 25, 1882, 4; January 23, 1883, 4; February 6, 7, 14, 22, 1883, all 4.

73. See DCB, March 13, 1883, 4. Leonard and Scott defiantly responded to Barton in the *Cairo Gazette*, quoted in DCB, March 22, 1883, 4. Leonard eventually moved to Washington, D.C., in mid-1884, where he got a job at the Government Printing Office (WB, June 21, 1884, 3; August 9, 1884, 4).

74. DCB, April 4, 1883, 4.

75. DCB, January 12, 1884, 4. ORPO, 1885, 702, lists Bird's salary as $400, certainly part time. Only two of the five employees at the post office worked full time, but the two other White part-time workers made $650 per year.

76. DCB, January 19, 1884, 3.

77. DCB, January 25, 1884, 4.

78. DCB, June 12, 1883, 4.

79. DCB, April 6, 1884, 3; May 25, 1884, 3.

80. ISJ, April 6, 1884, 4; CG, April 26, 1884, 1; IO, April 17, 1884, 1, 2; CT, April 17, 1884, 2; Joens, *From Slave*, 93–95.

81. DCB, April 6, 1884, 3; June 19, 21, 1884, both 4. The DCB itself attacked Scott and his followers, March 27, 1884, 3 and 4; March 28, 1884, 3.

82. Grossman, *Democratic Party*, 107–15; Plummer, *Lincoln's Rail-Splitter*, 185–86.

83. CC, July 22, 1886, 4; July 29, 1886, 5.

84. CC, January 14, 1886, 5.

85. Munn had been a Republican colleague of Bird from 1870 until January 1875, when he moved to Chicago (cf. BP, January 8, 1875, 1).

86. A. M. Green to Governor Richard J. Oglesby, February 3, 1885. Richard James Oglesby (3rd term) Correspondence, ISA, record series 101/020. Green mentions the penitentiary position in his letter. John J. Bird to Governor Richard J. Oglesby, February 11, 1885. Oglesby (3rd term) Correspondence, ISA, record series 101/020. The relative modesty evident in this letter seems confirmed by an earlier letter Bird sent to Governor John M. Hamilton in 1883, in which he recommended Warren Wims, a colleague in Cairo, for a position at the Chester Penitentiary, even though Bird was much more qualified for such a job than Wims. John J. Bird to Governor John M. Hamilton, November 22, 1883. John M. Hamilton Correspondence, ISA, records series 101/019.

87. Joens, *From Slave*, 109–12.

88. IO April 3, 1885, 3; Joens, *From Slave*, 112–15; Dale, "'Social Equality,'" 311–39.

89. On Wheeler and Harrison, see Joens, *From Slave*, 102.

90. See John J. Bird to Governor Richard J. Oglesby, August 14, 1885, which includes the letter from Mitchell. Oglesby responded to Bird on August 22. See Oglesby (3rd term) correspondence, ISA, record series 101/029. Bird took the opportunity at the beginning of his letter to remind the governor that he was still interested in a state job.

91. ISJ, October 16, 1885, 4.

92. CC, October 15, 1885, 5.

93. ISJ, October 16, 17, 18, 1885, all 4; CT, October 16, 1885, 2; October 17, 1885, 6.

94. ISJ, October 17, 1885, 4.

95. Joens, *From Slave*, 117–23.

96. CC, July 22, 1886, 4; July 29, 1886, 5.

7. "More Entitled to Recognition than Any Other One of His Race"

1. Senechal de la Roche, *In Lincoln's Shadow*, 56, 60, 79–82; Black voters in the First Ward may have impacted the ward's alderman elections, see 79. Compare these figures with 1890 Cairo's Black population of 3,689 out of 10,324 (35.7%) and 1900's 5,000 of 12,566 (39.7%), *Compendium of the Eleventh Census: 1890*, 544; *Compendium of the Twelfth Census:1900*, 613. On Springfield's Democratic

leaning, see election results in ISR November 6, 1884, 3; November 8, 1888, 1; November 9, 1892, 1, 8.

2. Anderson, *Education of Blacks*, 33–57; Gaines, *Uplifting the Race*, 67–96; Gates, Jr, *Stony the Road*, 55–157.

3. Beatty, *Revolution Gone Backward*, 169–72.

4. Senechal de la Roche, *In Lincoln's Shadow*, 16–17; 66–73.

5. CC, September 2, 1886, 5. On the Cleveland guidelines, see Grossman, *Democratic Party*, 121–22.

6. CC, January 13, 1887, 1.

7. CT, February 19, 1887, 1; ISJ, February 16, 1887, 2. For Bird's two appointments, JS, 1888, 48, 278–79, 343–44, and Statement: Expenses of the Thirty-Fifth General Assembly, viii and xiii.

8. Emmerson, *Blue Book*, 112; DCSSC, 1886, 276.

9. SCDSCG, 1887, 46; DCSSC, 1888, 44, 308.

10. See, e.g., its criticism of Senator M. S. Quay (SC, August 8, 1891, 1); and President Harrison's State Department (SC, August 22, 1891, 1).

11. Penn, *Afro-American Press*, 256, 258. Cf. also the DDR, May 11, 1895, 1; ISR, October 28, 1888, 1.

12. DCSSC, 1888, 44, 308, lists only Bird as editor. ISR, January 4, 1889, 3, mentions R. O. Lee, "who is at present publishing the *State Capital*," and S. B. Turner, "late of the *State Capital*." Later in the year, the *Directory of the City of Springfield Illinois*, 44 and 294, once again has both as editors. Turner was the sole editor in 1890 and 1891, see *Springfield Duplex City Directory 1890–91*, 461; 1891–92, 539.

13. Turner moved back to Chicago in the late 1890s and eventually served six terms in the Illinois House from the First District (between 1915 and 1927); cf. Penn, *Afro-American Press*, 256, 258; Emmerson, *Blue Book*, 112.

14. CT, September 23, 1887, 2; IO, July 31, 1888, 3; ISR, June 29, 1888, 3.

15. On the Fifer rally, see CT, August 23, 1888, 3; IO, August 23, 1888, 5; CC, August 23, 1888, 4. CT is almost certainly wrong in suggesting that Bird and Fifer met in Cairo in August 1863 when the wounded Fifer was transferred from a ship to a train there on his way home. No other paper reports this incident. Fifer had different memories of an encounter with an African American in Cairo, which does not seem to be Bird. See *"Private Joe" Fifer*, 69–71. Bird's participation in other political events is discussed in ISJ, May 31, 1887, 4; February 23, 1888, 4; IO, August 22, 1888, 3; ISJ, August 23, 1888, 4; CC, August 30, 1888, 1, 4; ISR, October 28, 1888, 1.

16. ISJ, May 6, 1887, 4; ISR, February 18, 1888, 1.

17. ISR, January 4, 1889, 3. CT, January 31, 1889, 6, describes a delegation that called on Fifer urging his appointment of Bird. IO, January 25, 1889, 12,

supported Bird over Ferdinand Barnett for the appointment to the penitentiary position.

18. Senator Shelby Cullom to Governor Joseph Fifer, January 9, 1889, Fifer Correspondence, ISA, record series 101/021.

19. Robert Allyn to Governor Joseph Fifer, January 7, 1889, Fifer Correspondence, ISA, record series 101/021.

20. John J. Bird to Governor Joseph Fifer, January 6, 1889, Fifer Correspondence, ISA, record series 101/021.

21. John J. Bird to Governor Joseph Fifer, March 18, 1889, Fifer Correspondence, ISA, record series 101/021.

22. R. H. Obryan to Governor Joseph Fifer, April 1, 1889; N. B Thistlewood to Governor Joseph Fifer, August 10, 1889; Alexander Lane to Governor Joseph Fifer, September 3, 1889; William N. Butler to Governor Joseph Fifer, September 11, 1889; E. W. Moore to Governor Joseph Fifer, October 15, 1889; Austin Carter to Governor Joseph Fifer, October 6, 1889; Peoria Illinois Fifer Republican Club Executive Committee to Governor Joseph Fifer, November 3, 1889; John R. Lynch to Governor Joseph Fifer, October 12, 1889, Fifer Correspondence, ISA, record series 101/021.

23. John J. Bird to Governor Joseph Fifer, August 12, 1889, Fifer Correspondence, ISA, record series 101/021.

24. DCD, 1890, 270; *Twelfth Census of the United States*, Supervisor's District No. 116, Enumeration District 94, Wayne County, Schedule 1—Wayne County, City of Detroit, MI 9th Ward, sheet 1, 661, 1900. John appears in *Twelfth Census of the United States,* Supervisor's District No. 11, Enumeration District 86, Sangamon County, Springfield City, IL sheet 15, 302, June 12, 1900.

25. J. V. Cheneworth to Governor Joseph Fifer, September 27, 1889, Fifer Correspondence, ISA, record series 101/021.

26. On the value of Annie's estate, see the DFP, November 12, 1903, 7.

27. IO, October 8, 1889, 3.

28. Ap, October 12, 1889, 1 and 2; NYA, October 12, 1889, 2. Cf. IO, July 28,1891, 7. Wright would become one of the most important Black politicians in Chicago from the 1890s to the 1920s. See Branham, "Transformation," 51–61, 165–235.

29. ISJ, October 9, 1889, 4. On the impact of the four Illinois African American conventions during the 1880s, see Joens, "Illinois Colored Conventions," 305–24.

30. Alexander, *Army of Lions*, 23–29; Thornbrough, "National Afro-American League, 1887–1908," 494–500. See Fortune's thoughts on the nature of the league in NYF, June 4, 1887, 2. On the convention, see IO, January 16, 1890, 8; January 17, 1890, 5; January 18, 1890, 3; January 19, 1890, 7. A supportive editorial appeared in IO, January 20, 1890, 4.

31. IO, January 16, 1890, 8.

32. ISR, November 19, 1889, 3; ISJ, November 20, 1889, 4; December 13, 1889, 4; IO, January 16, 1890, 8.

33. IO, January 5, 1890, 7.

34. Alexander, *Army of Lions*, 23–65; Thornbrough, "National Afro-American League, 1887–1908," 494–512. The state league apparently merged into the new organization, IO, July 28, 1891, 7.

35. Bird had written another impassioned letter to Fifer on January 19, 1890, shortly before Fifer acted. Fifer Correspondence, ISA, record series 101/021.

36. Sixth Biennial Report Bureau Labor Statistics, XIII–XIV.

37. CC, February 6, 1890, 4.

38. CT, July 29, 1891, 2.

39. Quoted in ISJ, February 8, 1890, 4.

40. George W. Smith to Governor Joseph Fifer, June 18, 1890. Fifer Correspondence, ISA, record series 101/021.

41. ISJ, September 21, 1890, 5.

42. SC, May 9, 1891, 4, mentions a speech he gave in Springfield and he spoke again at St. David's Emancipation Day celebration, SC, September 26, 1891.

43. SC, August 22, 1891, 4; September 26, 1891, 4.

44. Cf. SC, September 26, 1891, 1 and 4.

45. PSCD, 1904, 87. This is the last directory in which he is identified as a lawyer.

46. ISJ, May 3, 1892, 1

47. PD, May 6, 1892, 1; ISJ, June 1, 1892, 1; ISR, June 1, 1892, 1. Cf. Alexander, *Army of Lions*, 57–59.

48. SC, August 13, 27, 1892, both 4; IO, October 17, 1892, 3; SC, October 29, 1892, 1; November 19, 1892, 4.

49. CT, September 23, 1892, 6; CT, October 5, 1892, 2; October 7, 1892, 2; ISJ, October 10, 1892, 5; IO, October 9, 1892, 2. Bird was back in DuQuoin on November 3. IO, November 4, 1892, 6.

50. ISJ, April 1, 1894, 4; June 17, 1894, 6; September 11, 1894, 4; October 4, 11, 1894, both 5; April 2, 1895, 4; ISR, October 11, 1894, 8.

51. CT, June 5, 1892, 10; Mouser, *For Labor*, 70–78.

52. DFP, July 25, 1892, 1; IJ, September 22, 24, 1892, both 4; IN, September 23, 1892, 2. Both NYT, September 23, 1892, 8, and IJ, September 26, 1892, 4, reported that only about twenty people attended the convention.

53. IF, October 22, 1892, 8; October 29, 1892, 5.

54. IJ, October 20, 1892, 2.

55. IO, June 27, 1893, 13; June 28, 29, 1893, both 7; CT, June 28, 1893, 8. See Mouser, *For Labor*, 78.

56. ISJ, March 1, 1893, 4; ISR, March 18, 1893, 1.

57. On the sales of the paper, see ISR, January 31, 1894, 8. Otis B. Duncan is mentioned in several surviving issues of SC, including January 30, 1892, 1; February 6, 1892, 4; February 27, 1892, 6; August 13, 1892, 1; November 5, 1892, 4. In 1902, he joined the Eighth Infantry Regiment of the Illinois National Guard, an all-African-American unit, and saw brief service in Mexico during the U.S. military's expedition against Pancho Villa in 1916. The Eighth Infantry was sent into action in World War I, where Duncan served as lieutenant colonel, the highest-ranking African American officer in the entire American Expeditionary Forces. He and his unit served with distinction, and he received the Croix de Guerre from the French Army for his service. Editor, "Col. Otis B. Duncan," October 29, 2013, Sangamon County Historical Society, http:// sangamoncountyhistory.org/wp/?p=2333.

58. ISJ, February 1, 1894, 1. Yancey appears to have been a con man and a spectacularly unsuccessful businessman. See ISR, April 11, 1894, 1; IF, July 7, 1894, 8; PWB, February 6, 1897, 4; February 13, 1897, 1; August 6, 1898, 4.

59. ISJ, April 10, 1894, 4; ISR, April 11, 1894, 6.

60. ISR, December 7, 1894, 6.

61. DDR, May 12, 1895, 1.

62. The last time SC appears in PSCD's list of newspapers is 1904, 779. Murray is still listed as its editor, 483.

63. OE, December 14, 1895, 2; and ISJ, December 8, 1895, 2.

64. E.g., ISJ, March 22, 1896, 5; May 11, 1896, 6; CG, December 19, 1896, 1; and OE, October 24, 1896, 2. Other cases occur where it is not clear whether a newspaper is quoting from Bird's *Springfield Republican* or from a commonly cited White paper of the same name from Springfield, Massachusetts.

65. No references to the *Springfield Republican* in 1897 can be definitively attributed to the Illinois paper.

66. DCD, 1889, 350; 1891, 252 (Annie Bird) and 305 (John W. Byrd);1893, 320.

67. The number of stories about Annie in the *Plaindealer* and the *Appeal* contrasts sharply with the single reference to her in the *Cairo Bulletin* during all the years she and John lived there (CB, February 9, 1875, 3, which noted that "Mrs. Bird has been teaching at the Grammar Colored School in place of Miss Nelle Banks, who is sick"). This notice shows that Annie was also active in the Cairo community while John was involved in politics, but her contributions (like those of most women) were not of interest to the city's newspapers. On her visits to St. Louis, see PD, September 20, 1889, 5; October 25, 1889, 5; September 5, 1890, 4; August 25, 1891, 8; SC, October 24, 1891, 4; Ap, October 17, 1891, 1. For Annie's activities with the Willing Workers, see PD, November 20, 1891, 5; and cf. February 7, 1890, 4.

68. Arena's first husband and Annie's father, Samuel Venerable, had died in 1873 (see Bird's eulogy for him in CR, December 25, 1873, 8; and the editor's note on 4). Sometime thereafter, Arena married Inge. She appears in Detroit in PD, December 13, 1889, 5. Already in her late seventies, she stayed actively involved in the African American community, serving, for example, as president of the Helping Hands Society at the Bethel AME Church (PD, July 17, 1891, 5). She also traveled on business, May 15, 1891, 5. In the 1895 DCD, 726, Arena appears as the widow of "Peter H.," a mistake for Patrick. She lived with the Byrds until her death on December 3, 1899, at age eighty-seven (DCD, 1900, 827).

69. PD, January 30, 1891, 5.

70. John J. Bird to Governor Joseph Fifer, January 27, 1891, Fifer Correspondence, ISA, record series 101/021.

71. See the Return of Marriages 1892, 449, Record No. 11529.

72. PD, July 8, 1892, 5, provides the official announcement of the wedding, which mentions Annie, as mother of the groom, but not his father. John W. is described as "one of our most highly esteemed youths of favorite circles," and the coverage of the wedding suggests that Annie and her son had a relatively high status within the Detroit community.

73. Return of Deaths 1894, 368–69, No. 1912. In this record, Laurette's first name is spelled "Loretta."

74. Return of Marriages 1925, 95, Record No. 285965.

75. He died on November 24, 1951, in Detroit. See Michigan, US, Death Records, 1867–1952, Record No. 434242.

76. Cha-Jua, "'Warlike Demonstration': Legalism, Armed Resistance," 67n2.

77. "Appendix: Lynchings in the Northeast, Midwest, and West," in Pfeifer, *Lynching beyond Dixie*, 278.

78. On this movement, see Redkey, *Black Exodus*, esp. 150–251.

79. On the Bush lynching and Woodford's role in the aftermath, see Cha-Jua, "'Cry of the Negro,'" 165–89; and Cha-Jua, "'Warlike Demonstration,'" 591–629.

80. The DDR, May 12, 1895, 1; DH, May 15, 1895, 3.

81. Waldron, "'Lynch-law Must Go!,'" 50–77; Armfield, "Fire on the Prairies," 185–200.

82. IO, August 13, 1895, 2.

83. ISJ, August 8, 1895, 1; IO, August 9, 1895, 1.

84. IO, August 10, 1895, 2. Altgeld's representatives were not very helpful. George Schilling, his leading investigator, blamed the entire riot on the African Americans, referring to them as "the scum of the earth." See ISJ, August 10, 1895, 2; IO, August 25, 1895, 3; CT, August 25,1895, 2.

85. Keiser, "Black Strikebreakers," 313–26. Strike-related violence would again appear in Virden and Pana in 1898–99. See also Hicken, "Virden and Pana," 263–78. No attack similar to that of Spring Valley would occur again in Illinois until the 1908 Springfield Riot.

86. On Buckner's political career, see Branham, "Transformation," 18–20.

87. IO, August 13, 1895, 2.

88. IO, August 17, 1895, 1.

89. IO, September 1, 1895, 1, and September 3, 1895, 8. It seems that Delmargo never stood trial. See MCD, October 11, 1895, 2.

90. IO, November 1, 1895, 1.

91. IO, October 29, 1895, 2.

92. IO, November 2, 1895, 1; November 3, 1895, 11.

93. IO, November 13, 17, 1895, both 2; November 20, 21, 1895, both 1.

94. IO, August 17, 1895, 1; ISR, August 27, 1895, 4.

95. ISJ, September 24, 1895, 5; September 25, 1895, 1–2; IO, September 25, 1895, 1.

96. IO, October 21, 1895, 3.

97. CT, July 10, 1896, 14.

98. IO, July 9, 1896, 15; July 10, 1896, 6.

99. WB, September 11, 1897, 5; IO, November 20, 1897, 16.

100. IR, November 27, 1897, 1.

101. Ap, January 8, 1898, 1. On the convention, see OWH, August 17, 1898, 8; August 18, 1898, 4 and 5; August 19, 1898, 5; OAAS, August 20, 1898, 1; Peavler, "African Americans in Omaha," 345–52.

102. IR, November 27, 1897, 1; December 4, 1897, 1.

103. IR, July 2, 1898, 2; September 3, 10, 1898, both 2; DDR, September 17, 1898, 2.

104. BP, September 29, 1898, 7; November 24, 1899, 5; IR, October 1, 1898, 1, 2, 3.

105. ISR, November 27, 1898, 4; ISJ, November 10, 1899, 5.

106. ISJ, November 10, 1899, 5. On the Eighth Illinois Volunteers, see Goode, *"Eighth Illinois"*; and McCard and Turnley, *History of the Eighth.*

107. BP, November 24, 1899, 5; ISJ, December 3, 1899, 5. The temporary position was a five-day assignment at Camp Lincoln in Springfield. See *Biennial Report of the Adjutant General,* 245.

108. Alexander, *Army of Lions,* 89–134.

109. WB, January 4, 1902, 11; IO, April 8, 1902, 2.

110. DH, October 15, 1903, 4.

111. Cf. Beatty, *Revolution Gone Backward,* 169–70.

112. See the *Springfield Republican* editorials republished in ISJ, February 2, 1896, 3; March 22, 1896, 5. On Bird's support of Cullom, see also February 4, 1896, 5; February 5, 1896, 1 and 2; IO, February 5, 1896, 1.

113. DH, April 1, 1896, 2. Neilson, *Shelby M. Cullom,* 162–70.

114. See the "Republican Party Platform of 1896," American Presidency Project, University of California at Santa Barbara at http://www.presidency.ucsb.edu /ws/index.php?pid=29629.

115. ISJ, June 21, 1896, 5; July 17, 1896, 6; July 24, 1896, 3; August 26, 1896, 3; September 23, 1896, 5; October 7, 1896, 3; October 21, 1896, 3; November 1, 1896, 3.

116. ISJ, April 14, 1897, 6; DH, April 16, 1897, 2; ISJ, May 5, 1897, 1.

117. DH, June 30, 1898, 2; ISR, June 30, 1898, 5; October 15, 1898, 5. John Gladney was also on the reception committee.

118. IR, November 13, 1897, 2; JS, 1896: Statement of Expenses, xv; 1897, 1139.

119. ISJ, July 14, 1898, 6; December 1, 1898, 3.

120. JS, 1899, 4–5.

121. BP, November 24, 1899, 5.

122. Garb, *Freedom's Ballot*, 107–12; 137–53.

123. Wheeler, "Together in Egypt," 126–28; Pimblott, *Faith in Black Power*, 43–52, 219–27.

124. Senechal de la Roche, *In Lincoln's Shadow*, 55–73; Ward, "Specter of Black Labor," 273–76.

125. On Rose's relationship to the African American community, see AC, March 2, 1912, 1.

126. ISJ, February 6, 1900, 1; February 13, 1900, 1–2.

127. ISR, May 29, 1900, 5; ISJ, September 22, 1900, 3; October 19, 1900, 3; ISR, October 19, 1900, 5. Cf. ISJ, July 4, 1900, 6.

128. IF, March 15, 1902, 4; ISJ, January 13, 1905, 6; January 24, 1907, 2; February 22, 1907, 5; ISR, July 2, 1908, 13; February 11, 1909, 12.

129. ISJ, April 20, 1902, 14.

130. ISR, February 2, 1906, 7.

131. ISR, January 30, 1907, 5. On Springfield's corrupt city government, see Senechal de la Roche, *In Lincoln's Shadow*, 73–76.

132. Forum, July 18, 1908, 8; May 22, 1909, 1.

133. JHR, 1903, 1194; 1906, 205; 1907–8, 90.

134. PSCD, 1902, 80 (listed as pension agent); 1904, 87 (lawyer); 1905, 87 (no listing); 1906, 93 (no job indication); 1907, 94 (porter).

135. ISJ, December 21, 1902, 6; Oak Ridge Cemetery Interment Records, vol. 3, 146. The grave was located in Block 4, Range 2, Grave 138. After Augustus's death in 1878, Catherine's stepson Richard A. Green had moved to Vicksburg, where she lived, and practiced medicine until his death in 1890 (see CR, December 23, 1880, 2; Mississippi Wills and Probate Records, Warren County, Administrator's Bonds and Letters, 1890, 97, number 3624). She moved to Springfield shortly thereafter.

136. DFP, October 31, 1903, 12. Vital Statistics Division, Michigan Department of State, Lansing, MI, Transcript of Certificate of Death, Wayne County, Detroit, 1903, Registered No. 4478. John W. signed her death certificate, not John J.

137. On the riot, see Senechal de la Roche, *In Lincoln's Shadow*, 93–157; Crouthamel, "Springfield Race Riot," 164–81.

138. PSCD, 1907, 94; 1908, 251.

139. PSCD, 1910, 101, 116. The *Advance Citizen*, founded in 1894, had become the leading African American newspaper in Springfield by the early 1900s, particularly after the demise of SC in 1904.

140. See *Thirteenth Census of the United States*, Supervisor's District No. 12, Enumeration District No. 155, Sangamon County, Springfield, Illinois, Seventh Ward, Sheet 1, April 15, 1910. This census sheet is filled with errors, including most of Bird's details. On the Sallies, see Forum, July 18, 1908, 8; ISJ, February 16, 1909, 5; PSCD, 1912, 822. On the Sallies's losses in the riot, see ISR, August 21, 1908, 5.

141. ISR, August 4, 1910, 5, 11; ISJ, August 5, 1910, 2.

142. JHR, 1911, 1464; cf. 320.

143. JHR, 1912, 75.

144. ISJ, May 30, 1912, 1, 2, 6; ISR, May 30, 1912, 1, 4.

145. For the story connecting Magee's death to that of Rose, see ISJ, May 30, 1912, 2. A more conventional obituary is in ISR, May 30, 1912, 2.

146. Bird's old friend John Gladney had died in Springfield on March 12, 1908 (ISJ, March 13, 1908, 6).

147. ISR, June 2, 1912, 3.

148. ISR, June 2, 1912, 3; ISJ, June 4, 5, 1912, both 2.

149. Oak Ridge Cemetery Interment Records, vol. 4, 109.

150. JHR, 1912, 78.

151. ISR, June 9, 1912, 12; ISJ, June 9, 1912, 4;

152. JHR, 1911, 617; also 320.

153. For these two, see JHR, 1911, 3, District 45.

154. Mouser, *Black Gambler's World*, 111–14.

155. ISR, June 10, 1912, 11.

156. AC, June 21, 1912, 2.

157. WB, July 6, 1912, 1.

Epilogue

1. CT, January 14, 1951, pt. 3, p. 7 (227); January 21, 1951, pt.3, p. 8 (175). On Simmons, see Kaye, "Colonel Roscoe Conkling Simmons," 79–93.

2. Horney and Keller, "Negro's Two Hundred Forty Years," 435–37.

3. See Hodges and Levene, *Illinois Negro Historymakers*, 23–25; Harris, *Generations of Pride*, 6–8; Burkett, Burkett, and Gates, Jr., *Black Biography, 1790–1950*; Gates Jr. and Higginbotham, *African-American Lives*.

4. Solberg, *University of Illinois 1867–1894* (1968), 120; Bridges, "Equality Deferred" (1981); and Wheeler, "Together in Egypt" (1982). More recently, Hays, "Way Down" (1996) and "African American Struggle" (1997); Joens, *From Slave* (2012); Mouser, *Black Gambler's World* (2014); and Bigham, *On Jordan's Banks* (2015).

5. TAC, March 1, 1889, 1. On the relative impact of the few great national leaders, such as Frederick Douglass, Sojourner Truth, Martin Delany, and others, on individual communities compared with the local leadership, cf. Horton and Flaherty, "Black Leadership," 71.

6. On many of the ideology's problematic aspects in the twentieth century, see Gaines, *Uplifting the Race*, 41–46, 234–60. On its more positive effects, see Pimblott, *Faith in Black Power*, 54–87; Alexander, *Army of Lions*, 262–296. Cf. Garb, *Freedom's Ballot*, 187–220.

Abbreviations

General

AME   African Methodist Episcopal (Church)

ARUI   James Herbert Kelley, ed., *Alumni Record of the University of Illinois.* Urbana: University of Illinois, 1913.

BDW   Boyd, William H., ed., *Boyd's Directory of Washington & Georgetown: Together with a Business Directory of Alexandria, VA.* Washington, DC: Hudson Taylor, 1867–70.

BTIIU   *Report of the Board of Trustees of the Illinois Industrial University.* Springfield, IL: State Journal Printing Office, 1874–80; H. W. Rokker, 1881–85.

BTUI   *Report of the Board of Trustees of the University of Illinois.* Springfield, IL: H. W. Rokker, 1892–96.

DCD   *Detroit City Directory.* Detroit: R. L. Polk, 1889–1900.

DCSSC   *Babeuf's Directory of the City of Springfield and Sangamon County 1886–7.* Springfield, IL: J. Babeuf, 1886, 1888.

GSLD   *Gould's St. Louis Directory.* St. Louis: Gould, 1874–87.

ISA   Illinois State Archives, Springfield, IL.

JHR   *Journal of the House of Representatives of the State of Illinois.* Springfield: Phillips Bros., 1903–1908; Illinois State Journal Co., 1911–12.

JS   *Journal of the Senate of the State of Illinois.* Springfield, IL: State Journal Steam Print, 1873–74; Weber & Co., 1879; Springfield Printing Co., 1888; Edward F. Hartman, 1896; Phillips Bros., 1897–99.

ORPO   *Official Register of the United States Containing a List of Officers and Employés.* Vol. 2, *Post Office Department.* Washington, DC: Government Printing Office, 1879, 1885.

PSCD   *Polk's Springfield City Directory.* Springfield, IL: R. L. Polk, 1898–1912.

SCAR   *Semi-Centennial Alumni Record of the University of Illinois.*
          Urbana, 1918.
SCDSCG   *Springfield City Directory and Sangamon County Gazette.*
          Springfield, IL: Fitzpatrick, 1887.

Newspapers

AC   *Advance Citizen*
Ap   *The Appeal*
BP   *Bloomington Pantagraph*
CB   *Cairo Bulletin*
CC   *Cairo Citizen*
CCG   *Champaign County Gazette*
CCons   *Chicago Conservator*
CD   *Columbus* (KY) *Dispatch*
CDB   *Cairo Daily Bulletin*
CDD   *Cairo Daily Democrat*
CDG   *Champaign Daily Gazette*
CEB   *Cairo Evening Bulletin*
CES   *Cairo Evening Sun*
CG   *Cleveland Gazette*
CR   *Christian Recorder*
CT   *Chicago Tribune*
DCB   *Daily Cairo Bulletin*
DDR   *Decatur Daily Review*
DDRep   *Decatur Daily Republican*
DFP   *Detroit Free Press*
DH   *Decatur Herald*
DMD   *Daily Missouri Democrat* (St. Louis)
Forum   *The Forum* (Springfield, IL)
IF   *Indianapolis Freeman*
IJ   *Indianapolis Journal*
IN   *Indianapolis News*
IO   *Inter Ocean* (Chicago)
IR   *Illinois Record*
ISJ   *Illinois State Journal*
ISR   *Illinois State Register*
LDT   *Leavenworth* (KS) *Daily Times*
MCD   *Marion County Democrat* (Salem, IL)

MG	*Mattoon Gazette*
MT	*Macon* (MO) *Times*
NDA	*Nashville Daily American*
NR	*National Republican* (Washington, DC)
NYA	*New York Age*
NYF	*New York Freeman*
NYT	*New York Times*
OAAS	*Omaha Afro-American Sentinel*
OE	*Omaha Enterprise*
OWH	*Omaha World Herald*
PD	*Plaindealer* (Detroit)
PET	*Philadelphia Evening Telegraph*
PF	*Provincial Freeman*
PWB	*Parsons* (KS) *Weekly Blade*
RA	*Republican Advocate*
SC	*State Capital*
TAC	*Topeka American Citizen*
WB	*Washington Bee*
WT	*Washington Times*

Alexander, Shawn Leigh. *An Army of Lions: The Civil Rights Struggle before the NAACP*. Philadelphia: University of Pennsylvania Press, 2012.

Anderson, James D. *The Education of Blacks in the South, 1860–1935*. Chapel Hill: University of North Carolina Press, 1988.

Andrews, Daryl Lamar. *Masonic Abolitionists: Freemasonry and the Underground Railroad*. Chicago: Andrews, 2011.

Armfield, Felix L. "Fire on the Prairies: The 1895 Spring Valley Race Riot." *Journal of Illinois History* 3 (2000): 185–200.

Arnett, Benjamin W. "Historical and Semi-Centennial Address." In *Proceedings of the Semi-Centenary Celebration of the African Methodist Episcopal Church of Cincinnati Held in Allen Temple, February 8th, 9th, and 10th, 1874*, edited by Benjamin W. Arnett, 9–77. Cincinnati: H. Watkin, 1874.

Bailey, Julius H. *Race Patriotism: Protest and Print Culture in the AME Church*. Knoxville: University of Tennessee Press, 2012.

Ball, Erica L. *To Live an Antislavery Life: Personal Politics and the Antebellum Black Middle Class*. Athens: University of Georgia Press, 2012.

Bateman, Newton, Paul Selby, and J. Seymour Currey. *Historical Encyclopedia of Illinois with Commemorative Biographies*. Vol. 1. Chicago: Munsell, 1926.

Beatty, Bess. *A Revolution Gone Backward: The Black Response to National Politics, 1876–1896*. New York: Greenwood, 1987.

Belles, A. Gilbert. "The Black Press in Illinois." *Journal of the Illinois State Historical Society* 68, no. 4 (1975): 344–52.

Benford, Robert D., and David A. Snow. "Framing Processes and Social Movements: An Overview and Assessment." *Annual Review of Sociology* 26 (2000): 611–39.

Bennett & Co.'s Cairo City Directory for 1887–'88. Evansville, IN: Bennett, 1887.

Bergeron, Paul H. *Andrew Johnson's Civil War and Reconstruction*. Knoxville: University of Tennessee Press, 2011.

Berlin, Ira, et al. *Free at Last: A Documentary History of Slavery, Freedom, and the Civil War*. New York: New Press, 1992.

Bernstein, Samuel. "American Labor in the Long Depression, 1873–78." *Science & Society* 20 (1956): 59–83.

Biennial Report of the Adjutant General of Illinois, 1899–1900. Springfield, IL: Phillips Bros., 1900.

Bigham, Darrell E. *On Jordan's Banks: Emancipation and Its Aftermath in the Ohio River Valley*. Lexington: University Press of Kentucky, 2015.

Biographical Encyclopedia of Illinois of the Nineteenth Century. Philadelphia: Galaxy, 1875.

Bledstein, Burton J., and Robert D. Johnston, eds. *The Middling Sorts: Explorations in the History of the American Middle Class*. New York: Routledge, 2001.

Bloom, Khaled J. *The Mississippi Valley's Great Yellow Fever Epidemic of 1878*. Baton Rouge: Louisiana State University Press, 1993.

Blum, Edward J. *Reforging the White Republic: Race, Religion, and American Nationalism, 1865–1898*. Baton Rouge: Louisiana State University Press, 2005.

Blumin, Stuart M. *The Emergence of the Middle Class: Social Experience in the American City, 1760–1900*. Cambridge: Cambridge University Press, 1989.

Bonner, Christopher James. *Remaking the Republic: Black Politics and the Creation of American Citizenship*. Philadelphia: University of Pennsylvania Press, 2020.

Branham, Charles Russell. "The Transformation of Black Political Leadership in Chicago, 1864–1942." PhD diss., University of Chicago, 1981.

Bridges, Roger D. "Equality Deferred: Civil Rights for Illinois Blacks, 1865–1885." *Journal of the Illinois State Historical Society* 74, no. 2 (1981): 82–108.

Brown, Elizabeth Gaspar. "The Initial Admission of Negro Students to the University of Michigan." *Michigan Quarterly Review* 2 (1963): 233–36.

Burkett, Randall K., Nancy Hall Burkett, and Henry Louis Gates, Jr., eds. *Black Biography, 1790–1950*. 3 vols. Alexandria VA: Chadwick-Healey, 1991.

Bushman, Richard L. *The Refinement of America: Persons, Houses, Cities.* New York: Alfred A. Knopf, 1992.

Carlson, Shirley J. "Black Migration to Pulaski County, Illinois 1860–1900." *Illinois Historical Journal* 80 (1987): 37–46.

Census of Canada West 1861. Essex County, Town of Windsor, Ontario West.

Cha-Jua, Sundiata Keita. *America's First Black Town: Brooklyn, Illinois 1830–1915.* Urbana: University of Illinois Press, 2000.

———. "'The Cry of the Negro Should Not Be Remember the Maine, but Remember the Hanging of Bush': African American Responses to Lynching in Decatur, Illinois, 1893." In *Lynching beyond Dixie: American Mob Violence outside the South,* edited by Michael J. Pfeifer, 165–89. Urbana: University of Illinois Press, 2013.

———. "'A Warlike Demonstration': Legalism, Armed Resistance, and Black Political Mobilization in Decatur, Illinois, 1894–1898." *Journal of Negro History* 83 (1998): 52–72.

———. "'A Warlike Demonstration:' Legalism, Violent Self-Help, and Electoral Politics in Decatur, Illinois, 1895–1898." *Journal of Urban History* 26 (2000): 591–629.

Chas. O. Ebel & Co's Cairo City Directory for 1884–85. Terre Haute, IN: Chas. O. Ebel, 1884.

Cheek, William, and Aimee Lee Cheek. *John Mercer Langston and the Fight for Black Freedom, 1829–65.* Urbana: University of Illinois Press, 1989.

———. "John Mercer Langston and the Cincinnati Riot of 1841." In *Race and the City: Work, Community, and Protest in Cincinnati, 1820–1970,* edited by Henry Louis Taylor, Jr., 29–69. Urbana: University of Illinois Press. 1993.

Cincinnati: A Guide to the Queen City and Its Neighbors. Compiled by workers of the Writer's Program of the WPA. Cincinnati: Wiesen-Hart, 1943.

Cist, Charles. *Cincinnati in 1841: Its Early Annals and Future Prospects.* Cincinnati: E. Morgan, 1841.

———. *Sketches and Statistics of Cincinnati in 1851.* Cincinnati: W. H. Moore, 1851.

Coffin, Levi. *Reminiscences of Levi Coffin, the Reputed President of the Underground Railroad.* 2nd ed., with appendix. Cincinnati: Robert Clarke, 1880.

Compendium of the Ninth Census: 1870. Pt. 1, "Population." Washington, DC: Government Printing Office, 1872.

Compendium of the Tenth Census (June 1, 1880). Rev. ed. Pt. 1, "Population." Washington, DC: Government Printing Office, 1885.

Compendium of the Eleventh Census: 1890. Pt. 1, "Population." Washington, DC: Government Printing Office, 1892.

Compendium of the Twelfth Census: 1900. Pt. 1, "Population." Washington, DC: Government Printing Office, 1901.

Condensed Report of the Twelfth Annual Communication of the Most Worshipful Grand Lodge of the State of Illinois. Chicago: George W. Blair, 1878.

Crouthamel, James L. "The Springfield Race Riot of 1908." *Journal of Negro History* 45, no. 3 (1960): 164–81.

Dabney, Wendell P. *Cincinnati's Colored Citizens: Historical, Sociological and Biographical.* New York: Negro Universities Press, 1970. Reprint of the 1926 original.

Dale, Elizabeth. "'Social Equality Does Not Exist among Themselves, nor among Us': *Baylies vs. Curry* and Civil Rights in Chicago, 1888." *American Historical Review* 102, no. 2 (1997): 311–39.

Davis, Hugh. *We Will Be Satisfied with Nothing Less: The African American Struggle for Equal Rights in the North during Reconstruction.* Ithaca, NY: Cornell University Press, 2011.

Delany, Martin R. *The Condition, Elevation, Emigration and Destiny of the Colored People of the United States, Politically Considered.* Philadelphia: Privately published, 1852.

Dickens, Charles. *American Notes: A Journey.* New York: Fromm International Publishing, 1982.

Directory of the City of Springfield Illinois. Springfield, IL: Hendrix, 1889.

Du Bois, W. E. B. *Black Reconstruction in America.* New York: Atheneum, 1973.

Emmerson, Louis L., ed. *The Blue Book of the State of Illinois, 1921–22.* Springfield: Illinois State Journal Company, 1921.

Erickson, Leonard E. "The Color Line in Ohio Public Schools, 1829–1890." PhD diss., Ohio State University, 1959.

Finkelman, Paul, ed. *Encyclopedia of African American History, 1896 to the Present: From the Age of Segregation to the Twenty-First Century.* Oxford: Oxford University Press, 2009.

First Annual Report of the Board of Trustees, for the Colored Public Schools of Cincinnati, for the School Year, ending June 30, 1855. Cincinnati: Moore, Wilstach, Keys, 1855.

Flood, Theodore L., and John W. Hamilton, eds. *Lives of Methodist Bishops.* New York: Phillips & Hunt, 1882.

Foner, Eric. *Freedom's Lawmakers: A Directory of Black Officeholders during Reconstruction.* New York: Oxford University Press, 1993.

———. *Reconstruction: America's Unfinished Revolution, 1863–1877.* Updated ed. New York: HarperPerennial, 2014.

Foner, Philip S., and Robert J. Branham, *Lift Every Voice: African American Oratory, 1787–1900*. Tuscaloosa: University of Alabama, 1998.

Foner, Philip S., and George E. Walker. *Proceedings of the Black State Conventions, 1840–1865*. Vol. 1. Philadelphia: Temple University Press, 1980.

Gaines, Kevin K. *Uplifting the Race: Black Leadership, Politics and Culture in the Twentieth Century*. Chapel Hill: University of North Carolina Press, 1996.

Garb, Margaret. *Freedom's Ballot: African American Political Struggles in Chicago from Abolition to the Great Migration*. Chicago: University of Chicago Press, 2014.

Gardner, Eric. *Black Print Unbound: The* Christian Recorder, *African American Literature, and Periodical Culture*. Oxford: Oxford University Press, 2015.

Gardner and Gaines Cairo City Directory for 1875–76 (publication data missing from copy at Cairo Public Library).

Gates, Henry Louis, Jr. *Stony the Road: Reconstruction, White Supremacy and the Rise of Jim Crow*. New York: Penguin, 2019.

Gates, Henry Louis, Jr., and Evelyn Brooks Higginbotham, eds. *African-American Lives*. Oxford: Oxford University Press, 2004.

Gerber, David A. *Black Ohio and the Color Line 1860–1915*. Urbana: University of Illinois Press, 1976.

Gibson, Campbell. "Population of the 100 Largest Cities and Other Urban Places in the United States, 1790 to 1990." U.S. Census Bureau, 1995. https://www .census.gov/library/working-papers/1998/demo/POP-twps0027.html.

Goode, W. T. *The "Eighth Illinois."* Chicago: Blakely, 1899.

Green, Alfred M. *Letters and Discussions on the Formation of Colored Regiments, and the Duty of the Colored People in Regard to the Great Slaveholders' Rebellion in the United States of America*. Philadelphia: Ringwalt & Brown, 1862. Reprinted by Rhistoric Press, Afro-American History Series, 1969.

Green, Augustus R. *A Discourse for the Times, on Our Condition as It Is and Might Be: Or Duty Rewarded*. Philadelphia: Hughes, 1853.

Green, Augustus R., and Samuel Venable. *A Brief Account of the Re-Organization of the B. M. E. Church in B. N. A.* Detroit: O. S. Gulley's, 1872.

Griffith, Cyril E. *The African Dream: Martin R. Delany and the Emergence of Pan-African Thought*. University Park: Pennsylvania State University Press, 1975.

Grossman, Lawrence. *The Democratic Party and the Negro: Northern and National Politics, 1868–92*. Urbana: University of Illinois Press, 1976.

Harris, Kathryn M. *Generations of Pride: African-Americans in Illinois: A Select Chronology*. Springfield: Illinois Historic Preservation Agency, 1995.

Harrison, Victoria. *Fight like a Tiger: Conway Barbour and the Challenges of the Black Middle Class in Nineteenth-Century America*. Carbondale: Southern Illinois University Press, 2018.

Hart, Richard E. *The Colored Section, Oak Ridge Cemetery, Springfield, Sangamon County, Illinois*. Springfield, IL: Richard E. Hart, n.d.

Hays, Christopher K. "The African American Struggle for Equality and Justice in Cairo, Illinois, 1865–1900." *Illinois Historical Journal* 90 (1997): 265–84.

———. "Way Down in Egypt Land: Conflict and Community in Cairo, Illinois 1850–1930." PhD diss., University of Missouri, Columbia, 1996.

Heinzel, Sally E. "Liberty Protected by Law: Race, Rights and the Civil War in Illinois." PhD diss., University of Illinois at Urbana-Champaign, 2015.

Hicken, Victor. "The Virden and Pana Mine Wars of 1898." *Journal of the Illinois State Historical Society* 52 (1959): 263–78.

Hodges, Carl G., and Helene H. Levene. *Illinois Negro Historymakers*. Chicago: Illinois Emancipation Centennial Commission, 1964.

Hollis, Andrew Philip. *The Contribution of the Oswego Normal School to Educational Progress in the United States*. Boston: D. C. Heath, 1898.

Holt, Thomas C. *Children of Fire: A History of African Americans*. New York: Hill and Wang, 2010.

Horney, Helen, and William E. Keller. "The Negro's Two Hundred Forty Years in Illinois: A Chronology." *Journal of the Illinois State Historical Society* 56, no. 3 (1963): 433–38.

Horton, James Oliver, and Stacy Flaherty. "Black Leadership in Antebellum Cincinnati." In *Race and the City: Work, Community, and Protest in Cincinnati, 1820–1970*, ed. Henry Louis Taylor, Jr., 70–95. Urbana: University of Illinois Press. 1993.

Howard, Robert P. *Mostly Good and Competent Men: Illinois Governors, 1818–1988*. Springfield, IL: Sangamon State University & Illinois State Historical Society, 1988.

Howe, Samuel Gridley. *The Refugees from Slavery in Canada West: Report to the Freedmen's Inquiry Commission*. Boston: Wright & Potter, 1864.

Illinois Industrial University Catalogue and Circular 1873. Urbana: Illinois Industrial University, 1873.

Illinois State Census 1865, County of Alexander, City of Cairo (colored). Illinois U.S. State Census Collection, 1825–1865. Accessed on Ancestry.com.

Jack, Bryan M. *The St. Louis African American Community and the Exodusters*. Columbia: University of Missouri Press, 2007.

Jenkins, Jeffrey A., and Justin Peck. *Congress and the First Civil Rights Era, 1861–1918*. Chicago: University of Chicago Press, 2021.

Joens, David A. *From Slave to State Legislator: John W. E. Thomas, Illinois' First African American Lawmaker.* Carbondale: Southern Illinois University Press, 2012.

———. "Illinois Colored Conventions of the 1880s." *Journal of the Illinois State Historical Society* 110: 3–4 (2017): 305–24.

Jones, Absalom, and Richard Allen. *A Narrative of the Proceedings of the Black People during the Late Awful Calamity in Philadelphia in the Year 1793.* Philadelphia: William W. Woodward, 1794.

Katzman, David M. *Before the Ghetto: Black Detroit in the Nineteenth Century.* Urbana: University of Illinois Press, 1973.

Kaye, Andrew M. "Colonel Roscoe Conkling Simmons and the Mechanics of Black Leadership." *Journal of American Studies* 37, no. 1 (April 2003): 79–93.

Keiser, John H. "Black Strikebreakers and Racism in Illinois, 1865–1900." *Journal of the Illinois State Historical Society* 65 (1972): 313–26.

Kionka, T. K. *Key Command: Ulysses S. Grant's District of Cairo.* Columbia: University of Missouri Press, 2006.

Lacy, Karyn R. *Blue-Chip Black: Race, Class, and Status in the New Black Middle Class.* Berkeley: University of California Press, 2007.

Lansden, John M. *A History of the City of Cairo, Illinois.* Chicago: R. R. Donnelley, 1910. Reprinted by Southern Illinois University Press, Carbondale, 1976.

Lantz, Herman R. *A Community in Search of Itself: A Case History of Cairo, Illinois.* Carbondale: Southern Illinois University Press/Feffer & Simons, 1972.

LaRoche, Cheryl J. *Free Black Communities and the Underground Railroad: The Geography of Resistance.* Urbana: University of Illinois Press, 2014.

Lee, Albert R. "The University of Illinois Negro Students: Data Concerning Negro Students at the State University." Unpublished manuscript, 1940. University of Illinois Archives, box 2/9/16.

Lentz, Eli G. *Seventy Five Years in Retrospect from Normal School to Teachers College to University: Southern Illinois University 1874–1949.* Carbondale: Southern Illinois University, 1955.

Levine, Robert S., ed. *Martin R. Delany: A Documentary Reader.* Chapel Hill: University of North Carolina Press, 2003.

Litwack, Leon F. *Been in the Storm So Long: The Aftermath of Slavery.* New York: Alfred A. Knopf, 1979.

Louisiana Compiled Marriage Index, 1718–1925, New Orleans, Louisiana.

Luckett, Judith Ann Blodgett. "Protest, Advancement and Identity: Organizational Strategies of Northern Free Blacks, 1830 to 1860." PhD diss., Johns Hopkins University, 1992.

Lusk, David W. *Politics and Politicians of Illinois*. 2nd ed. Springfield, IL: H. W. Rokker, 1886.

Manning, Chandra. *Troubled Refuge: Struggling for Freedom in the Civil War*. New York: Alfred A. Knopf, 2016.

Map of the City of Cairo Containing the Additions and Houses. Cairo: S. Staats Taylor & E. Parsons, Trustees, 1872.

Materson, Lisa. *For the Freedom of Her Race: Black Women and Electoral Politics in Illinois, 1877–1932*. Chapel Hill: University of North Carolina Press, 2009.

McCard, Harry Stanton, and Henry Turnley. *History of the Eighth Illinois United States Volunteers*. Chicago: E. F. Harman, 1899.

McCaul, Robert L. *The Black Struggle for Public Schooling in Nineteenth-Century Illinois*. Carbondale: Southern Illinois University Press, 2009.

Michigan, US, Death Records, 1867–1952. State of Michigan Vital Records Department. Accessed on Ancestry.com.

Mississippi Wills and Probate Records. Warren County, MS, Administrator's Bonds and Letters, 1872–1903. Warren County Court House. Accessed on Ancestry.com.

Morris, Aldon D. *The Origins of the Civil Rights Movement: Black Communities Organizing for Change*. New York: Free Press, 1984.

Mouser, Bruce L. *A Black Gambler's World of Liquor, Vice and Presidential Politics: William Thomas Scott of Illinois, 1839–1917*. Madison: University of Wisconsin Press, 2014.

———. *For Labor, Race, and Liberty: George Edwin Taylor, His Historic Run for the White House and the Making of Independent Black Politics*. Madison: University of Wisconsin Press, 2011.

Neilson, James W. *Shelby M. Cullom: Prairie State Senator*. Urbana: University of Illinois Press, 1962.

Newberry, J. S. *The Sanitary Commission in the Valley of the Mississippi, during the War of the Rebellion, 1861–1866: Final Report*. Sanitary Commission No. 96. Cleveland: Benedict Fairbanks, 1871.

Ninth Census of the United States. Schedule 1–County of Alexander, North Cairo Precinct, June 1870.

Noyes, Edward. "The Contraband Camp at Cairo, Illinois." In *Selected Papers of the Sixth Northern Great Plains History Conference*, edited by Lysle E. Meyer, 203–17. University of Minnesota Moorhead, 1971.

Nuwer, Deanne Stephens. *Plague among the Magnolias: The 1878 Yellow Fever Epidemic in Mississippi*. Tuscaloosa: University of Alabama Press, 2015.

Oak Ridge Cemetery Interment Records. Springfield, IL. Illinois Digital Archives, http://www.idaillinois.org/digital/collection/linl3.

Oberly, John H., ed. *Cairo City Directory for 1872*. Cairo, IL: Daily Bulletin Steam Job Print, 1872.

Ohio, County Marriage Records, Hamilton County, 1789–2013: reference v B7, 218, no. 477. Accessed on Ancestry.com.

Ohio, County Marriage Records, Montgomery County, 1838–1844. Accessed on Ancestry.com.

Painter, Nell Irvin. *Exodusters: Black Migration to Kansas after Reconstruction*. New York: Alfred A. Knopf, 1977.

Payne, Daniel A. *History of the African Methodist Episcopal Church*. Nashville: Publishing House of the AME Sunday-School Union, 1891.

Peavler, David J. "African Americans in Omaha and the 1898 Trans-Mississippi and International Exposition." *Journal of African American History* 93, no. 3 (2008): 337–61.

Penn, I. Garland. *The Afro-American Press and Its Editors*. Springfield, MA: Wiley, 1891.

Perrin, William H., ed. *History of Alexander, Union and Pulaski Counties, Illinois*. Chicago: O. L. Baskin, 1883.

Pfeifer, Michael J., ed. *Lynching beyond Dixie: American Mob Violence outside the South*. Urbana: University of Illinois Press, 2013.

Pimblott, Kerry. *Faith in Black Power: Religion, Race, and Resistance in Cairo, Illinois*. Lexington: University Press of Kentucky, 2017.

Plummer, Mark A. *Lincoln's Rail-Splitter: Governor Richard J. Oglesby*. Urbana: University of Illinois Press, 2001.

Pope, William A. *History of the First Half Century of the Oswego State Normal and Training School, Oswego, New York*. Oswego, NY: Radcliffe Press, 1913.

Power, J. L. *The Epidemic of 1878, in Mississippi: Report of the Yellow Fever Relief Work*. Jackson, MS: Clarion Steam, 1879.

Prince, Bryan. *My Brother's Keeper: African Canadians and the American Civil War*. Toronto: Dundurn, 2015.

"Private Joe" Fifer. Bloomington, IL: Pantagraph Printing & Stationery, 1936.

Private Laws of the State of Illinois. Vol. 1. Springfield, IL: Baker, Bailhache, 1867.

Proceedings of the Colored National Convention Held in Rochester, July 6th, 7th and 8th, 1853. Rochester, NY: Office of Frederick Douglass' Paper, 1853.

Proceedings of the Eighteenth Annual Communication of the Most Worshipful Grand Lodge, Ancient, Free and Accepted York Masons, State of Illinois. Chicago: Thorpe, West, 1885.

Proceedings of the Illinois State Convention of Colored Men Assembled at Galesburg, October 16th, 17th, and 18th. Chicago: Church, Goodman and Donnelley, 1867.

Proceedings of the National Conference of Colored Men of the United States Held in the State Capitol at Nashville, Tennessee, May 6, 7, 8, and 9, 1879. Washington, DC: Rufus H. Darby, 1879.

Proceedings of the National Emigration Convention of Colored People Held at Cleveland, Ohio 1854. Pittsburgh: A. A. Anderson, 1854.

Proceedings of the Twenty-First Annual Communication of the Most Worshipful Grand Lodge, Ancient, Free and Accepted Masons, State of Illinois. Sparta, IL: Plaindealer, 1888.

Rael, Patrick. *Black Identity & Black Protest in the Antebellum North.* Chapel Hill: University of North Carolina Press, 2002.

Records of the Assistant Commissioner for the State of Arkansas Bureau of Refugees, Freedmen and Abandon Lands, 1865–1869, M979, roll 6.

———. Bureau Record Book 1865, M979, roll 51.

Redkey, Edwin S. *Black Exodus: Black Nationalist and Back-to-Africa Movements, 1890–1910.* New Haven, CT: Yale University Press, 1969.

Reidy, Joseph P. "The African American Struggle for Citizenship Rights in the Northern States during the Civil War." In *Civil War Citizens: Race, Ethnicity and Identity in America's Bloodiest Conflict,* edited by Susannah J. Ural, 213–31. New York: New York University Press, 2010.

Return of Marriages in the County of Wayne, Michigan for the Quarter Ending June 30th A.D. 1892, 1925.

Return of Deaths in the County of Wayne Michigan for the Year Ending December 31, A.D. 1894.

Riddleberger, Patrick W. *1866: The Critical Year Revisited.* Carbondale: Southern Illinois University & Feffer & Simons, 1979.

Rittenhouse, Maud. *Maud.* Edited by Richard Lee Strout. New York: Macmillan, 1939.

Robinson & Jones' Cincinnati Directory for 1846. Cincinnati: Robinson and Jones, 1846.

Schneider, Norris F. *Y Bridge City: The Story of Zanesville and Muskingum County, Ohio.* Cleveland: World Publishing, 1950.

Schwalm, Leslie A. *Emancipation's Diaspora: Race and Reconstruction in the Upper Midwest.* Chapel Hill: University of North Carolina Press, 2009.

Senechal de la Roche, Roberta. *In Lincoln's Shadow: The 1908 Race Riot in Springfield, Illinois.* Carbondale: Southern Illinois University Press, 1990.

Seventh Census of the United States. District No. 60, Schedule I—Free Inhabitants in the 9th Ward of Cincinnati in the County of Hamilton, State of Ohio, 1850.

———. Free Inhabitants of Pitt Township in the County of Allegheny, Schedule 1—State of Pennsylvania, 1850.

Sheard, John J. "Notes on the African Methodist Episcopal Church in Cairo, Illinois." The Illinois Writers Project: "Negro in Illinois" Papers, box 17, folder 3, Vivian G. Harsh Research Collection of Afro-American History and Literature, Chicago Public Library, 1941.

Shotwell, John B. *A History of the Schools of Cincinnati.* Cincinnati: School Life, 1902.

Simmons, William J. *Men of Mark: Eminent, Progressive and Rising.* Cleveland: George M. Rewell, 1887. Reprinted Arno Press & New York Times, 1968.

Sixteenth Census of the United States, Supervisor's Dist. 13, Enumeration Dist. No. 84, Population Schedule, Wayne County, Michigan, Detroit City, Ward 6, 295, 1940.

Sixth Biennial Report of the Bureau of Labor Statistics of Illinois 1890. Springfield, IL: H. W. Rokker, 1891.

Skocpol, Theda, Ariane Liazos, and Marshall Ganz. *What a Mighty Power We Can Be: African American Fraternal Groups and the Struggle for Racial Equality.* Princeton, NJ: Princeton University Press, 2006.

Slap, Andrew L. *The Doom of Reconstruction: The Liberal Republicans in the Civil War Era.* New York: Fordham University Press, 2006.

Smith, Charles S. *A History of the African Methodist Episcopal Church.* Supplemental vol. Philadelphia: Book Concern of the A. M. E. Church, 1922.

Smith, J. Clay, Jr. *Emancipation: The Making of the Black Lawyer 1844–1944.* Philadelphia: University of Pennsylvania Press, 1993.

Snow, David A., E. Burke Rochford, Jr., Steven K. Worden, and Robert D. Benford. "Frame Alignment Processes, Micromobilization, and Movement Participation." *American Sociological Review* 51, no. 4 (1986): 464–81.

Solberg, Winton U. *The University of Illinois 1867–1894: An Intellectual and Cultural History.* Urbana: University of Illinois Press, 1968.

The Southern Loyalists: The Tribune Tracts—No. 2. New York: New York Tribune(?), 1866.

Springfield Duplex City Directory. St. Louis, MO: Benson Bros., 1890–91, 1891–92.

Taylor, Amy Murrell. *Embattled Freedom: Journeys through the Civil War's Slave Refugee Camps.* Chapel Hill: University of North Carolina Press, 2018.

Taylor, Henry Louis, Jr., ed. *Race and the City: Work, Community, and Protest in Cincinnati, 1820–1970.* Urbana: University of Illinois Press, 1993.

Taylor, Henry Louis, Jr., and Vicky Dula. "The Black Residential Experience and Community Formation in Antebellum Cincinnati." In *Race and the City: Work, Community, and Protest in Cincinnati, 1820–1970,* edited by Henry Louis Taylor, Jr., 96–125. Urbana: University of Illinois Press, 1993.

Taylor, Nikki M. *Frontiers of Freedom: Cincinnati's Black Community, 1802–1868.* Athens: Ohio University Press, 2005.

Tenth Census of the United States. Supervisor's District No. 17, Enumeration District No. 69, Schedule 1–Inhabitants in Washington City, District of Columbia, June 1880.

———. Supervisor's District No. 8, Enumeration District No. 2, Schedule 1–Inhabitants in the City of Cairo, Alexander County, Illinois, June 1880.

Thirteenth Census of the United States. Supervisor's District No. 12, Enumeration District No. 155, Sangamon County, Springfield, Illinois, 1910.

Thornbrough, Emma Lou. "The National Afro-American League, 1887–1908." *Journal of Southern History* 27, no. 4 (1961): 494–512.

Trefousse, Hans L. *Andrew Johnson: A Biography.* New York: W. W. Norton, 1989.

Trollope, Anthony. *North America.* Vol. 2. Philadelphia: J. B. Lippincott, 1862.

Twelfth Census of the United States. Supervisor's District No. 11, Enumeration District No. 102, Schedule 1–Sangamon County, City of Springfield, Illinois, 1900.

———. Supervisor's District No. 116, Enumeration District 94, Schedule 1–Wayne County, City of Detroit, Michigan, 1900.

Tye, Larry. *Rising from the Rails: Pullman Porters and the Making of the Black Middle Class.* New York: Henry Holt, 2004.

Ullman, Victor. *Martin R. Delany: The Beginnings of Black Nationalism.* Boston: Beacon, 1971.

United States Biographical Dictionary and Portrait Gallery of Eminent and Self-Made Men. Illinois ed. Chicago: American Biographical Publishing, 1883.

Vital Statistics Division, Michigan Department of State, Lansing, MI.

Waldron, Caroline A. "'Lynch-law Must Go!': Race, Citizenship, and the Other in an American Coal Mining Town." *Journal of American Ethnic History* 20, no. 1 (Fall 2000): 50–77.

Walker, Clarence E. *A Rock in a Weary Land: The African Methodist Episcopal Church during the Civil War and Reconstruction.* Baton Rouge: Louisiana State University Press, 1982.

Walker, Juliet E. K. "The Promised Land: The *Chicago Defender* and the Black Press in Illinois, 1862–1970." In *The Black Press in the Middle West, 1865–1985*, edited by Henry Lewis Suggs, 9–50. Westport, CT: Greenwood, 1996.

Walsh, Justin E. "Radically and Thoroughly Democratic: Wilbur F. Storey and the *Detroit Free Press* 1853 to 1861." *Michigan History* 47, no. 3 (1963): 193–225.

Ward, Alonzo. "The Specter of Black Labor: African American Workers in Illinois before the Great Migration, 1847–1910." PhD diss., University of Illinois at Urbana-Champaign, 2017.

Wentzell, Tyler. "Mercenaries and Adventurers: Canada and the Foreign Enlistment Act in the Nineteenth Century." *Canadian Military History* 23 (2015): 57–77.

Wheeler, Joanne. "Together in Egypt: A Pattern of Race Relations in Cairo, Illinois, 1865–1915." In *Toward a New South? Studies in Post-Civil War Southern Communities*, edited by Orville Vernon Burton and Robert C. McMath, Jr., 103–34. Westport, CT: Greenwood, 1982.

Will Record. *Alexander County Court House, Cairo, Ill.* Vol. A: *1880–1894*.

Williams' Cincinnati Directory, City Guide, and Business Mirror, 1853. Cincinnati: C. S. Williams, 1853.

Williamson, Joy Ann. "The Snail-like Progress of Racial Desegregation at the University of Illinois." *Journal of Blacks in Higher Education* 42 (2003–2004): 116–20.

Winks, Robin W. *The Blacks in Canada: A History*. Carleton Library Series 192. Montreal: McGill-Queen's University Press, 1997.

Woodson, C. G. "The Negroes of Cincinnati Prior to the Civil War." *Journal of Negro History* 1, no. 1 (1916): 1–22.

trip to Illinois and Missouri (1864),
35, 38, 39; and Underground
Railroad, 9, 25, 26, 29, 33, 222n26;
and Wilbur Storey, 223n50, 224n56
Green, Catherine Bird (John J.'s
mother), 9, 19, 23, 25, 29–31, 38, 39,
136–37, 208, 225n68, 258n135
Green, Elizabeth, 29, 31, 225n5
Green, infant son, 30–31
Green, James A. D., 29, 30, 31, 34,
223n51, 225n5
Green, Rebecca J. N. (Augustus's first
wife), 25, 221n20
Green, Richard A., 30, 34, 38, 39,
221n20, 225n68, 258n135
Green, William, 30, 225n5
Gregory, John Milton, 100, 101, 105

Hadley, Job, 42, 226n15
Hall, Abraham, 47
Halliday, William P., 71, 165
Hampton Normal Institute,
Virginia, 182
Harewood, Richard, 248n40
Harlan, Robert, 187
Harlow, George, 150, 236n10
Harmon, John Q., 91
Harrell, A., 240nn87–88
Harrell, Moses B., 65, 84, 85, 245n30
Harris, William F., 116
Harrison, Benjamin, 194
Harrison, Carter, 159, 179
Harrison, Victoria, 220n16
Hartzell, William, 111, 126, 127
Hatch, Frank L., 209
Hayes, Rutherford B., 99, 128, 130, 136,
140, 142, 143–44
Hays, Christopher K., 14, 229n62
Hendricks, William, 175

Henry Act (1874), 110–11, 118, 119, 154,
238nn41–42, 240n72
Hertz, Henry, 202
Hoar, George, 246n1
Hollinger, J. H., 148
Home Mission Society (Baptist),
62, 67
Horner, Moses, 34
Howe, Samuel Gridley, 224n55
Hurd, Daniel, 84
Huston (or Houston), Jeff, 50, 62, 81

Illinois Bureau of Labor Statistics,
191–93
Illinois Central Railroad, 40, 75, 101,
102, 174
Illinois Constitutional Conventions,
45, 82
Illinois General Assembly, 47, 74, 83,
101–2, 181, 183, 210–12, 238n42
Illinois Industrial University, xiii, xiv, 1,
11, 97, 100–6, 165–67, 169–70
Illinois Record (Springfield), 17, 203
Illinois school laws, 60, 62, 66, 83–84,
110–11, 118, 119
Illinois State Convention of Colored
Men, Galesburg (1866), 37, 51–52
Illinois State Convention of Colored
Men, Springfield (1879), 148
Illinois State Convention of Colored
Men, Springfield (1880), 150–54
Illinois State Convention of Colored
Men, Springfield (1883), 167–70
Illinois State Convention of Colored
Men, Springfield (1885), 177, 179
Illinois State Convention of Colored
Men, Springfield (1889), 189–90
Illinois State Journal (Springfield), 17,
102, 156, 196, 202, 208, 211

Washington Bee (Washington, D. C.), 17, 213
"Watchman, Tell Us of the Night" (Bowring), vii, 3–4, 76, 97, 117, 214, 216
Waterfield, Fred M., 195
Wayman, Alexander, 135
Webb, William, 28
Wells-Barnett, Ida B., 13, 202, 215
Wheeler, Joanne, 14, 226n13
Wheeler, Lloyd G., 167, 179, 232n99
White, Laura, 198
Wilberforce University, 51, 121
Wilson, Frances, 136
Wilson, Laurette E., 198
Wilson, Thomas, 91, 185
Wims, Warren, 184, 251n86

Windsor, Ontario (Canada West), 18, 20, 29–33, 35, 38, 39, 46, 50, 53, 74, 170
Winston, Claiborne, 80, 94, 235n56
Winter, Henry, 128, 135
Wood, John, 107, 109–10
Woodford, Wilson, 198
Wright, Edward H., 189, 190, 192, 253n28
Wright, Jonathan J., 109

Yancey, W. L., 195, 255n58
Yates, Richard, 40, 186, 193, 207, 208
yellow fever epidemic of 1878, 125, 129, 136–38, 171, 243n149
Young, Henry, 50

Zanesville, Ohio, 20, 29, 137

WAYNE T. PITARD is professor emeritus at the University of Illinois at Urbana-Champaign. Between 1983 and 2016 he taught Hebrew Bible and ancient Near Eastern religions in the Department of Religion at Illinois and for nine years was director of the University's Spurlock Museum of World Cultures. He is author of *Ancient Damascus* and coauthor with Mark S. Smith of *The Ugaritic Baal Cycle Volume II: Text, Translation and Commentary on KTU 1.3–1.4*, as well as sixty academic articles and chapters. His research focus has been on the ancient Canaanite literary texts from the city of Ugarit, Syria, dating to the thirteenth century BCE.